Succession

Succession and Trusts

Alex Gibb

Lecturer in Law, North East Scotland College

W. GREEN

First Edition   2017

Published in 2017 by Thomson Reuters, trading as W. Green, 21 Alva Street, Edinburgh EH2
4PS. Registered in England & Wales, Company No.1679046. Registered Office and address
for service: 5 Canada Square, Canary Wharf, London, E14 5AQ.

Typeset by Letterpart Limited, Caterham on the Hill, Surrey, CR3 5XL.

Printed and bound in Great Britain by CPI Group (UK) Ltd, Croydon, CR0 4YY.

No natural forests were destroyed to make this product: only farmed timber was used and
re-planted.

A CIP catalogue record of this book is available from the British Library.

http://www.wgreen.co.uk

ISBN: 978-0-414-01811-2

Thomson Reuters and the Thomson Reuters logo are trademarks of Thomson Reuters.

Crown copyright material is reproduced with the permission of the Controller of HMSO and
the Queen's Printer for Scotland.

Preface

The law of succession is fundamental to any legal system. The question of what ought to be done with a person's property upon their death demands an answer in order to facilitate the efficient transfer of rights over that property to those entitled to it, therefore ensuring that its value can continue to be enjoyed. The purpose of this book is to provide an overview of the rules governing such rights as determined by the law of Scotland. In keeping with the tradition of the *Greens Concise Scots Law* series, I have attempted to strike a balance between providing comprehensive coverage of the subject and presenting the material in a comprehensible format; the reader will, of course, be the ultimate judge of my success in achieving this.

At the time of writing, a new Succession (Scotland) Act has recently come into force. Whilst this Act did not herald a fundamental shift in the approach taken to succession under Scots law, it did introduce a number of welcome amendments that have accordingly been given treatment where relevant in the text. The Scottish Law Commission have long proposed a far more extensive overhaul of the rules of succession, and indeed the Scottish Government have on occasion hinted that this might yet come to pass. It is important to note that the outset, as it is with many areas of law, that succession is a dynamic subject, which remains liable to change.

Whilst writing is a solitary occupation, it is not an endeavour undertaken in complete isolation. It is essential for me to acknowledge the tremendous assistance I have received from others, whether directly or indirectly, during the process of bringing this book to completion. I owe an immense debt of gratitude to the many who have written on the subject of succession, but in particular to the work of Ross MacDonald, who produced the previous title on succession in the *Greens Concise Scots Law* series, and also to Alasdair Gordon, who originally prepared the *Succession LawBasics* title of which I am now lead author. Indeed, readers of the *LawBasics* volume will recognise one or two of the examples included in the current text; to the fascinating illustrations from the experiences of Dr Gordon I have added some from my own family's history. I also offer my heartfelt thanks to the editorial team at W. Green, whose guidance during the preparation of the text, and expertise in the publication of the book itself, has been invaluable. On a personal note, I would like to thank my wife, Amanda, for the support she has provided, and the admirable patience she has demonstrated, throughout this project.

PREFACE

My aim has been to state the law as at 31 March 2017. Any errors or omissions are entirely my own responsibility.

Alex Gibb
Aberdeen, April 2017

TABLE OF CONTENTS

CONTENTS

3. Property and Persons

4. Intestate Succession

CONTENTS

CONTENTS

CONTENTS

TABLE OF CASES

TABLE OF CASES

TABLE OF CASES

TABLE OF CASES

TABLE OF STATUTES

TABLE OF SCOTTISH STATUTES

TABLE OF STATUTORY INSTRUMENTS

TABLE OF SCOTTISH STATUTORY INSTRUMENTS

Table of Common Citations and Abbreviations

Erskine	Erskine, J., *An Institute of the Law of Scotland*, 8th edn (Edinburgh: Bell & Bradfute, 1871)
Stair	Dalrymple, J., (Viscount Stair) *Institutions of the Law of Scotland*, Tercentenary edn, (Edinburgh: Edinburgh University Press, 1981).
Bankton	Bankton, A., *An Institute of the Laws of Scotland in Civil Rights* (1751–1753).
McLaren	McLaren, J., *The Law of Wills and Succession as Administered in Scotland*, 3rd edn (Edinburgh: Bell and Bradfute, 1894).
Mackintosh Report	Mackintosh, Lord C., *Law of Succession in Scotland Report of the Committee of Inquiry* (Scottish Home Department, 1950).
Scot. Law Com. No.215	Scottish Law Commission, *Report on Succession* (Scot. Law Com. No.215, 2009).
The 1800 Act	Accumulations Act 1800.
The 1855 Act	Intestate Moveable Succession (Scotland) Act 1855 (c.23).
The 1921 Act	Trusts (Scotland) Act 1921 (c.58).
The 1961 Act	Trusts (Scotland) Act 1961 (c.57).
The 1964 Act	Succession (Scotland) Act 1964 (c.41).
The 1977 Act	Presumption of Death (Scotland) Act 1977 (c.27).
The 1982 Act	Forfeiture Act 1982 (c.34).
The 1990 Act	Law Reform (Miscellaneous Provisions) (Scotland) Act 1990 (c.40).
The 1995 Act	Requirements of Writing (Scotland) Act 1995 (c.7).
The 2005 Act	Charities and Trustee Investment (Scotland) Act 2005 (asp 10).
The HTSA 2006	Human Tissue (Scotland) Act 2006 (asp 4).
The 2006 Act	Family Law (Scotland) Act 2006 (asp 2).
The 2016 Act	Succession (Scotland) Act 2016 (asp 7).

CHAPTER 1

Introduction and Basic Concepts

GENERAL INTRODUCTION

Succession is the area of law that regulates the passing of a person's property   **1–01**
after their death. It is an area that is relevant to everyone, since even a person of
the most modest means will leave behind a certain amount of property, and it is
only logical that something must be done with these belongings.

Sometimes, the value of the property that a deceased has left behind will be
very high, and sometimes it will be very low; most often, the value falls
somewhere in the middle of these two extremes. Regardless of the sums
involved, the principles behind the law of succession remain the same; to
determine who has the right to take ownership of the deceased's property, and to
calculate exactly what these entitlements amount to.

Broadly speaking, the law of succession is divided into two parts, the main
distinguishing factor between the two being whether or not the deceased person
made any provision for the disposal of their property after death. Where the
deceased left a will, this is called "testate" succession, and where the deceased
left no will, it is called "intestate" succession. The rules governing the two areas
are very different indeed, as will become clear in due course.

HISTORY AND BACKGROUND

Every legal system acknowledges some form of the law of succession. Ever since   **1–02**
civilisations developed to the point where there was respect for the personal
ownership of property, there has been the question of who should get what when
a person dies. In most modern democratic legal systems, the law has had to
maintain a balance between giving effect to the wishes of the deceased, and
treating the survivors (particularly close family members) in a fair and equitable
manner. This spirit has informed the law of succession in Scotland since its
earliest days of development.

Historical context

It is generally agreed that the formalisation of Scots law began during the 12th   **1–03**
century, before which the law was based on a combination of customs and local
charters. Little in the way of documentation from the earliest periods of

1

development exists, although there are limited surviving written records such as the *Regiam Majestatem*, a collection of Scots law from various sources, including statutes of the 12th and 13th centuries.[1]

Despite the relative lack of formal writings, there can be no doubt that succession has always occupied a crucial role within Scots law. The venerable institutional writer Stair stated that "succession to defuncts is the most important title in law",[2] and offers the rules of succession as an example of common law derived from "our ancient and immemorial customs ... anterior to any statute".[3] Indeed, as will be seen the substantive rules directing distribution of property after death were firmly based in common law until the mid-19th century; even then it was not until the 20th century that significant statutory reform was effected.

For the greater part of its history, succession in Scotland was focused in similar manner to many other countries in that emphasis was on the continuation of the family line. To this end, identification of an "heir" (person entitled to inherit) was of paramount importance. Due to the patriarchal nature of traditional Western societies, males would always be favoured over females, and the first-born son would often inherit the majority of his deceased father's "estate" (property left behind upon death). The claims of female family members were secondary to this, and more commonly involved occupation rights than a right to actually take ownership of property.

Of course, in modern times such gender inequality is viewed as entirely unacceptable, and significant steps have been taken in many areas of the law towards ensuring parity of treatment between the sexes. Discussion of whether or not such advancements have created the desired equality is far beyond the scope of this book, but what can certainly be said is that the rules of succession in Scotland nowadays make no distinction between males and females in terms of inheriting property. In an interesting side note, the rules of succession relating to the throne of the UK have until very recently always favoured the first-born male over any female heir, and were among the final remnants of the traditional notion that males' birthrights should be superior to females'. However, this preference was abolished by the Succession to the Crown Act 2013, which implemented the "Perth Agreement" that had been reached by the heads of government of the Commonwealth states in October 2011.[4]

Succession in modern times

1–04   Nowadays, with the fading importance of identifying a single heir to one's estate, succession is more concerned with the distribution of property among the deceased person's "beneficiaries", of which there may be any number. Broadly speaking, the rules of succession are divided into two distinct areas; those that regulate the situation where the deceased left no will (called "intestate

---

[1] See White R., Willock I. and MacQueen H., *The Scottish Legal System*, 5th edn (Edinburgh: W. Green, 2013).
[2] Stair, III, 4, 2.
[3] Stair, I, 1, 16.
[4] House of Commons Political and Constitutional Reforms Committee, *Rules of Royal Succession* (Report HC1615, October 2011).

succession") and those that regulate the situation where the deceased did leave a will (called "testate succession"). A person who has left a will is called the "testator" or, if female, the "testatrix".

Both testate and intestate succession present their own specific challenges to the legal practitioner, from the rigid and generalised rules of intestate succession, to the sometimes surprising (and often unpalatable) provisions that are contained in some wills. It is probably, on balance, the preferable situation where the deceased has left at least some indication of what he wished done with his property, though in reality it is still a minority of the population who actually leave any precise instructions by will as to the disposal of their estate.

As alluded to above, anyone who inherits property under succession can be referred to as a "beneficiary". Other commonly encountered terms which, although similar in ultimate effect, are more precise and therefore only applicable to certain contexts, are "claimant" and "legatee". The former term is used where someone is pursuing an entitlement other than as endowed upon them in a will; the latter is used where someone has been identified as being entitled to receive property under the terms of a will itself. There can be little doubt that, whether distribution of an estate is to be affected according to the rules of testacy or intestacy, close family members occupy the most favourable positions in terms of inheritance. Although there is no longer any preference between male and female heirs, the position of children is still (in many circumstances) a very powerful one. The position of spouse (or, more recently, civil partner[5]) is also much stronger now than in previous times, particularly in terms of intestate division, and inroads have also been made into increasing the succession rights of cohabiting partners. The intention behind many rules of succession is to achieve a fair balance between these competing interests, but it must be said that succession is an area of law that can be very divisive among members of a family, where perceptions of what is "fair" are often clouded by what one actually stands to inherit.

SUCCESSION AND RELATED LEGAL AREAS

It is fair to say that succession straddles a number of areas of law. Whilst the rules directing distribution of property upon death are self-contained and relatively well-defined, those rules are informed by principles from many other fields. An obvious example is that succession grants a considerable range of rights to certain close family members of the deceased; but the rules determining who actually occupies those positions are laid down by family law.

Application of the many rules of succession requires consideration of various other legal principles, drawn from areas including property, trusts and private international law, to name just but a few. Of course no area of law operates in isolation, and the complete compartmentalisation of any field of legal study is therefore inappropriate, but succession more than most is a discipline that crosses boundaries; both legal and geographical.

1–05

---

[5] Under the Civil Partnership Act 2004; see related commentary at appropriate points throughout.

Property

1–06   Property is of paramount significance to the law of succession. Whilst expertise in property law is not required in order to understand succession (although doubtless it greatly helps), it is necessary to appreciate some basic property law principles. Fundamentally, it is very important to understand that not all property is the same, and that a typical estate is likely to be composed of several different types of property, often with distinct rules relating to each.

   The most important distinction is between "heritable" and "moveable" property. By way of simple overview, heritable property refers to land and to items permanently attached to land, such as buildings, houses and trees growing in the ground. All property that is not heritable is counted as moveable, and there is an almost endless list of possible examples; some of the most relevant to succession include furniture, vehicles, jewellery and, of course, money itself. This is the most important classification of property for succession purposes because it can have a significant bearing on the calculation, and so the value, of certain rights.

   Also relevant is the distinction between "corporeal" and "incorporeal" property. Again to put it simply, corporeal property is anything that has a physical body to which our five senses can, in theory at least, be applied. Examples include land, buildings, furniture and vehicles. Incorporeal property is anything that lacks a physical body but nevertheless has value, usually by conferring some right or benefit on the owner. Examples include leases, shares in a company, and the funds in a bank account. Whilst the distinction between corporeal and incorporeal property was historically of quite significant importance, it is probably fair to say that it has less direct relevance in modern times.

   A final common distinction is that made between "fungible" and "non-fungible" property. Fungible property is something that, by its nature, is consumed through use, and can be easily replaced with a similar quantity of the same property that is also of the same quality. This may sound complicated, but it is actually quite simple; commercial commodities such as oil and coal are good examples of fungibles, as are ingredients such as sugar and grain. Money is also classed as fungible, though there is an argument as to the extent that it is actually "consumed" in use; the notes and coinage are not of course destroyed, but their value to the person spending them is relinquished. Non-fungible property is anything that, by its nature, is not consumed in use, and has a specific inherent value which sets it apart from property that is similar in type. A work of art is a common example of a non-fungible, as is a motor vehicle which, although it has a finite working life and *could* be said to be very gradually "used up", is obviously very different from the general nature of fungibles otherwise. This distinction is relevant in certain areas, most notably in testate succession, where a will might direct that certain property be used in certain ways.

   The distinction between heritable and moveable property is, along with other issues related to property law, explored in greater detail in Ch.3. The various applications of rights in succession to property are, of course, considered throughout the text. An issue that *is* universal across different types of property is monetary value. Succession practice is almost entirely focused on the calculation of the value of property rights, so it is essential that a deceased's assets are accurately valued. This can lead to problems in practice, and various solutions exist; these are also explained at appropriate points throughout the text.

Debts

Debt is obviously related to rights in property. The right of one person to receive property invariably requires the obligation on another person to deliver it; this is the nature of debt. An oft-asked question in the area of succession is, do a deceased's debts die with him? The answer to this is not entirely straightforward, partly because the legal existence of a debt and the fact of that debt actually being paid are not always the same thing, and also because death itself creates debts of various types. There are, however, a number of important points to note which, when taken together, help to make the full situation clear.

First, it can be stated without doubt that the vast majority of existing debts accrued during a person's lifetime do not simply "disappear" upon his death. Instead, they become debts liable to be paid out of the deceased's estate. (An exception to this is student loans, which will usually be cancelled if they remain unpaid upon the borrower's death.) Secondly, death and the need to deal with the deceased's estate will create a number of "new" debts, such as potential claims by surviving family members, and the expenses of the administration itself. Thirdly, all debts due by the estate must be paid, so far as is possible, in accordance with a pre-determined "rank" outlined by statute; the value of any estate that remains after all debts have been settled then passes on to the beneficiaries by function of inheritance. If the total estate is exhausted by the payment of outstanding debts, any remaining debts are written off; they do not pass on to be paid by the deceased's descendants.

A further point worth noting is that many people make arrangements for certain debts to be paid upon their death. For example, many homeowners who are required to repay a secured loan on their house will also take out a life assurance policy with sufficient proceeds to cover the outstanding balance of the secured loan. Upon death, the insurance policy effectively negates this particular debt, although the mechanism by which this occurs is actually more complicated than that. Debts are further considered alongside other matters relating to the deceased's estate in Ch.3.

1–07

Inheritance tax

It has been said that there are only two certainties in life; death and taxes. True or false, the two can certainly be connected. Since the 17th century, successive governments have realised that death can be a convenient time to tax a person's estate.[6] Various terminology has been used since then, with the term "inheritance tax" coming into common usage during the 1980s.[7] Although various different mechanisms have been applied over the years, the central principle has always been the same; that a certain portion of an estate is due to be paid over to the public purse, rather than it passing to the beneficiaries in its entirety.

1–08

---

[6] See, e.g. the Stamp Acts of 1694 (introduced in England) and 1712 (which applied to the then recently-united kingdoms of England and Scotland).
[7] See, e.g. the Inheritance Tax Act 1984 and the Finance Act 1986.

It is fair to say that inheritance tax has long attracted criticism, and the debate over its merits and demerits continues.[8] In practice, relatively few estates are actually liable to inheritance tax, due to the nil-rate band by which no tax is payable on the first portion of an estate. At the time of writing this threshold is £325,000,[9] although recent developments have opened up the possibility of increasing this in certain circumstances. Where an estate's net value (i.e. after deduction of debts and funeral expenses) is higher than the nil-rate threshold, the portion in excess of the threshold is taxed at 40 per cent. For example, if the net value of an estate is £340,000, only £15,000 is liable to be taxed (at 40 per cent), so the amount charged would be £6,000.

Inheritance tax is a relevant consideration when valuing an estate and paying debts, so is mentioned alongside these matters in Ch.3. It is also mentioned in certain other contexts as appropriate. However, it must be said that inheritance tax is a specialist discipline in its own right and is, generally speaking, beyond the scope of this book.

Trusts and executry law

1–09 It is a practical reality of succession that, upon a person's death, someone is required to take responsibility for the deceased's property. The matters referred to above in respect of the deceased's estate all require practical human intervention, as does the distribution of the estate to the appropriate beneficiaries. The person responsible for doing this is called the "executor" or, if female, the "executrix".[10] The executor must prepare an "inventory" of the deceased's estate, which in most cases must be submitted to the court in order to gain "confirmation", i.e. legal authority to "intromit with" (administer) the estate for the benefit of those entitled to inherit.

The executor therefore takes control of the deceased's property, and will often retain it in his possession whilst dealing with matters such as payment of debts, and the calculation of rights of the various beneficiaries. It is important to note, however, that the executor does not own this property free of obligations, and has no rights over it other than those that are necessary for the carrying out of his duties. The executor is said to hold the property "in trust" for the benefit of the deceased's survivors, and there is therefore a strong link between the law of succession and the law of trusts (i.e. the area of law regulating property that is held and administered by one person for the benefit of another). Further coverage on trusts is provided in Ch.12, and the role of the executor himself is fully considered in Ch.11.

---

[8] See, e.g. Seely, A., *Inheritance Tax* (House of Commons Library Briefing Paper 15/93, 29 September 2015).

[9] Originally set for the tax year 2009–2010 by the Finance Act 2006 s.155, and maintained by subsequent legislation.

[10] The male form is used for sake of brevity throughout this text, except when the context requires otherwise.

Private international law

As mentioned earlier in this chapter, succession in Scotland has largely been developed through custom and common law, with statutory formalisation being a relatively recent innovation. The result is that Scotland's succession laws are distinct from that of any other country, and whilst assistance on certain matters has at times been sought from other jurisdictions, there is no legal system whose regime in this area is entirely comparable. Of particular note is the fact that, despite Scotland's long-standing constitutional union with England, and the resulting similarities in many guiding principles and opinions, the rules of succession between the two countries are actually quite different.

1–10

This diversity of approaches can occasionally lead to problems where two legal systems claim jurisdiction over the same estate. This is particularly relevant in the UK, where it is very possible for the same individual to have property interests in both Scotland and England, Wales or Northern Ireland. Indeed, in this modern age of globalisation and increased workforce mobility, it is increasingly common for people to have property interests that expand beyond the borders of the UK into Europe and even farther afield. The resolution of such disputes can be an exceptionally complicated matter.

To consider the issue briefly, there are two general rules as developed by Scottish common law. The first is that the Scots law of succession applies to moveable property owned by any person who is "domiciled" in Scotland. Domicile is a difficult term to define; it is distinct from residence, which can be a more transient concept, and it is different also from place of birth that, although fixed, need not have much significance to a person's current circumstances. Domicile is perhaps best taken to mean the place where a person makes his permanent home. Therefore, regardless of where moveable property is located at any particular time, if it is owned by a person domiciled in Scotland, the Scots law rules of succession apply to it. The second rule is that any "immoveable" property situated in Scotland is also subject to the Scottish laws, regardless of where the owner is domiciled. The term "immoveable" is not exactly the same as heritable, since the latter is broader, but for practical purposes means something very similar, i.e. land and buildings. Private international law is another very specialist area, and as such is beyond the scope of this book.

SUCCESSION AND LAW REFORM

Like any area of law, succession is a dynamic field of study which is subject to ongoing development. Indeed, owing partly to the range of other disciplines it pulls into its orbit, succession experiences fairly regular amendment, and keeping abreast of these changes is a challenge for academics and practitioners alike. As society's views alter on matters as diverse as family, morality and ownership of property, so too must various legal rules and doctrines relevant to succession.

1–11

Despite its strong, and still-felt, common law influence, the modern legal basis for succession is statutory, in the form of the Succession (Scotland) Act 1964 (the 1964 Act). This statute marked a different approach to the law of succession than had previously been seen in Scotland, by establishing rights for various family members. Perhaps of greatest significance was the development of a surviving spouse's "prior rights" to claim major portions of an intestate estate, and establishing (to a very much lesser extent) statutory rules relevant to the "legal rights" of a surviving spouse and children, which previously had been governed exclusively by common law. These concepts are given full consideration in Ch.4 in respect of intestate succession, and the application of legal rights in testate estates is considered in Ch.6.

Since its passing, the 1964 Act has been regularly amended and updated, commonly for practical purposes such as increasing certain financial limits to correspond with inflationary rises. In addition, the general statutory regime regulating succession has been altered and contributed to by various other pieces of legislation, such as the Civil Partnership Act 2004 and the Family Law (Scotland) Act 2006. From time to time, the Scottish Law Commission undertakes reviews of the law relating to succession (as they do with many other areas) and makes recommendations as to how the law should be developed. The most recent such review culminated in the publication of a report in 2009,[11] in which a number of major changes were suggested, one example being considerable reform of the rules governing distribution of intestate estates. Although the Scottish Government's response to many of the recommendations was positive, at the time of writing only a relatively small portion of these changes have been implemented.

That said, of no small significance is the Succession (Scotland) Act 2016 (the 2016 Act), which was passed following a major consultation process which concluded in 2014.[12] The 2016 Act introduced various amendments regarding primarily technical areas such as survivorship, forfeiture and the effects of divorce on succession rights. The affected areas are consequently diverse, and are referred to as appropriate throughout this book.

There is no doubt that the 2016 Act was welcomed among the legal community. However, it was not the sweeping overhaul of succession that many, the Scottish Law Commission included, had perhaps envisioned. There is speculation that this is to be only the first of a number of amendments to the law of succession in Scotland that will be implemented over the coming years. At the time of writing no further formal plans have been published, but it seems likely that further change is yet to come. It will be very interesting to see how the matter develops in the near future.[13]

---

[11] Scottish Law Commission, *Report on Succession* (Scot. Law Com. No.215).
[12] Wheelhouse, P., *Consultation on the Law of Succession* (Scottish Government, 26 June 2015).
[13] Updates available at *http://www.gov.scot/Topics/Justice/law/damages/succession* [Accessed 5 May 2017].

CHAPTER 2

Practical Matters Upon Death

INTRODUCTION

Succession can only operate when someone has died. This may sound obvious in   **2–01**
the extreme, but it is actually a very important issue that can give rise to a number
of problems. The exact moment of death can sometimes be difficult (or even
impossible) to identify. It might even be the case that the very fact of death
cannot be established, for example where someone has gone missing without
apparent trace. Either of these situations can leave the law of succession
struggling somewhat to regulate the passing of the deceased's property. There are
also significant problems when two or more people die at or around the same
time, especially if they are the beneficiaries of each other's estate; although
recent legislative developments have simplified this particular issue. Even in the
absence of such complications, death obliges a number of practical matters to be
dealt with.

DEATH

Death is, arguably, a less precise concept now than it was historically. Modern   **2–02**
science has devised ingenious methods of preserving and extending life, and
whilst of course these efforts are to be commended, their results are not entirely
without problem. One such issue is the somewhat fluid state that life and death
increasingly occupy, and the consequently subjective perspective from which
they are viewed. This lack of clarity can frustrate the application of legal
principles.

The fact of death

When considering the nature of death it seems logical to turn first to a medical   **2–03**
definition. The Academy of Medical Royal Colleges states that death involves
"the irreversible loss of the capacity for consciousness, combined with
irreversible loss of the capacity to breathe".[1] Whilst this may appear
straightforward, and indeed is perfectly sound from a medical practitioner's point
of view, it does give rise to problems for the legal practitioner. This is because

---

[1] Academy of Medical Royal Colleges, "A Code of Practice for the Diagnosis and Confirmation of
Death" (AOMRC, October 2008).

Scots law, like most legal systems, is still coming to terms with the distinction between actual death and states that fall short of this, such as "brain" death.

The main problem concerns the primary purpose of succession, which is to transfer property rights from the dead to the living, so that the latter can enjoy them once the former no longer can. However, in the modern day there is the potential for a person to be kept technically (some might even say artificially) "alive", but in a state whereby he cannot possibly enjoy use of his property, and the likelihood of him ever doing so again is negligible. Among the myriad ethical questions to be considered in such a situation is that of what ought to be done with the person's property. At present, the answer appears to be elusive, but what can be said is that it shall not pass by virtue of succession until nature takes its course, or until life-preserving medical treatment is withdrawn, and the individual actually dies.[2]

It must be said that the above situation is very rare. In the vast majority of cases, the fact and broad circumstances of a person's death can be determined without difficulty and, accordingly, confirmed by a medical practitioner.

It is also relevant here to make mention of so-called "living wills". An increasing number of people have put in place instructions regarding how they might wish to be treated in the event of a debilitating illness or life threatening trauma, e.g. whether or not they would wish to be resuscitated. This is a complex area of law, far beyond the scope of this book, and so it is sufficient to state that the term "living will" is a contradiction in terms. It is not a testamentary provision, and so does not, despite its name, come under the auspices of the law of succession.

Proof of death

2–04   Before any actings can be made in relation to a deceased's estate, the date and place of death must be established. This is most commonly achieved by registering the death according to the procedure outlined in Pt 3 of the Registration of Births, Deaths and Marriages (Scotland) Act 1965. It is worth noting that the oft-used term "death certificate" is potentially confusing, as it can actually refer to either of two different (but closely related) documents. These are distinguished in the passage below by use of their more exact descriptions according to the relevant legislation.

To briefly summarise the requirements, a medical practitioner must, within seven days of either the death or discovery of the body, issue a "medical certificate of cause of death".[3] This must, within *eight* days of either death or discovery, be registered with the Registrar of Births, Deaths and Marriages by a person duty-bound to do so.[4] The Registrar must then issue an extract "certificate of registration of death", which is provided free of charge to the person effecting the registration.[5] This extract is regarded as "sufficient" evidence of death.[6]

---

[2] For an in-depth consideration of this issue, and of related topics, see Laurie G.T. et al, *Mason and McCall Smith's Law and Medical Ethics*, 10 edn (Oxford: Oxford University Press, 2016).

[3] Registration of Births, Deaths and Marriages (Scotland) Act 1965 s.24.

[4] Registration of Births, Deaths and Marriages (Scotland) Act 1965 s.23(1); such persons include relatives of the deceased, anyone present at the death, and the executor or legal representative of the deceased.

[5] Registration of Births, Deaths and Marriages (Scotland) Act 1965 s.27(1).

Largely motivated by concerns raised following the Harold Shipman case,[7] the issuing of medical certificates of cause of death is now subject to stricter scrutiny.[8] This is another topic far beyond the scope of this book, but common sense dictates that at the very least a medical practitioner must have an opportunity to examine identified human remains before issuing a medical certificate of cause of death. This is simple enough when a death has occurred in hospital or when a doctor has been called following the discovery of a death at home. However, where there is no such opportunity, death will have to be proven by other means. Two possible situations are cases of missing persons, and cases where someone is believed to have died but their remains have not been recovered.

Presumption of death

Under common law, if the fact of someone's death could not otherwise be established, there was no presumption other than that his life continued to the extremes of old age. This upper limit was considered by Stair to be 80 years old,[9] and by Bankton to be 100.[10] In *Bruce v Smith*,[11] the descendants of one Alexander Bruce were in dispute over family property. The particular issue was whether Bruce, who was born in 1768 and had not been heard from since 1825, would have still been alive in 1849, at which time an agreement relating to this property was signed by his grandchildren. The court held that Bruce could be presumed to have died by 1849, at which point he would have been aged around 81. However, it was remarked that this decision was influenced by the fact that the question was being considered a further 22 years after the relevant date; a decision actually taken by the court in 1849 might have been decided differently.[12]

Anyone seeking to rebut the presumption of life required proof beyond reasonable doubt, a much higher standard than normally expected in civil cases.[13] The rigid application of this can be seen in *Secretary of State for Scotland v Sutherland*,[14] in which a wife sought declarator of death in respect of her husband, who had disappeared and not been heard of for 42 years. The court adhered to the presumption that he was still alive, now aged 72, and refused the wife's claim.

That said, if circumstances suggested that the individual's life would have been considerably shorter than normal, this could be taken into account. In *Greig v Merchant Company of Edinburgh*,[15] a wife sought declarator of death so that she might claim her husband's pension. He had not been seen or heard of for around 20 years prior to the action, and at the time of the case being heard would have been aged around 63 years; far below the limits previously applied.

2–05

[6] Registration of Births, Deaths and Marriages (Scotland) Act 1965 s.41A.
[7] See, e.g. Smith J., *The Shipman Inquiry third report: death certification and the investigation of deaths by coroners* (Cm 5854, 2003).
[8] In Scotland the relevant legislation is the Certification of Death (Scotland) Act 2011.
[9] Stair, IV, 45, 17.
[10] Bankton, IV, 34, 1.
[11] *Bruce v Smith* (1871) 10 M. 130.
[12] *Bruce v Smith* (1871) 10 M. 130 at 132, per Lord President Inglis.
[13] See, e.g. *McGeachy v Standard Life Assurance Co*, 1972 S.C. 145.
[14] *Secretary of State for Scotland v Sutherland*, 1944 S.C. 79.
[15] *Greig v Merchant Company of Edinburgh*, 1921 S.C. 76.

However, there was convincing evidence that he had succumbed to alcoholism, and reliable medical opinion that his life expectancy would have extended no more than 10 years beyond his disappearance. The court granted declarator of death, with the date of death established in accordance with this 10-year estimate.

In time, legislation was passed to provide a greater degree of consistency. Some headway was made in the late 19th century with the Presumption of Life Limitation (Scotland) Acts of 1881 and 1891, but these were very technical and somewhat limited in scope, reducing their usefulness in application. For example, in *Murray v Chalmers*[16] a petition taken under the 1891 Act was rejected because the petitioner's rights were dependent upon the *date* of death, rather than the *fact* of death itself, and consequently he had no title to present the petition. Related measures, such as the Divorce (Scotland) Act 1938, allowed death to be declared for certain other purposes, but the piecemeal approach led to a complex, and at times inconsistent, legislative landscape.[17]

2–06   A uniform approach was established by the Presumption of Death (Scotland) Act 1977 (the 1977 Act). Under s.1(1) of this Act, anyone having an interest to do so may raise an action to have a person declared legally dead. This applies in two main circumstances.

First, it may be that someone is thought to have died at or around a particular time. An example would be where an air accident occurred over the ocean and no human remains have been recovered. Secondly, someone may not have been known to be alive for a period of at least seven years. To put it another way, the person has simply disappeared. With modern forms of communication and computer databases, it is much more difficult for a living person to disappear, but it is still possible.

Proof of death under the 1977 Act is on balance of probabilities, as would be normal in civil cases. If it cannot be proved exactly when death took place, but that it must have occurred within a certain time period, the end of that period will be the date on the court decree. If the deceased has simply disappeared, death will be deemed to have taken place at the end of the day seven years after he was last known to be alive.[18]

The decree is conclusive in absence of any appeal, and for most purposes is the equivalent of death being established by more traditional means. Its effects include the dissolution of any marriage or civil partnership to which the deceased was a party, and also any property rights,[19] though the jurisdiction of foreign legal systems in relevant questions is explicitly retained.[20] The decree therefore allows the estate to be dealt with exactly as if death had been established as a matter of fact. It is worth noting that insurance companies need not allow payment of a life policy proceeds purely on the evidence of a declarator of death although, in practice, most do.

Although it is very rare, should the "deceased" reappear, it is necessary for him (or an interested party) to apply for recall of the decree.[21] In such cases, any

---

[16] *Murray v Chalmers*, 1913 1 S.L.T. 223.
[17] For further commentary see Scottish Law Commission, *Presumptions of Survivorship and Death* (SLC Memorandum No.11, 1969).
[18] Presumption of Death (Scotland) Act 1977 s.2(1).
[19] Presumption of Death (Scotland) Act 1977 s.3(1).
[20] Presumption of Death (Scotland) Act 1977 s.3(2).
[21] This is known as a "variation order"; Presumption of Death (Scotland) Act 1977 s.4.

marriage or civil partnership remains dissolved,[22] and property rights acquired as a result of the decree are unaffected.[23] However, where an application is made within five years of the decree, such property rights can be varied by the court according to what is "fair and reasonable" in the circumstances, which can include an order to repay capital sums.[24] This is obviously very complicated in practice, so to simplify matters somewhat it is necessary to effect an insurance policy (at the expense of the estate) to safeguard against such a possibility.[25] Finally here, any criminal liability on the part of the reappearing "deceased" remains.[26]

TREATMENT OF HUMAN REMAINS

This is an area that perhaps falls more squarely within the area of medical ethics, but it is worthy of brief mention due to certain relevant legal principles. The essential issue is legal regulation of the manner in which human remains can be dealt with, regarding first what rights can be exercised over the body itself, and secondly of how that body might lawfully be disposed. These considerations, whilst macabre and unpalatable to some, have been the subject of no small number of legal disputes.

2–07

Rights in respect of a cadaver

The central principle here is fairly simple; no one has ownership rights over a dead body. It was stated with authority by Alison that "our practice acknowledges no property in the remains of deceased relations after they have been committed to the grave".[27] Prior to burial, the position is not, in a material sense, any different; a number of people might of course have lawful possession of the body, and might be entitled to have a say in respect of what is to be done with it, but they do not own it.[28] Indeed, there are a number of very seriously regarded criminal acts that might be committed in respect of how someone interacts with human remains, both prior to and after interment,[29] including the spectacularly titled offence "violation of sepulchres".[30]

2–08

An area that is perhaps more difficult, and certainly one that is very sensitive, is the question of using the deceased's body for purposes of organ donation. At common law, this was an area regulated more through the operation of civil law principles rather than criminal matters of theft or other related offences. Based on the ancient Roman law principles of *actio injuriarum* (a claim for hurt feelings

[22] Presumption of Death (Scotland) Act 1977 s.3(3).
[23] Presumption of Death (Scotland) Act 1977 s.5(1).
[24] Presumption of Death (Scotland) Act 1977 s.5.
[25] Presumption of Death (Scotland) Act 1977 s.6.
[26] Presumption of Death (Scotland) Act 1977 s.3(4).
[27] Alison, A., *Principles of the Criminal Law of Scotland* (Edinburgh: Law Society of Scotland/Butterworths, 1989), p.461.
[28] *Robson v Robson* (1898) 5 S.L.T. 351.
[29] See, e.g. *Dewar v HM Advocate*, 1945 J.C. 5.
[30] Hume, D., *Commentaries on the Law of Scotland Respecting Crimes* (Michigan: Gale, 2010), p.i, 85; see also *HM Advocate v Coutts* (1899) 3 Adam 50.

and affront to honour), it was possible to sue for damages as a result of unauthorised removal of organs from the body of a deceased. It can be observed that such cases were not commonly successful, though at times this was due to failures of a technical rather than ideological nature.[31]

At the turn of the 21st century, it emerged in highly-publicised circumstances that organs had been routinely removed from deceased infants at a number of hospitals across the UK, without the consent of parents. In Scotland, this ultimately resulted in the case of *Stevens v Yorkhill NHS Trust*,[32] in which the brain of a deceased one month-old child had been removed by doctors without their seeking consent from the child's parents. The mother sought a remedy against the health authority, and among a number of rulings, it was held that a claim for compensation based on the principles of *actio injuriarum* was still competent. The same surrounding events led to the passing of the Human Tissue (Scotland) Act 2006 (the HTSA 2006).

The HTSA 2006 has now been in force for some years, but it is still relatively new and as yet has been subject to little judicial interpretation. To briefly outline its relevant provisions, the general effect of the HTSA 2006 is that organ removal is permitted for the purposes of transplantation, research or education, provided that removal is conducted according to various requirements.[33] The most relevant of these is that authorisation must be obtained, either through the deceased having given this in life,[34] or through his nearest relative giving it in death.[35] "Nearest relative" is defined as the highest ranking person on a subscribed list, the first rank being occupied by a spouse, civil partner, or someone living with the deceased in the nature of such a relationship for a period of at least six months prior to death.[36] There are specific rules regulating authority in respect of children.[37]

The basic purpose of the HTSA 2006 is to ensure that the deceased's wishes about donation are respected, or in the case of children that parents are given the opportunity to decide. A person can, during life, express his wishes in various ways, such as through the use of a donor card, an entry on the National Health Service Organ Donor Register, an express provision in his will, or other written or verbal instructions. In the absence of this, a member of medical staff will timeously approach the nearest relative to enquire as to whether or not authorisation will be given. If there is either such authorisation, the hospital staff may proceed to harvest the organs according to the procedure outlined by the HTSA 2006.[38]

It remains competent to instruct that one's remains are to be donated to medical research or, more officially, for anatomical examination. This is regulated by statute under the Anatomy Act 1984, as amended, which requires that the request must have been made in writing, signed and witnessed.[39] The

---

[31] See, e.g. *Pollok v Workman* (1900) 2 F. 354 and *Conway v Dalziel* (1901) 3 F. 918.
[32] *Stevens v Yorkhill NHS Trust*, 2006 S.L.T. 889.
[33] Human Tissue (Scotland) Act 2006 s.3.
[34] Human Tissue (Scotland) Act 2006 s.6
[35] Human Tissue (Scotland) Act 2006 s.7.
[36] Human Tissue (Scotland) Act 2006 s.50.
[37] Human Tissue (Scotland) Act 2006 ss.8–10.
[38] Human Tissue (Scotland) Act 2006 s.11.
[39] Anatomy Act 1984 s.4(1A).

most common method by which this is achieved is to include instructions in a will, but the same wish could be expressed by some other means provided the requirements were complied with.

Disposal of human remains

There are a number of ways in which it is lawful to dispose of human remains. The traditional method, and the only one recognised at common law, is burial, although its regulation is now statutory and there are other methods that can lawfully be effected. It is, of course, possible to make a request regarding how one's remains are to be disposed of after death; such requests tend to be written into wills, or can even be agreed in meticulous detail through prepaid funeral plans. It is a matter of potential dispute that the wishes of the deceased, or those of relatives, in this regard will not necessarily be followed; who precisely is entitled to make a request regarding disposal, or indeed to ensure that one is carried out, is uncertain. There is currently no outright authority establishing who has the final say where there is disagreement, though the wishes of the deceased's spouse have been given significant weight in reported cases.[40]

2–09

Although burial is the traditional method, cremation is increasingly being employed as an efficient means of disposal. This is most likely influenced by a number of factors, such as a decrease in the availability of funeral plots (or "lairs"), and the associated rising costs of those that can be secured. Both involve legal formalities, as one would expect, though in-depth discussion of the specifics of these is beyond the scope of this book. Burial was previously regulated by the Burial Grounds (Scotland) Act 1855, and cremation was regulated by the Cremation (Scotland) Regulations 1935–1967. The current legislation on both is gradually being replaced by the Burial and Cremation (Scotland) Act 2016 which, although not yet fully in force, has been designed to provide a comprehensive legislative framework.

To consider another long lasting tradition among certain portions of the population, it is still legitimate for a body to be committed to the sea. This practice (known as "burial at sea") is regulated by statute[41] and supervised and administrated by Marine Scotland, an agency of the Scottish Government. A licence is required and the burial can only be carried out at an authorised site. Certain other conditions must be met, such as there being no immediate risk to the environment so, for example, a medical certificate requires to be issued confirming that the deceased was free of diseases that might give rise to water-born infection concerns.[42] Failure to comply with the requirements can have both criminal and civil consequences.[43]

If no one has made funeral arrangements in respect of a deceased, disposal of the body becomes the responsibility of the local authority.[44]

---

[40] See, e.g. *Robson v Robson* (1898) 5 S.L.T. 351.
[41] Food and Environment Protection Act 1985 Pt II.
[42] Further information can be obtained from the Marine Scotland website, available at: *http://www.gov.scot/Topics/marine* [Accessed 5 May 2017].
[43] See, e.g. *Herron v Diack*, 1973 S.L.T. (Sh Ct) 27.
[44] National Assistance Act 1948 s.50; this is set to be replaced by the Burial and Cremation (Scotland) Act 2016 s.87, but currently no date of commencement has been appointed.

SURVIVORSHIP

2–10   The basic rule of succession is that rights pass only to those who survive the deceased.[45] This is only logical, and in the vast majority of cases poses no problem, as it is not normally difficult to prove that one person has outlived another. However, complications can arise where more than one person dies at or around the same time, for example where two people are killed in the same car accident. Such "common calamities" often present difficult questions regarding inheritance, especially where, as is often the case, the parties involved are related or are close friends. Where it can actually be proved that one party survived the other, even by seconds, then rights may pass. However, in the absence of such proof, certain presumptions may have to be employed.

Common law

2–11   There is no minimum period required for which one party must have survived another. Under common law such survivance, however brief, required to be proven, and no presumptions would be made in the absence of relevant evidence. The result was that failure to prove survivance resulted in the failure of any claim that depended upon it. In *Drummond's JF v HM Advocate*,[46] a husband, wife and two children were killed in a bomb blast during the Second World War. Both husband and wife died intestate, the former survived by several siblings and the latter without surviving relatives. The result was that if the husband could be proven to have survived his wife and children, his siblings could claim both his estate *and* that of his wife. However, there was no evidence regarding survivorship between the couple, leading the husband's siblings to submit a claim, based on principles drawn from other legal jurisdictions, that he should be presumed to have survived his wife and children. The court rejected this claim, with the result that his estate passed to the Crown as *ultimus haeres*.[47] In the oft-quoted words of Lord Justice-Clerk Cooper:

> "Survivance is in every case a matter of proof, and … when a claimant … is unable to establish the fact of survivance, his claim necessarily fails."[48]

The application of the common law rule was strict, even if the result was clearly contrary to that intended by the deceased parties. In *Ross's JF v Martin*,[49] two sisters had "mirror-image" wills, with each leaving everything to the other, or to a named charity if the other sister predeceased. Both died as a result of a gas leak, and there was no indication as to whom had died first. Because, at common law, neither had survived the other, the "whom failing" provision of their wills could not operate. Both of their estates had to be divided according to intestate succession, which meant that the charity had no claim. Clearly this interpretation did not achieve the result the sisters would have wished.

---

[45] McLaren, 108.
[46] *Drummond's JF v HM Advocate*, 1944 S.C. 298.
[47] The operation of this particular principle is discussed in Ch.4.
[48] *Drummond's JF v HM Advocate*, 1944 S.C. 298 at 302 per Lord Justice-Clerk Cooper.
[49] *Ross's JF v Martin*, 1955 SC (HL) 56.

Statute

The severity of the common law in time gave way to somewhat kinder **2–12**
presumptions under statute. Until recently, legislation provided that where two
people die in circumstances that suggest simultaneous death, or that make the
order of death uncertain, the general rule is that the younger person is presumed
to have survived the elder.[50] This was subject to two exceptions.

First, where the parties were spouses or civil partners, the presumption is that
they died simultaneously and that neither survived the other. In effect, this means
that their estates are divided as though they had been single people. Secondly, if
the older person made a bequest in favour of the younger person, "whom failing"
to a third party,[51] and the younger person is intestate (or partially intestate), the
older party is presumed to have survived the younger, but for the purpose of that
bequest only. Although this provision seems complicated, its application is in fact
very logical, since it protects the position of the third party rather than allowing
the elder party's bequest to go to the younger party's heirs in intestacy; which, of
course, was not the elder's intention.

The 2016 Act introduced significant changes in this area. Most importantly, it
removes the basic presumption of younger surviving elder in a common calamity,
stating that where order of death is uncertain, each deceased is to be treated as
having failed to survive the other.[52] This, in effect, extends the previous exception
for spouses and civil partners to *all* persons. Further provision explicitly extends
the previous exception for destinations-over to *all* situations,[53] and no longer just
where the younger person is intestate. Although in some ways this seems to be a
reversion to the common law position, the additional provisions and subtle
difference in application would serve to avoid problems such as those
encountered in the *Ross* case. However, it would have no impact on a situation
such as encountered in the *Drummond* case, so perhaps this most recent
legislative change is best viewed as a compromise between the two previous
regimes. In any case, many modern wills provide that a beneficiary must survive
the testator for a certain period, often 30 days, to avoid most complicated
problems of survivance. To provide further clarity, the 2016 Act also states that
where there is any uncertainty regarding whether or not someone *has* survived for
a required period, they are deemed to have failed to do so.[54]

There is also provision in the 2016 Act for legacies that depend on the order of
death of beneficiaries within a defined group, for example, property that is
bequeathed to the "last surviving child" of the testator. If the only remaining two
or more members of the group die in common calamity, the benefit is to be
divided equally between their estates.[55] This section does *not* apply, however,
where the testator himself dies in common calamity with the remaining member
or members of the group; in such a case the legacy would simply fail.

[50] Succession (Scotland) Act 1964 s.31 (now repealed).
[51] Such a provision is known technically as a "destination-over"; see Ch.6.
[52] Succession (Scotland) Act 2016 s.9(1).
[53] Succession (Scotland) Act 2016 s.9(2).
[54] Succession (Scotland) Act 2016 s.11.
[55] Succession (Scotland) Act 2016 s.10.

CHAPTER 3

Property and Persons

INTRODUCTION

It is often remarked that a central question in the law of succession is "who gets   **3–01**
what?" This neatly summarises the purpose of this area of law, and strikes at the
two issues that form its very essence; property and persons. The deceased's
property is, of course, the subject of the law's concern, and the object is to ensure
that this property passes to the persons so entitled to inherit it.

There are a great many associated legal principles relevant to these two issues.
Due to the diversity of areas it is not possible to provide an exhaustive account of
them all in a book of this size. However, the following should provide sufficient
information to understand their context within the law of succession.

THE DECEASED'S ESTATE

A number of basic concepts regarding the deceased's estate were discussed in   **3–02**
Ch.1. To summarise briefly, in terms of classification the most significant
distinction is that made between heritable property, which for most practical
purposes means land and buildings, and moveable property, which incorporates
everything that is not heritable. All property, regardless of classification, is
relevant to the deceased's estate to the extent that it has a monetary value. The
payment of debts and liability to inheritance tax are also relevant here.

Classifications of property

In the majority of cases, it is easy to identify into which category any given item   **3–03**
of property falls. Most property is obviously either heritable or moveable by its
nature; the most simple example being land. That said, there can occasionally be
problems in this regard. The definition of heritable property requires that
anything other than the land itself must "accede" to (meaning, loosely, become
part of) the land, in terms of factors such as the degree of physical joining,
subordination of purpose and permanent attachment. So, a house is heritable
because it "accedes" to the land.

However, there is a question regarding structures that do not have the same
characteristics of permanence, such as a garden shed or a summer house. These
structures can be dismantled and moved without necessarily damaging them, but
many people would view it as common sense that they are buildings that

accompany a house in the same plot. There is physical joining in the sense that they are fixed to the land (at least to an extent), they serve a purpose that is subordinate to the land generally (i.e. storage or temporary occupation) and there is a degree of permanent attachment. There is, therefore, an argument in favour of either classification. Where there is such a question over whether property is one thing or another, cases are judged individually, on their own merits. For example, in *Christie v Smith's Executor*,[1] a summer house was deemed to have acceded to the land due to its weight and the contribution it made to a boundary wall; it was therefore heritable. The test applied in *Elitestone Ltd v Morris*[2] was whether or not the "secondary" property (i.e. the property in question) could be separated from the "principal" property (i.e. the heritage) without damage being done to either; although an English case, the same principle is relevant in Scotland.[3]

Fixtures and fittings

3–04   A common term used in this regard, particularly when referring to houses and their contents, is "fixtures and fittings". Fixtures are items that were moveable but have become part of the heritable property through accession, as described above. Fittings, on the other hand, are moveable property that can more easily be removed from the heritage. This is very relevant to succession because many wills direct that a house is to be inherited by one person, while the contents are to be inherited by another. This means that whoever is entitled to the house takes it inclusive of all fixtures but *not* the fittings; as these are moveable they are claimable by those entitled to the contents. It is similarly relevant to intestate succession (where there is no will) because different rights apply to different classifications of property.

The same questions apply as before; how to deal with situations where the exact nature is not clear? The principles above, which concentrate mainly on the physical relationship between the principal and secondary properties, are of course still relevant; in addition other considerations have been added to the tests by subsequent case law. There is strong authority for this by way of *Scottish Discount Co v Blin*,[4] where a bench of seven judges in the Court of Session held that the question of whether an item is a fixture should be decided on the basis of a number of considerations, including the intentions of the parties. Although this is perhaps more directly relevant to commercial contracts,[5] it is not difficult to see how it can also be applied to the law of succession by, if possible, examining the will to establish if the matter has been dealt with directly, or otherwise attempting the determine the intention of the deceased. In the absence of any such determination each case, again, would have to be decided according to its individual circumstances.

---

[1] *Christie v Smith's Executor*, 1949 S.C. 572.
[2] *Elitestone Ltd v Morris* [1997] 2 All E.R. 513.
[3] Both jurisdictions follow the leading case of *Brand's Trustees v Brand's Trustees* (1876) 3 R. (HL) 16.
[4] *Scottish Discount Co v Blin*, 1985 S.C. 216.
[5] See, e.g. the old case of *Syme v Harvey* (1861) 24 D. 202.

Conversion

One troublesome area is that of "conversion". This relates to the possibility that **3–05** the inherent nature of an item of property can be fundamentally altered so as to change its classification from one type to another. A simple example is naturally growing trees, which are heritable as long as they remain rooted in the ground.[6] If these trees are felled, however, then the timber they yield is obviously moveable; i.e. its essential nature has been altered. Of course, that timber could then be built into the structure of a house, facilitating another conversion (or perhaps a reversion?) to heritable property through the rules of accession.

Conversion becomes particularly problematic when the deceased's death causes an interruption to a planned process of how property is to be used. There is, in the law of succession, a particular legal fiction that allows certain moveable property to be "constructively" converted into heritage. This allows a change in its classification. Thus, money required for the completion of an unfinished building counts as heritage and heirs would not be able to claim legal rights out of it. In the old case of *Johnston v Dobie*,[7] it was held that building materials piled on the ground beside an incomplete structure counted as heritable property.

Goodwill

Certain other examples of property also give rise to complications. A useful **3–06** example is the goodwill of a business, which is incorporeal property as it lacks a physical body to which the five senses can be applied. As explained in Ch.1, this element of its nature is not really relevant for succession, but what *is* very relevant is whether it should be classed as heritable or moveable. Goodwill is an elusive concept at the best of times,[8] yet anyone buying or selling a business is well aware that it can be a valuable asset.[9] In fact, goodwill may be heritable or moveable, or a mixture of the two. If the business is closely associated with particular premises, such as a well-known and established hotel, the goodwill will generally count as heritable. If the reputation of the business relied mainly on the deceased's skill and personal reputation, the goodwill will be moveable. Obviously, there are times where the goodwill will be a mixture of the two and a precise apportionment between heritable and moveable may well be problematic. A related rule regarding businesses can be found under s.22 of the Partnership Act 1890, which states that a partner's share in a firm's assets count as moveable, even if some or all of these assets are actually heritable, such as a farming partnership.

---

[6] *Paul v Cuthbertson* (1840) 2 D. 1286. This can be contrasted with cultivated crops which are more likely to be considered moveable; *Begbie v Boyd* (1837) 16 S. 232.

[7] *Johnston v Dobie* (1783) Mor. 5443.

[8] For a recent case in which the nature of goodwill was considered for tax purposes see *Greenbank Holidays Ltd v Revenue and Customs Commissioners* [2011] UKUT 155 (TCC).

[9] Mentioned in the recent English case of *Petterson v Ross* [2013] EWHC 2724 (Ch).

Valuation of the deceased's estate

3–07   As explained in Ch.1, the person tasked with "ingathering" the deceased's estate is called the executor. It is a very important requirement of this office that all relevant property, howsoever classified, is identified and included in the deceased's estate. The executor is also responsible for arranging valuation of the estate. Many of the rules regarding valuation are derived from rules of inheritance tax, since this is a matter of significant consideration. It is worth noting that there are also various specialist rules that relate directly to valuation for taxation purposes, some of which are distinct from the "general" rules of valuation.

There are various specialist rules that relate directly to valuation for taxation purposes, some of which are distinct from the "general" rules of valuation.

The most basic rule is that property is valued according to the price that it might reasonably be expected to achieve if sold on the open market.[10] Some assets will require to actually be sold before those entitled to inherit can actually derive their benefit; it is often the case, for example, that a deceased has directed that a house be sold and the proceeds divided amongst various beneficiaries. In other, admittedly rarer cases, there can be a bar to the actual transfer of assets, such as might be imposed on the sale of certain company shares, or the assignation of a lease. These assets must still be valued, however, with the relevant valuation being as if they are to be the subject of a "hypothetical" sale.[11]

There are, inevitably, some potentially difficult areas here. One that gives rise to particular problems is heritable property; this is, of course, significant primarily because the deceased's house will, if it forms part of the estate, likely be the most valuable single asset by some margin. It is also liable to cause trouble because the deceased's death can interrupt the completion of some legal or financial process, very commonly the repayment of a loan secured on a house or, perhaps even more problematic, a transfer of heritable property that is only partially complete.

3–08   If the deceased had agreed to sell heritable property but, at the time of death, the transaction had not been settled, the heritage would count as a heritable asset with a nil-value but the amount of the price unpaid would be a moveable asset, as would any sum already paid to account. If the deceased had, conversely, agreed to buy heritable property but had not paid for it, that property would count as a heritable asset and the unpaid price would be a moveable debt. In a point worthy of reiteration, this is not merely an academic distinction, because different rights can be claimed against different classifications of property; the legal right to claim a portion of an estate that in actuality has a nil-value is, of course, of no practical use.

If the deceased's heritable property was mortgaged, i.e. if funds had been provided for its purchase subject to a standard security being taken by the lender, the debt, or outstanding loan amount, counts as heritable and is deducted from the value of the heritage. If the deceased was a creditor in a standard security over another person's property, the value of the security counts as moveable but not in respect of legal rights or taxation, where it counts as heritable (this simply means that legal rights cannot be claimed out of the value of the standard security). The word "mortgage" is used popularly to describe a loan advanced to a buyer of

---

[10] *IRC v Crossman* [1937] A.C. 26.
[11] *Baird's Executorr v IRC*, 1991 S.L.T. (Lands Tr) 9.

heritable property, though strictly speaking this term is inaccurate; this is a technical matter far beyond the scope of this book, and the term is used here for reasons of convenience.

Many people who have received a loan secured over their property will have some form of mortgage protection policy to pay off the outstanding capital sum in the event of death. It is important to note that, in general, the secured loan is a heritable debt and the proceeds of the policy count as a moveable asset, although the latter actually depends on the terms of the policy and the agreements that has been made. The point, however, is that the heritable debt is not automatically extinguished by the moveable asset, even if in practice this is what will ultimately be effected. This is considered further later in this chapter.

If the loan is an endowment mortgage, the debtor pays interest only but, in addition, pays premiums on an endowment insurance policy which, at the end of its term or on the earlier death of the insured, will produce (in theory!) at least an adequate sum to repay the original amount borrowed. In a traditional endowment mortgage, the debt is doubly secured. There will be a standard security over the heritable property and the insurance policy will have been assigned to the lender and that assignation duly intimated to the insurance company. In such a case, the debt would be deducted from heritable and moveable estate in proportion to the respective values of the heritage and the policy. If the policy has not been properly assigned to the lender, the debt is not doubly secured and all the proceeds simply count as a moveable asset. It is probably fair to say that this, again, is a very technical area on which the reading of specialist texts is to be advised.

Inheritance tax

As mentioned in Ch.1, inheritance tax is a specialist field which is generally beyond the scope of this book. However, it is an important area in succession and executry practice so brief consideration is warranted, even if it is with the caveat that governments can, and do, change their minds.

Taxing a deceased's estate is a method of revenue-raising that has existed for centuries. A number of different mechanisms were imposed during the 1700s and 1800s, resulting in a piecemeal and complicated system, the focus being on what a deceased owned at the time of his death. This allowed an obvious form of avoidance whereby an older person could transfer the bulk of his property before death. By the late 19th century a more integrated system was being introduced[12] that, among many other things, led to the extension of the rules of taxation to include the value of disposals made during the few years preceding death. For most of the 20th century, the main tax payable upon death was called "estate duty",[13] replaced briefly by capital transfer tax.[14] In 1986, this was replaced by "inheritance tax".[15]

3–09

---

[12] See, e.g. the Customs and Inland Revenue Act 1881.
[13] Under various Finance Acts passed between 1894 and 1969.
[14] Under the Finance Act 1975.
[15] Under the Inheritance Tax Act 1984 and the Finance Act 1986.

Under the current legislation, inheritance tax is charged on the loss of value caused to an estate when a transfer is made,[16] unless it is an exempt transfer[17]; death counts as a transfer of the entire estate.[18] If a transfer is made more than seven years before death, it is exempt and no inheritance tax is paid on that property. Thus, if someone gives his son £100,000 and dies 10 years thereafter, no tax is payable on that sum. But if he dies one year after making the transfer, the result is different because tax is payable; although even when a transfer is made within the seven year period, the tax actually due may be reduced by "taper relief" depending on when, within that period, the gift was made.[19]

It was also stated in Ch.1 that no inheritance tax is payable until the value of an estate exceeds a certain "threshold", and there are certain transfers of property on which no inheritance tax is due[20]; debts and funeral expenses can also be deducted from the total value of the estate in calculating inheritance tax. By way of reminder, at the time of writing the threshold is £325,000 (for tax year 2017/2018),[21] though in October 2007 a mechanism was introduced to allow any unused exemption from a deceased's estate to be transferred to a surviving spouse or civil partner, effectively increasing the survivor's threshold to (potentially) £650,000.[22] Further, an additional nil-rate band is currently being phased in which allows transfer of a single heritable property to descendants, provided it has been used as a residence by the deceased. As of April 2017 this band is £100,000, and is set to increase annually until it reaches £175,000 in 2021.[23] Also by way of reminder, inheritance tax is payable at the rate of 40 per cent of any excess in the net estate over the exemption threshold. In practice, executors may well have to obtain some form of credit, such as an overdraft or bridging loan, to pay the tax.

PAYMENT OF DEBTS

3–10   As far as creditors are concerned, the executor is the same person as the deceased, in accordance with the Latin maxim *"eadem persona cum defuncto"*. The executor is liable to the creditors to the same extent as the deceased was. However, the liability of the executor is clearly limited to the amount of the deceased's estate, provided he has first obtained confirmation, i.e. the court's authority to administer the estate. By the same principle, beneficiaries are technically liable for the deceased's debts up to the value of their inheritance, but in practice this is very rarely relevant since the debt will be paid as far as possible from the estate before any distribution is made to beneficiaries; so if the beneficiaries receive nothing (or a reduced amount) they may not even realise that this was because money they *might* have been entitled to has been used to

---

[16] Inheritance Tax Act 1984 s.1.
[17] Inheritance Tax Act 1984 s.2.
[18] Inheritance Tax Act 1984 s.4.
[19] Inheritance Tax Act 1984 s.7.
[20] See Ch.9.
[21] Inheritance Tax Act 1984 s.7 and Sch.1, as amended by the Finance Act 2014.
[22] Inheritance Tax Act 1984 ss.8A–8C, inserted by the Finance Act 2008.
[23] Inheritance Tax Act 1984 ss.8D–8M, inserted and amended variously by the Finance (No.2) Act 2015 and the Finance Act 2016.

pay off debts. That said, on occasion the rule is relevant, as demonstrated by *Menzies v Poutz*.[24] Here, a widow succeeded to her late husband's entire estate, and four years later was declared bankrupt and her estate sequestrated. It transpired that her late husband has also been bankrupt, and an action was brought by *his* creditors for sequestration. The court held that any action against the husband's estate was no longer competent since it had vested in his widow, but the husband's creditors *were* given a preferential claim in the widow's sequestration.

Schemes of payment

The executor must pay all known debts before anything, even income, goes to beneficiaries.[25] It is common for the payment of lawful debts to be directed in a will, but this is unnecessary; the payment of debts is a legal requirement, not something which falls to the discretion of the deceased, the executor or beneficiaries.

3–11

Historically, the deceased's creditors were paid on a "first come, first served" basis. This of course raised the possibility that creditors who had not timeously received word of the deceased's passing, or were otherwise slow to affect their claims, might find the estate already exhausted and have to write off their debt. There is an inherent unfairness in this, and with the emergence of modern bankruptcy law the rule was altered so that all creditor claims made within six months of the date of the deceased's death rank equally with each other, or "pari passu".[26] Payment cannot be compelled within this six-month period, and if the executor does so he risks being held personally liable if it transpires that the estate has insufficient funds to pay other creditors as well. After the six-month period the executor is no longer personally liable to later claimants, provided he has acted in good faith.[27] There are, however, certain creditors who *may* safely be paid during the six-month period, if the debt is regarded as "privileged", since these require to be paid before other creditors. Most significant here are funeral expenses and the categories of "preferred debts" as outlined below. Unless an executor is satisfied that the estate can meet all debts in full, he would be most unwise to pay any ordinary unsecured creditor until six months have expired from the date of death.

Even after the six month period has expired, the executor is still bound to pay any valid claim from a creditor, assuming he still has funds in hand to do so. If the executor is aware that valid debts have not been paid and he still distributes the whole estate to beneficiaries, he can find himself personally liable to pay such debts. Beneficiaries under wills frequently complain that they have to wait too long for their money. In fact, this is often due more to perception than to reality. Having paid out all debts, an executor may, a year at most after the death, start paying the beneficiaries.

The payment of debts is an area that was developed by common now, but is now regulated by statute, specifically by bankruptcy legislation. This might seem

---

[24] *Menzies v Poutz*, 1916 S.C. 143.

[25] *Heritable Securities Investment Association Ltd v Miller's Trustees* (1892) 20 R. 675.

[26] Act of Sederunt, Act anent Executors-Creditors, 28 February 1662.

[27] *Stewart's Trustees v Eans* (1871) 9 M. 810.

confusing at first glance, because of course most estates are *not* consumed entirely by debts; in other words most estates are solvent rather than insolvent. However, it is actually very logical since there are in reality very few situations where a person's debts require to be assessed and paid en masse; bankruptcy is one and death is the other.

Order of payment

3–12   The current law is contained within the Bankruptcy (Scotland) Act 2016, which recently overhauled bankruptcy law in Scotland; that said, it did not fundamentally alter the principles to be applied here. In keeping with older versions of the legislation,[28] creditors are arranged according to a statutory "rank",[29] based on the nature of the debt owed. The executor must pay the creditors in each rank in full before moving onto the next. If at any point it is not possible to settle a debt in full, certain rules of insolvency apply; these are considered below.

(1)   Deathbed and funeral expenses are payable before all others. They cover reasonable medical expenses of the deceased's last illness as well as funeral expenses, subject again to the reasonableness test. Also included are the expenses of confirmation and the executry administration.

(2)   Secured debts speak for themselves. A secured creditor is in a good position in that he can generally enforce his debt at any time. If the secured property is worth more than the debt (including interest), the creditor must account for the surplus to the estate. If the security is worth less than the debt, the creditor can rank for the deficit against the estate, but only as an ordinary creditor in respect of that proportion. A security covers any valid security granted by the deceased over his own property or implied by law, such as a landlord's hypothec.

(3)   Preferred debts, which in practice most commonly means wages owed to employees (up to certain statutory limits).

(4)   Ordinary unsecured debts also speak for themselves.

(5)   Inheritance tax (IHT), in practice, is paid first, often by means of a temporary overdraft, since confirmation cannot be obtained until it is paid. Nevertheless, it actually ranks last in order of priority. The point is academic; it stands to reason that if there is no estate, no IHT is payable.

Insolvent estates

3–13   Insolvency is a financial state of affairs whereby there are insufficient assets to pay all debts in full. It is a concept that can be applied to any person or legal entity; when applied to an individual, the term commonly used is "bankruptcy". The legal process by which a bankrupt person's assets are distributed to creditors is called "sequestration". The same terminology is applied to a deceased's estate which can, therefore, either be solvent or insolvent.

---

[28]   Previously the matter was governed by the Bankruptcy (Scotland) Act 1985, as amended.

[29]   Bankruptcy (Scotland) Act 2016 s.129(1).

In terms of payment of debts, broadly speaking the same rules apply regardless of whether an estate is solvent or insolvent. There is one important addition to the ranks in the latter case; any expenses of sequestration must be paid before any other debts are considered. The difference is also relevant to the process of paying out funds. If, at any point, payment of a rank exhausts the estate, no further debts can be paid and must be written off. Hence, those creditors who are ranked in higher positions are safer than those ranks in lower positions as they are more likely to receive the full value of their debts. Claimants in each class rank pari passu, so if there are insufficient funds to pay all creditors within a rank, their payments are reduced proportionately so that each receives an equal percentage of the debt owed.[30]

If an executor has reason to believe that there will be insufficient funds to cover the debts of the deceased, he should be advised, at the earliest date possible, to have a judicial factor or a trustee in bankruptcy appointed. If an executor knows, or clearly ought to know, that an estate is insolvent and he fails to take appropriate steps, the executor's intromissions (i.e. actions in respect of the estate) may count as vitious (i.e. unauthorised). In such a situation, the executor becomes personally liable for the debts of the deceased.

Incidence of debts

Another matter to be addressed is what is called the "incidence" of debts. It was mentioned in the Ch.1 that the distinction between heritable and moveable estate is still crucial in the law of succession. It was also alluded to earlier in this chapter that the question is bound to arise as to which parts of the estate are liable for which debts. The basic rule is simple: heritable debts are paid out of heritage and moveable debts out of the moveable estate. In a solvent estate, the incidence of debts is almost certain to affect various rights that can be exercised against different parts of the estate.

3–14

A debt is heritable if it is secured over heritable property. Nowadays, such a charge would be effected by a standard security recorded in the General Register of Sasines or registered in the Land Register. Other debts are paid out of moveable property, unless the will provides otherwise.

It has already been noted that problems can, and do, frequently arise when a heritable debt exists but the amount of the debt is covered by an insurance policy. Many mortgages have the capital sum covered by life assurance. Borrowers are often under the impression that, should they die during the life of the mortgage, the capital sum will automatically be repaid. It is necessary to underline the fact that a mortgage is a heritable debt and the proceeds of an insurance policy count as a moveable asset. The two do not automatically cancel one another out. A surviving spouse, under intestate succession, can take the matrimonial home (subject to certain rules and upper limits), but takes it subject to any existing security. Since the proceeds of the policy are moveable, these may be subject to other claims with the result that the funds available to the surviving spouse are diminished, and might not be sufficient to pay the outstanding debt over the house. In effect, the spouse may have inherited the house but not the funds with

---

[30] Bankruptcy (Scotland) Act 2016 s.129(5). For an old illustration of the historical approach see, e.g. *Peter v Monro* (1749) Mor. 11852.

which to pay for it. This can lead to the situation where a house must be sold, which is often not the desired result of anyone concerned.

The matter becomes more complicated if there are two securities for the one debt. The heritable property will have been validly mortgaged to the lender by a standard security. (In the case of security granted prior to the Conveyancing and Feudal Reform (Scotland) Act 1970, this would have been effected by a bond and disposition in security or by an ex facie absolute disposition. These obsolete forms of security are of declining significance, but might still be encountered occasionally.) However, in some mortgages, a life insurance policy will also be formally assigned in security to the lender. To put this another way, the debt is doubly secured. In such a case, the debt must be deducted from the heritable and moveable property in proportion to the values of the two securities.

If any asset in the estate, whether heritable or moveable, is subject to a creditor's right of security, the beneficiary can only take that asset subject to the debt. In *Stewart v Stewart*,[31] a beneficiary was left the proceeds of an insurance policy. As the policy had been assigned to a creditor as security for a loan, the beneficiary was only entitled to the net proceeds.

If the will is well drafted, it may specify its own incidence of debts. So, if a house is left to a beneficiary "free of debt", then any outstanding mortgage has to be paid off out of the residue of the estate.

ENTITLEMENT TO INHERIT

3–15
As will be demonstrated when considering will provisions in Ch.6, the law of succession is generally very liberal; the law does not lightly seek to intrude on the personal wishes of what someone wants done with their property after death. It will be seen that there are certain purposes or conditions that the law will not allow, but there are far fewer restrictions on whom may benefit under a will. So, if someone decides to leave the bulk or, in some cases, the entirety of their estate to an unexpected beneficiary, there is a good chance that this will be followed.

However, the above is significantly qualified by certain indefeasible rights enjoyed by close family members to the deceased. It was mentioned in Ch.1 that a spouse or civil partner and any children of the deceased occupy the strongest positions in terms of succession. Indeed, it is only these limited relations who can be said to have anything close to a guaranteed entitlement to inherit. Other family members, and even cohabitants of the deceased who are unrelated (at least in a formal sense) to the deceased, might enjoy certain rights under intestate succession, but these are very much subordinate to those of spouse, civil partner or children and can be defeated by a will.

The entitlements of these various parties are outlined in detail in the later chapters of this text; that is not the current matter at hand. The purpose of this section is to consider the circumstances in which someone might be barred from inheriting under a deceased's estate, due to them having been involved in certain nefarious activities. The following rules can even bar from inheriting someone who would enjoy otherwise indefeasible rights.

---

[31] *Stewart v Stewart* (1891) 19 R. 310.

Bars to inheritance

In many legal systems, certain factors are recognised which bar an individual   3–16
from inheriting, either under the rules of intestacy or under the terms of a will. It
is common in some jurisdictions for rules of formal validity to stipulate that
anyone involved in the drafting of a will, or witnessing its signing, must be
independent; there are obvious risks of fraudulence if such an individual stands to
benefit under a will, since he has a very real interest in its terms. In general,
however, Scotland does not impose quite so strict rules on entitlement to inherit
and, as a very general rule, only an "unworthy heir" is barred from inheriting.

The unworthy heir

Broadly speaking, a person may be deemed an unworthy heir if his conduct has   3–17
been such that it would be unlawful, or highly undesirable, for him to inherit
property. Under the very old Parricide Act 1594, a man who had "slain his father
or mother" could not inherit lands or title, and would also be deemed to have
surrendered the rights of his descendants.[32] However, the precise terms and scope
of this Act were unclear, resulting in difficulties regarding its interpretation and
application. One major hurdle was that a positive conviction for murder was
required. In *Oliphant v Oliphant*,[33] it had been established that a man had slain
his mother, but he fled and was legally deemed a fugitive. His brother sought a
declarator that he should be disbarred from inheriting in respect of their father's
heritable estate, and that his own heirs should also be so debarred. However, the
court held that the Act's terms could not be extended and that, in the absence of a
murder conviction, it therefore did not apply. Another problem with the Act,
again due to its limited scope, was that it did not preclude someone from
inheriting if they had murdered their spouse.

Public policy

A concept developed by English law, later adopted in Scotland, is that of "public   3–18
policy" preventing someone from inheriting as a result of their crimes.
Historically, this was a principle so rigorously applied that anyone convicted in
England of treason or felony would be deemed to have "forfeited" their property
to the Crown. Although this very broad rule was abolished,[34] the application of
the general policy continued in regards to unlawful killing. In the case of *Cleaver
v Mutual Reserve Fund Life Association*,[35] a woman who had murdered her
husband was debarred from taking the proceeds of a life assurance policy she
would otherwise have been entitled to.

There is also the notorious case of "Dr Crippen", who had inherited his wife's
estate upon her death but was convicted of her murder and executed. Prior to his
execution he made a will in sole favour of his mistress, which was successfully

---

[32] Parricide Act 1594 s.1.
[33] *Oliphant v Oliphant* (1674) Mor. 3429.
[34] Under the Forfeiture Act 1870.
[35] *Cleaver v Mutual Reserve Fund Life Association* [1892] 1 Q.B. 147.

challenged by his wife's family on the basis that his estate had been illegitimately enlarged by the inheritance of his wife's.[36] The "special circumstances" of the case were remarked upon.

There is a question of scope regarding the rule of public policy. Both the *Cleaver* and *Crippen* cases involved convictions for murder; more difficult are convictions for manslaughter or culpable homicide. In *Tinline v White Cross Insurance Association Ltd*,[37] a driver had been convicted of manslaughter after knocking down and killing a pedestrian. The question arose as to whether his conviction should bar him from claiming indemnity under his insurance policy upon being sued in respect of the losses caused; the court held that he had not lost his rights under the policy. However, in succession cases a stricter approach was taken, such as *Hall v Knight and Baxter*[38] in which a woman convicted of manslaughter was debarred from inheriting under the deceased's will. Similarly, in *Re Giles, Deceased*,[39] a woman convicted of the manslaughter of her husband could not inherit, despite significant evidence of diminished responsibility. In *Gray v Barr*[40] it was noted that manslaughter varies in seriousness and might not always bar a relevant claim, and that the logical test is whether the claimant was guilty of deliberate and unlawful violence resulting in death. Despite the emphasis placed on the *possibility* of manslaughter not being a bar to claiming, the result in this case was that the claimant was so debarred. A rare exception was made in *Re H, Deceased*,[41] where a husband had killed his wife whilst experiencing a psychotic episode, and had been convicted of manslaughter. The trial judge had held that he was not responsible for his actions and a treatment order had been made under mental health legislation; the forfeiture rule was held not to apply in the circumstances.[42]

To further illustrate the distinction of the public policy approach from the strict terms of the Parricide Act, it was also held that an actual conviction was not required for someone to be debarred. In *Re Dellow's Will Trusts*,[43] a husband and wife had been found to have both died from gas poisoning. Evidence indicated that the wife had unlawfully killed her husband, but of course a conviction was impossible; nevertheless it was held that her estate could not be enlarged through inheritance from his.

The Scottish position

3–19   In terms of the equivalent Scottish position, for many years it had been presumed that similar rules applied; it was part of the common law that an unlawful killer could not benefit from his crime and thus could not inherit from the person killed. Despite the wide range of English cases in point, the matter had not actually been

---

[36] *Crippen, in the Estate of* [1911] P. 108.
[37] *Tinline v White Cross Insurance Association Ltd* [1921] 3 K.B. 327.
[38] *Hall v Knight and Baxter* [1914] P. 1.
[39] *Re Giles, Deceased* [1972] Ch. 544.
[40] *Gray v Barr* [1971] 2 Q.B. 554.
[41] *Re H, Deceased* [1990] 1 F.L.R. 441.
[42] The rarity of this as an exception can be illustrated by the later case of *Jones v Roberts* [1995] 2 F.L.R. 422, which also involved a killing brought about by psychosis and in which the rule was strictly applied.
[43] *Re Dellow's Will Trusts* [1964] 1 All E.R. 771.

tried in the Scottish courts, and in practice estates had been administered on the understanding that the unlawful killer could not inherit.

The matter was first considered judicially in the sheriff court case of *Smith, Petitioner*.[44] Here, it was held that there was an absolute bar on inheriting if there was a conviction against the heir for murder or culpable homicide. Though this decision was not cited in the later case of *Burns v Secretary of State for Social Services*,[45] a similarly strict finding was reached. In *Burns*, a woman who had been the target of abuse at the hands of her husband for some years finally retaliated and stabbed him, pleading guilty at trial to culpable homicide. The Inner House of the Court of Session approved the test outlined in the English *Gray* case, and discussed at length the variable circumstances possible in cases of culpable homicide. Nevertheless, in the circumstances it was held that she was debarred from claiming a widow's allowance.

Statutory development

The position was altered in respect of both England and Scotland by way of later statutory development. The law first moved on as a result of the Forfeiture Act 1982 (the 1982 Act), which provided a statutory definition of the public policy rule, viz   **3–20**

> "the rule of public policy which in certain circumstances precludes a person who has unlawfully killed another from acquiring a benefit in consequence of the killing."[46]

It also extended the definition to explicitly include any person "who has unlawfully aided, abetted, counselled or procured the death of that other".[47]

It was recently remarked in judicial observation that this section did not necessarily serve to codify the rule or set it out in full, and that when applying it reference still required to be made to decided cases.[48]

The 1982 Act also gave the court a discretionary power to modify the extent of the forfeiture in the case of "unlawful killing" short of murder.[49] In Scotland, this would mean that forfeiture could, but need not be, modified in the case of culpable homicide. In *Gilchrist, Petitioner*,[50] a wife had been convicted of the culpable homicide of her husband. The evidence at her trial had shown that she had suffered emotional abuse due to her husband's adultery, and that she had been in a depressed and suicidal state of mind at the time of the offence. The offence itself had constituted two stab wounds, which had proved fatal due in large part to her husband having a chronic kidney disease. The wife had been admonished, essentially meaning she had been found guilty but, in the circumstances, would not be subjected to any substantive punishment. She then raised a petition seeking an order under the 1982 Act to modify the extent of the common law rule by which she could not benefit from her own crime. It was held that, in all the

---

[44] *Smith, Petitioner*, 1979 S.L.T. (Sh Ct) 35.
[45] *Burns v Secretary of State for Social Services*, 1985 S.L.T. 351.
[46] Forfeiture Act 1982 s.1(1).
[47] Forfeiture Act 1982 s.1(2).
[48] *Henderson v Wilcox* [2015] EWHC 3469 (Ch).
[49] Forfeiture Act 1982 s.2.
[50] *Gilchrist, Petitioner*, 1990 S.L.T. 494.

circumstances of the case, an order modifying the rule in respect of 80 per cent of the estate was appropriate; in effect, then, she forfeited 20 per cent of her inheritance.

Although the modification of the forfeiture is at the discretion of the court, it was held that the 1982 Act did not allow the court to modify the forfeiture to the extent of excluding it entirely. In *Cross, Petitioner*,[51] a man had pled guilty to the culpable homicide of his father. In light of the circumstances and considering psychiatric and social enquiry reports, the trial judge, Lord Cowie, had handed down a sentence of 18 months' imprisonment. The same judge presided over the claimant's petition for a modification of the forfeiture rule in respect of his father's estate and was of the opinion that, were it within his power, he would have excluded the operation of the rule entirely. However, he was persuaded that the court did not have this power; accordingly, he modified the forfeiture to the extent of 100 per cent in relation to the heritable estate and to 99 per cent in relation to the moveables.

Another troublesome aspect of the 1982 Act was that it did not prescribe the exact manner in which the person excluded from inheriting was to be treated for other succession purposes. In many jurisdictions the person debarred is treated as having predeceased. This was not the case in either England or Scotland, though under common law the correct approach was not clear. In the English case of *Re Calloway*[52] a woman had killed her mother, her son and then herself. She had been named as beneficiary in her mother's will. The Crown argued that her estate should be enlarged by the inheritance of her mother's before forfeiture, with the result of course that the Crown would be able to claim both. The court held, however, that the legacy simply lapsed, and so the mother's estate was declared intestate; it went to the excluded woman's brother rather than the Crown.

In the Scottish case of *Hunter's Executors, Petitioners*,[53] a wife had been killed by her husband. Her will made provision for her husband, naming alternative beneficiaries in the event that he should die before her. This is a very common will provision called a "destination-over".[54] As the husband had not, as a matter of fact, predeceased the alternative beneficiaries, the destination-over could not operate and the subjects of the provisions fell into intestate succession. Whilst it is difficult to fault the logic of this decision, and indeed it had the same effect as in the *Calloway* case, it is unlikely that the result favoured the wishes of the deceased.

Forfeiture under the Succession (Scotland) Act 2016

3–21   The Scottish Law Commission had long recommended that certain rules of forfeiture, the above areas included, be the subject of further statutory development.[55] This was achieved to an extent by way of the 2016 Act, under which three important amendments to the legal position are made.

---

[51] *Cross, Petitioner*, 1987 S.L.T. 384.
[52] *Re Calloway* [1956] 2 All E.R. 451.
[53] *Hunter's Executors, Petitioners*, 1992 S.L.T. 1141.
[54] These are given further consideration in Ch.6.
[55] Scottish Law Commission, *Report on* Succession (Scot. Law Com. No.215, 2009) paras 7.1–7.5.

First, the matter dealt with immediately above has been clarified. A person excluded from inheriting under the forfeiture rule is now deemed to have predeceased or, in the preferred term generally of the 2016 Act, "failed to survive".[56] This is a welcome change that addresses the problem highlighted by the *Hunter's Executors, Petitioners* case above. Secondly, the court is given discretion to modify the extent of the forfeiture rule so as to exclude it entirely where appropriate.[57] As illustrated by the *Cross* case above, the court had already engineered a way to allow near-exclusion of the rule anyway; still, it is convenient for statute to put the matter beyond doubt. Finally, the Parricide Act 1594 has at last been repealed.[58] Again, the practical implications of this are almost entirely non-existent, but it is probably fair to say that the removal of this archaic Act from the statute books is also to be welcomed; its value, such as it ever was, can safely be relegated to that of a historical curiosity.

The 2016 Act still does not provide a comprehensive statutory definition of the forfeiture rule, nor is the 1982 Act repealed under its provisions; although, of course, amendments and additions have been made. It would seem, then, that the common law principles relevant to this issue will continue to be applied where the legislation remains silent.

---

[56] Succession (Scotland) Act 2016 s.12.
[57] Succession (Scotland) Act 2016 s.15.
[58] Succession (Scotland) Act 2016 s.17.

CHAPTER 4

Intestate Succession

INTRODUCTION

As outlined in Ch.1, a person is said to be "intestate" when he dies without   **4–01**
leaving a will or other testamentary writing to direct how his estate is to be
distributed after his death. This is by far the most common situation to which the
rules of intestate succession are applied, but it is not the only one. It may be, for
example, that the deceased *has* left a testamentary expression of his wishes, but
for some reason this expression is wholly or partially ineffective. Or, the deceased
may have left a perfectly valid will, but which does not make provision for the
entire estate. It might also be the case that a beneficiary under a will simply
rejects his benefit, either for personal or financial reasons.

In any of these situations, the rules of intestate succession will determine how
the estate (or its effected part) is to be distributed. These rules are largely
inflexible, most having been laid down in statute by the 1964 Act, though there
remains a common law influence also. The lay person often assumes that the
division of an estate under the rules of intestate succession is likely to be more
complicated than where there is a will giving clear instructions. In fact, it is not
administratively any more difficult to divide an intestate estate, and in some ways
it is even easier; executors have no will to interpret, virtually no discretion, and
must simply apply the rules. Criticisms of intestate succession, and the
accompanying urging among the legal profession for people to make a will, come
instead from a far more social perspective, in that the inflexible rules of division
may not reflect what the deceased's wishes would actually have been.

BACKGROUND AND CONTEXT

The rules of intestate succession are of great significance. It is estimated that over   **4–02**
60 per cent of adults in Scotland do not have a valid will, and that even among
persons aged over 65 the figure for those not having made provision for their
estates upon death is around 30 per cent.[1] With a large proportion of the
population in this position, it is vital that the rules to be applied upon intestacy are
fair and equitable. Of course, any such rules can be circumvented by the simple
act of leaving a valid and comprehensive will, but since in practice these rules
will likely govern a significant number of estates, they must be fit for purpose.

---

[1] O'Neill, S., *Wills and Awareness of Inheritance Rights* (Scottish Consumer Council, 2006).

It is this task of identifying the proper purpose that first gives rise to a major problem for lawmakers. Those seeking to devise or amend rules of intestacy face an unenviable challenge, for there is not universal agreement as to what their proper purpose should be. It has long been widely accepted that making provision for those closest to the deceased is appropriate, but this inevitably raises the question of how "those closest to the deceased" ought to be defined. The view most widely supported historically is that the deceased's surviving family must be provided for, and so should take the majority (or even the entirety) of the estate.[2] This is an easily defended view, which is based in deep-rooted common law traditions regarding one's moral (and as a corollary, legal) responsibilities to support one's family. It also has the benefit of certainty because, at least in the majority of cases, it will be obvious who is connected to the deceased by family relationship.

However, it is certainly not without problems. There are a number of contentious issues to consider, such as which members of the family should be entitled to inherit, whose entitlement should take precedence over whose and, not least, the question of how "family" should even be defined in modern times. This last issue is an essential concept, since there can be no doubt that family dynamics have changed considerably over the past few decades.[3] Even finding an answer to the question of whom should have a valid claim, there remains the issue of determining exactly how much they should be entitled to inherit or, to look at the matter as a whole, how division should be effected among all of those so entitled.

It is clear, then, that this is an area fraught with ideological pitfalls. As will be seen, whilst the broad stance taken by the law of intestate succession in respect of the questions above has remained fairly consistent, there have been a raft of welcome advancements regarding application of the relevant principles. These have far from silenced the calls for reform, however, so it is perhaps fair to say that, despite centuries of jurisprudential development, it would appear that an ideal solution remains elusive.

The historical position

4–03   Prior to the major statutory developments affected during the 1960s, intestacy was regulated largely by the common law, peppered with sporadic and specialised legislative provisions. The result was a patchwork of rules affecting different parts of the deceased's estate, and under which various individuals could benefit. This piecemeal regulation, and the sometimes-complicated interaction between the various rules, makes presenting a concise summary challenging, but several significant points can be drawn out and subjected to useful analysis.

An appropriate starting point is the distinction between heritable and moveable property, which is of crucial importance since the rules and mechanisms governing their disposal were very different.[4] Also of significance

---

[2] Stair, III, 4, 2.

[3] See, e.g. Ellis, T., *Scotland's Population: The Registrar General's Annual Review of Demographic Trends* (National Records of Scotland, 2015).

[4] The distinction between these types of property is explained in Ch.3.

are the so-called legal rights that were enjoyed by certain family members. Finally, the minor statutory inroads that were made during the 19th and early 20th centuries are worthy of consideration.

Heritable property

The rules regarding heritage were derived from feudal traditions and dictated that heritable property should pass, directly and undivided, to a single person entitled to succeed, the so-called "heir-at-law". Historically, males were preferred over females for this, partly due to the patriarchical nature of traditional Western civilisations, but also (and perhaps more pragmatically) because of the common requirement in medieval times for military service to be performed as payment for tenure of land. The principles directing the identification of the heir-at-law heavily reflected this influence.

4–04

First in line to inherit were direct descendants of the deceased, with a preference for males as already mentioned, and also for the eldest, under the custom of "primogeniture", i.e. preference for the first born. This is why, in practice, it was most often the case that the deceased was succeeded by his eldest son, who would take all land and heritable titles that had belonged to his father. Thus, the continuation of the deceased's legacy was ensured in a majority of cases.

In absence of direct descendants, "collaterals" (siblings) of the deceased could inherit, again with a preference for males but *not* for the eldest. Instead, according to the rule "heritage descends", the deceased's immediate younger brother would be heir-at-law or, if the deceased himself was the last born, then his immediately elder brother would be. Half-blood siblings were eligible in absence of full-blood, provided the shared parent was the father; a half-blood sibling sharing a mother had no claim.

If there were no collaterals of the deceased, the final broad class of claimants was paternal ascendants, i.e. father, grandfather and so on. Again, collaterals within a particular generation required to be considered before ascending further, so the deceased's father's siblings would have a claim before the deceased's grandfather, whose siblings would have a claim before the deceased's great-grandfather, and so on. Among these, primogeniture applied, as did the male preference. Maternal ascendants were entirely excluded, as was the deceased's spouse.

To all of the above, the principle of "representation" applied, meaning that an heir who had predeceased (i.e. died before the deceased) could be "represented" by his or her own direct descendants. In other words, any descendant of someone who would have inherited as heir-at-law could take the place of that ancestor, even if this meant that a more distant relative inherited in favour of a closer one. For example, a child of a predeceasing eldest son (i.e. a grandchild of the deceased) would inherit rather than a younger child of the deceased. Primogeniture and male preference applied to these representatives in the same way as with other classes of claimant.

If no male heir could be identified, females were entitled to inherit, though they would not necessarily do so individually as a male would. Two or more females in the same, nearest degree of relationship to the deceased would share the heritage equally and were known as "heirs portioners". There was little regard for primogeniture, except in that the eldest had a right to any indivisible subjects as a *praecipuum* (a share or bonus), for example the principal mansion house of a landed estate. Representation applied to allow female descendants to inherit in the stead of their predeceasing ancestors, but the claim was only to that which would have been due to the predeceased. As a result, division could become somewhat complicated if the heirs portioners were spread across degrees of relationship to the deceased or, perhaps worse, somewhat contentious if claimants inherited inequally despite being in the *same* degree of relationship to the deceased. For example, if a deceased had two daughters, one of whom predeceased him but left two daughters of her own (i.e. granddaughters of the deceased), the surviving daughter would be entitled to half the heritable estate, and the surviving granddaughters to a quarter each. If, however, *both* daughters had predeceased, one having had two daughters and the other having had just one, then the division would be the same, with the lone granddaughter taking half, and the paired granddaughters taking a quarter each.[5]

Given the extent of potential claimants, it was very likely that a blood relation of the deceased, even if somewhat remote, could be identified as the heir-at-law. However, in the event that one could not, the Crown would inherit the heritage as *ultimus haeres* (last heir). The Crown's interests were represented by the Queen's and Lord Treasurer's Remembrancer, a position that still exists as part of the Crown Office[6] and still serves this function, in addition to dealing with all other ownerless property.

Moveable property

4–05   Under the old common law, moveables were treated quite differently from heritables. The principal rule was that the moveable estate would be inherited by the deceased's "next of kin", i.e. the person closest to him according to degree of relationship. At first glance, this may appear similar to the identification of the heir-at-law for purposes of heritage, but the principles directing who would be next-of-kin were very different.

Of foremost significance was the distinction that the moveable estate could far more readily be shared among a number of claimants. Because there were no responsibilities associated with it as there were with the heritage, there was no impetus for the moveable estate to remain intact, and therefore it was not necessary to identify a single heir. This meant that the deceased's next-of-kin could actually be composed of a number of people, comprising any and all surviving members of the *class* of relation closest to the deceased. In determining which class would be the next of kin, the rules of propinquity as applied to heritables were generally followed, i.e. children having the primary claim, followed by collaterals, then paternal ascendants.

Provided at least one survivor could be identified in a given class, that survivor would inherit the entire moveable estate, or share it equally with other survivors in the same class. The principles of primogeniture and male preference did not apply, meaning that younger members had as good a claim as elder, and

---

[5] It is worth noting that this latter rule did *not* apply to moveable property.
[6] The position is actually held by the Crown agent.

female members as good a claim as male. However, maternal ascendants were still excluded, as were half-blood collaterals who shared a mother with the deceased. Half-blood collaterals who shared a father with the deceased had full rights, but these were secondary to those of full-blood, even if this favoured a more remote class. So it was that in *Gemmil v Gemmils*,[7] a claim made by the children of a full-blood sister (i.e. by nephews and nieces of the deceased) was preferred to that made by a half-blood sister.

Representation did not apply to moveables at common law. Only surviving members within a class could succeed, and the rights of any predeceasing members were lost, serving only to increase the benefit to the survivors. This principle is well-illustrated by the case of *Ormiston v Broad*,[8] in which six first cousins of an intestate had claimed her entire moveable estate as next of kin. The pursuer was the son of a predeceasing first cousin who claimed, along with several others, that he should be entitled to a share as a representative under a recent statute[9] which had tentatively opened up the possibility of representation in moveable succession in limited circumstances. The court held that the statute did *not* open up representation to the extent pled by the pursuer, and that the common law position in his case remained unchanged. Thus, he and his co-claimants were not entitled to any share.[10]

Similarly as with heritable property, if no next of kin of the deceased could be found, the moveable estate would revert to the Crown as *ultimus haeres*.

Collation inter haeredes

Given the different rules that applied to identification of the heir-at-law and next of kin, it was entirely possible that a deceased's estate could be passed down two separate lines of succession. At the same time, it was also entirely possible for one individual to be identified as the rightful beneficiary of both the heritable and moveable property. Neither situation was particularly problematic.

4-06

A *third* possibility, however, was that an individual could be identified as heir-at-law, and also as next of kin, but alongside others for purposes of the latter. There was a perceived inequality in allowing the heir-at-law to share in the moveable estate in addition to being given the entire heritage, and so there emerged the doctrine of collation *inter haeredes*. This allowed, in certain circumstances, the combining of a mixed estate into a single fund, which would be distributed according to the rules of moveable property only.

The general principle in this circumstance was that the heir-at-law was barred from also sharing in the moveable estate as next of kin. This was illustrated in *Law v Law*,[11] in which the heritable heir of a deceased was prevented from also claiming moveable assets, which were to be shared equally between his brothers.

However, if the heir-at-law so chose, he could "collate" his heritable estate into a single common fund with the moveables. This fund would then be

---

[7] *Gemmil v Gemmils* (1729) Mor. 14877.
[8] *Ormiston v Broad* (1862) 1 M. 10.
[9] Intestate Moveable Succession (Scotland) Act 1855.
[10] The unanimous judicial construction given to the Act was that it allowed for representation only as regards descendants of siblings of the deceased, i.e. nieces and nephews.
[11] *Law v Law* (1553) Mor. 2365.

distributed among all members of the class constituting next of kin, including the heir-at-law. To paraphrase Balfour's report of the *Law* case above[12]:

> "No person succeeding as heir to his father's lands should have any part of moveable goods, except where he confers his whole heirship with the rest of the moveables, so that an equal parting might be made between him and the rest of the children."

It is worth noting that collation *inter haeredes* could not be invoked where the heir-at-law was *not* also a member of the class constituting next of kin. In *McCaw v McCaws*,[13] the heir-at-law was a nephew of the deceased, whilst the next of kin were the deceased's two sisters. The value of the moveable estate was far greater than the heritage, leading the heir-at-law to argue that he was entitled to collate the heritage and claim a rateable portion of the entire estate. This claim was unanimously rejected by the judges.

Legal rights

4–07   Operating alongside the rules governing heritable and moveable property generally were a number of protected entitlements called "legal rights". These were claimable by a surviving spouse and/or any children of the deceased, before the general rules of division were applied. Although subject to significant subsequent reform, certain of these rights survive in modern times, and as such are given separate treatment later in this chapter. Consideration here will, as a consequence, be brief and will focus chiefly on the historical aspects.

The first of these was the surviving spouse's right of "liferent" over a certain portion of the deceased's heritable property. Liferent itself is considered elsewhere,[14] but in essence means the right to use and derive financial benefit from property, without having the right to sell or otherwise dispose of it. A widow had the legal right of "terce", which entitled her to a liferent of one-third of the heritage owned by her husband at the time of his death. This right was based on the oft-encountered obligation placed upon a husband to provide for his family, but in practice was often of little real benefit, being a right only to net income after various deductions, and being subject to a number of exclusions. A widower had a corresponding right known as "courtesy", giving him a liferent of the *whole* heritage belonging to his wife at the time of her death, again subject to certain deductions and exceptions. The right of courtesy was dependent on their having been a child born of the marriage who was heir to the deceased. As such, courtesy can be observed as having developed less as the right of a husband than as the right of a father to an heir.[15]

The second category of legal rights comprised those claimable against the moveable estate. These were the widow's right of *jus relictae*, the widower's right of *jus relicti*, and the children's right of *legitim*. These rights remain in force. Worthy of mention here, however, is the fact that historically there was no

---

[12] Also quoted in *Law v Law* (1553) Mor. 2365.
[13] *McCaw v McCaws* (1787) Mor. 2383.
[14] See Ch.6.
[15] Stair, II, 6, 19.

representation permitted in legal rights, meaning that only surviving children of the deceased could claim *legitim*.[16] This is no longer the case.

The general nature of legal rights has not altered over time. Historically they have always been, and they remain, indefeasible except in certain rare circumstances. On the other hand, it has always been possible for them to be renounced by those entitled to them.

Statutory reform

In the mid-19th and early-20th centuries, a number of statutory provisions were introduced which altered certain rules of division, and gave additional rights to certain family members. Of foremost significance here was the Intestate Moveable Succession (Scotland) Act 1855 (the 1855 Act).

4–08

This Act provided the first statutory definition of representation, and allowed for representation in moveable succession with two important limitations.[17] First, those who could represent were limited to direct descendants of the deceased, and descendants of the deceased's collaterals.[18] Secondly, representation could only be made in terms of the moveable estate unaffected by legal rights,[19] and so it still did not apply to *legitim* claims.

The 1855 Act also improved the position of parents. Under s.3, the father of an intestate deceased had a right to claim one half of the moveable estate in preference to collaterals (or their descendants) claiming as next of kin, whilst under s.4 the mother was granted a right to one third of the moveable estate in the same circumstances, if the father had predeceased.[20]

A final change brought about by the 1855 Act was to allow claims on an intestate estate by half-blood siblings sharing a mother with the deceased.[21] This right was to one half of the moveable estate, and applied only where the deceased left no issue, had no collaterals of the full-blood or half-blood sharing a father, and had been predeceased by both parents. In the absence of other heirs, the remaining half of the estate went to the Crown.

A question did arise over the use of the term "next of kin". This matter came under judicial scrutiny in *Turner v Couper*,[22] concluding with the judgment that representation begins at the nearest class in which there are surviving members. The introduction of these statutory preferences, and the judicial interpretation given them, meant that in practice those who inherited moveable estate were not always limited to the "next of kin" as defined by common law.

---

[16] See, e.g. *McMurray v McMurray's Trustees*, 1852 4 D. 1048.

[17] Intestate Moveable Succession (Scotland) Act 1855 s.1.

[18] This was the matter at issue in the *Ormiston* case, discussed above.

[19] Intestate Moveable Succession (Scotland) Act 1855 s.9.

[20] This right was later made equal to that of the father, by the Intestate Moveable Succession (Scotland) Act 1919.

[21] Intestate Moveable Succession (Scotland) Act 1855 s.5.

[22] *Turner v Couper* (1869) 8 M. 222.

The present position

4–09 By the early 1900s it was widely accepted that reform was overdue. In 1911, spouses were given a limited protected right to inherit over and above their legal rights.[23] However, it was not until the Mackintosh Report in 1950 that a platform for major reform was outlined. This led, in time, to the passing of the 1964 Act, which has since been the cornerstone of succession law in Scotland. In outline, the process of intestate division involves three distinct stages, each of which must be calculated and deducted from the estate in turn. These stages are prior rights, legal rights, and rights to the free estate (also known as dead's part). These stages are now considered in turn.

PRIOR RIGHTS

4–10 "Prior rights" is the name given to the entitlement of a surviving spouse (or civil partner[24]) to make certain claims against a deceased's estate. The intention behind prior rights is to ensure that a surviving spouse's basic needs are provided for upon the death of his or her partner, and the specifics of the rights themselves are based on the assumption that if the deceased *had* left a will, at least part of its terms would have sought to achieve this aim.[25] However, this is only an assumption; if the deceased has actually left a will, even a will whose provisions are entirely contrary to the spirit of prior rights, then these assumptions are defeated and the rights do not apply. It is of utmost importance, then, to remember that prior rights only ever arise in intestate succession. This is unlike some other rights that are claimable by surviving family members, which will be considered in due course.

It should also be noted that cohabitees are not entitled to claim prior rights, although they can make an application to court to be awarded a capital payment or property transfer from the deceased's estate. This issue is considered in more detail later in this chapter.

General nature of prior rights

4–11 Prior rights were an innovation of the 1964 Act. Although there had previously been some tentative statutory inroads made regarding a spouse's rights, these were widely regarded among the legal community as inadequate in the circumstances of the times.[26] In an effort to address this inadequacy, three specific rights were set out by ss.8 and 9 of the 1964 Act, rights which endure to the present day. These allow a surviving spouse to claim ownership or tenancy of a dwelling-house, a share of relevant furniture and plenishings, and a certain sum

---

[23] Intestate Husband's Estate (Scotland) Act 1911.

[24] By virtue of the Civil Partnership Act 2004 Sch.28(1), the rights of a civil partner in this regard are identical to those of a spouse. For brevity, reference is made chiefly to the "spouse" throughout this chapter, but anything stated in this context can be taken to apply equally to civil partners. It should also be noted that same-sex couples are now permitted to marry under the Marriage and Civil Partnership (Scotland) Act 2014.

[25] Mackintosh Report, para.6.

[26] Mackintosh Report, para.10.

of money from the estate. Each of these three rights is subject to a prescribed maximum value, which is increased from time to time in line with inflation and other relevant factors.

There are a number of important points to note regarding prior rights. First, the three rights outlined by the Act are independent of each other. Whilst it would be logical for a surviving spouse to claim a dwelling-house in satisfaction of the first right, and its contents in satisfaction of the second, the application of these rights need not be so straightforward. For example, the claiming of furniture and plenishings from within a dwelling-house is not dependent on that dwelling-house having been claimed beforehand. Having said that, the rights *must* be applied in the statutory order, satisfying one (if possible) before considering the next; if at any point a right exhausts the *entire* estate, then the remaining rights are rendered worthless.

It should also be noted that representation does *not* apply to prior rights. Descendants of a predeceasing spouse have no entitlement to claim, which for practical purposes means that stepchildren have no claim on the deceased's estate. Also worthy of mention is that prior rights, if unclaimed, "prescribe" after 20 years, meaning they cease to be enforceable.[27]

Dwelling-house right

The first prior right, then, is the dwelling-house right. Regulated by s.8(1) of the 1964 Act, this entitles the surviving spouse to the ownership (or, in limited circumstances, tenancy) of any one "dwelling-house" owned (or tenanted) by the deceased at the time of his death. The intention behind this right is clearly to allow a surviving spouse to continue living in the family home, or at least to inherit a sufficient sum to make alternative living arrangements. At the time of its creation, this was a hugely important right, since historically there was a risk that one spouse (more often the wife) might be rendered homeless upon the death of the other, if the family home was owned by the deceased and then passed on to the heir-at-law. In modern times, with co-ownership between spouses being far more common, it is possible that the significance of this right has diminished somewhat; separate arrangements are often put in place regarding the transfer of ownership of a co-owned house upon the death of either party.[28]

Qualifying criteria

There are two main qualifying criteria that must be satisfied in order for a surviving spouse to claim under the dwelling-house right.

First, the deceased must have had a "relevant interest" in a "dwelling-house" for this right to apply. "Dwelling-house" is given a rather broad definition, being a building or

> "a part of a building occupied as a separate dwelling … including any garden or portion of ground attached to, and usually occupied with, the dwelling house".[29]

4–12

4–13

---

[27] Prescription and Limitation (Scotland) Act 1973 s.7 and Sch.1 para.2(f).
[28] See Ch.9.
[29] Succession (Scotland) Act 1964 s.8(6)(a).

Flatted residences are clearly intended to be included. "Relevant interest" is defined as the interest of an owner or a tenant,[30] both of which face potential complications. The interest of an owner is subject to any heritable debt secured on the property, for example a standard security granted in favour of a lender who provided the original purchase funds.[31] Any such debt will be deducted from the value of the property in determining the value of the relevant interest. In practice, such debts will almost always be offset to some extent by a life assurance policy over the deceased, though the effect of this will depend entirely on the policy's particular terms. The interest of a tenant is heavily restricted, specifically excluding tenancies regulated by the Rent (Scotland) Act 1984. In practice, various other common types of lease are also excluded, with succession rights being regulated by separate legislation, so it is actually very unusual for a lease to be taken over by virtue of this right.

Secondly, the surviving spouse must have been "ordinarily resident" in the dwelling-house on the date of the deceased's death.[32] "Ordinarily resident" is not defined by the 1964 Act, but seems to mean simply that the surviving spouse must have resided in the property at some point, even if only for a short time.[33] The definition would not include a property which was clearly not intended to be occupied by the surviving spouse, such as a premises used purely for business purposes, or a premises used solely as a holiday let; however these properties would always certainly qualify if they were *also* used as a personal residence. The residence of the deceased is not relevant, meaning that it *would* be possible for a surviving spouse to claim the dwelling-house right in respect of a property owned, but not occupied, by the deceased.

Where there are two or more properties that meet the qualifying criteria, the surviving spouse must, within six months of the intestate's death, elect only one to be the subject of the claim.[34] This choice is made entirely at the claimant's discretion, be it influenced by convenience, maximum financial benefit, or a compromise between the two. It need not be related to any similar election made in respect of the right to claim furniture and plenishings.

Value of the dwelling-house right

4–14   The 1964 Act places an upper limit on the value of property that can be claimed under the dwelling-house right, and indeed on the other prior rights. These upper limits effectively aid in striking a balance between the competing interests of, on the one hand, ensuring that a surviving spouse is adequately provided for and, on the other, allowing for inheritance by the deceased's heirs (in particular, issue).

In terms of the dwelling-house right, it seems it has always been the intention that all but the most valuable properties would fall within its prescribed sum. When the right was introduced in 1964, the upper limit was set as £15,000, whilst

---

[30] Succession (Scotland) Act 1964 s.8(6)(d).

[31] This is commonly known as a "mortgage", although strictly speaking that term is imprecise.

[32] Succession (Scotland) Act 1964 s.8(4).

[33] The test is most likely not as strict as that of "habitual residence", which itself is none too strict and is a question of fact in the circumstances; see, e.g. *Dickson v Dickson*, 1990 S.C.L.R. 692 and *Morris v Morris*, 1993 S.C.L.R. 144 which, although cases dealing residence of children, have on occasion been referred to in questions of succession.

[34] Succession (Scotland) Act 1964 s.8(2B)(a).

the average house price in the UK was around only £3,250.[35] The current prescribed sum for the dwelling-house right is £473,000,[36] which was set in February 2012 against an average UK house price of around £225,000.[37] Clearly, then, the sum has remained generous, in line with the intention that a surviving spouse should, in most cases, be able to claim the dwelling-house outright. Indeed, the likelihood of the prescribed sum being entirely sufficient is increased by the requirement to deduct any outstanding debt secured over the property, and by the increase in popularity of joint home ownership between couples. On this latter point, it is worth emphasising that the right is claimed over the *deceased's share* of the dwelling-house only. In cases of joint ownership, the surviving spouse already owns half the value, so in effect the *total* value of a qualifying dwelling-house could be as much as £946,000, i.e. twice the upper limit of £473,000.

There is, however, still a possibility that the dwelling-house in question might have a value greater than the prescribed sum. In such a case, the surviving spouse is *not* entitled to claim the dwelling-house outright, but is instead entitled to claim the prescribed sum from the estate. There are two potential issues in this regard.

The first issue is that of uncertainty regarding the nature of the debt owed under these circumstances. The wording of the Act does not make it clear whether the right to claim the prescribed sum constitutes a heritable or moveable debt on the estate. A monetary debt is typically moveable in nature, but here that monetary debt is intrinsically linked to heritable property; so which part of the estate is liable for it? This is not merely an academic distinction, as it could have a significant effect on the value of subsequent rights against the estate. Although the matter is debatable, compelling arguments have been made, based largely on considerations of private international law, for the debt to be heritable.[38]

The second issue, which may depend upon the resolution of the first, and also on the makeup of the estate otherwise, is that the dwelling-house in question might require to be sold in order to raise the necessary funds with which the payment will be made. There is an argument that this undermines the purpose of the dwelling-house right somewhat, and it has been considered that in such cases the surviving spouse should perhaps have a right to pay the "excess" value into the estate and claim the dwelling-house as a whole, hence preventing it having to be sold. Whilst this may well be a sensible suggestion, at present there is no such right, and any arrangement to this effect would have to be made with the co-operation of the executor.[39]

A final point worthy of note here is that, should there arise any question regarding the true value of the deceased's interest, this is to be answered by a single arbiter at arbitration. Where there is no agreement regarding the appointment of an arbiter, one shall be appointed by the sheriff responsible for the

---

[35] Scottish Law Commission, *Report on Succession* (Scot. Law Com. No.215), para.2.12.

[36] Succession (Scotland) Act 1964 s.8(1)(a), set by the Prior Rights of Surviving Spouse and Civil Partner (Scotland) Order 2011.

[37] Office of National Statistics, *Statistical Bulletin: House Price Index February 2012* (ONS, April 2012).

[38] Meston M., *The Succession (Scotland) Act 1964*, 5th edn (Edinburgh: W. Green, 2002), p.134.

[39] The Scottish Law Commission have most recently concluded that this is, on balance, unlikely to be necessary in practice; *Report on Succession* (Scot. Law Com. No.215), paras 2.17–2.18.

county of the deceased's domicile or, where this cannot be determined or where the deceased was domiciled outwith Scotland, by the Sheriff of the Lothians and Peebles at Edinburgh.[40]

Exceptions to the general rules

4–15 Section 8(2) of the 1964 Act provides for two exceptions where, despite the deceased having had a relevant interest of a value below the prescribed sum in a qualifying dwelling-house, the surviving spouse will *not* be permitted to claim that interest. Instead, the surviving spouse will be entitled to claim the value of the deceased's interest as a cash sum.[41] These exceptions are designed to deal with cases where there might be difficulties created by transferring the interest itself to the surviving spouse.

The first exception is relevant to tenanted properties only. It applies where the dwelling-house forms only *part* of the subjects comprised in one tenancy or lease under which the intestate was the tenant.[42] This is admittedly very rare in practice.

The second, and far more commonly encountered, exception is relevant to both ownership and tenancy interests. It applies where the dwelling-house forms the whole or part of subjects used by the intestate for carrying on a trade, profession or occupation, *and* the value of the estate as a whole would be substantially diminished if the dwelling-house were disposed of as a separate asset.[43] There are numerous examples where this might be the case in practice, but the one typically given is that of a working farm; clearly the value of the business as a whole would be significantly reduced if the farmhouse were removed from the estate.[44]

Dwelling-house right example

4–16 Alan has died intestate, survived by his wife Betty. Before Alan's death the couple lived together in their jointly owned marital home, which has a value of £300,000. Alan also solely owned a holiday cottage worth £160,000, in which the couple would spend a few months of the year.

It is likely that both these properties would qualify as "dwelling-houses", so Betty must choose one or the other in exercising her right. (She cannot claim both, even though the combined value would still be lower than the threshold sum.)

Claiming Alan's share of the marital home has the benefit of convenience, but would mean she receives a benefit of only £150,000 from her dwelling-house right. Claiming the holiday cottage would be more beneficial financially, since

---

[40] Succession (Scotland) Act 1964 s.8(5).
[41] Succession (Scotland) Act 1964 s.8(1)(a)(ii).
[42] Succession (Scotland) Act 1964 s.8(2)(a).
[43] Succession (Scotland) Act 1964 s.8(2)(b).
[44] It is worth noting that the 1964 Act now makes specific provision for the succession of leases relating to crofts, by virtue of the Crofting Reform etc. Act 2007; see Succession (Scotland) Act 1964 s.8(2A).

the right would be worth £160,000, but leaves a potentially troublesome situation regarding ownership of the marital home. It is up to Betty to balance these two considerations and make her decision.

Right to furniture and plenishings

The second prior right entitles the surviving spouse to claim furniture and plenishings belonging to the intestate. This is regulated by s.8(3) of the 1964 Act, and in many ways is a logical extension of the dwelling-house right. Indeed, its purpose is similar; to allow a surviving spouse to continue his or her present living arrangements, with minimum disruption. That said, the right to furniture and plenishings is not dependent on the dwelling-house right, and can be claimed regardless of whether or not the dwelling-house right has been exercised.

Qualifying criteria

There are, again, a number of qualifying criteria that must be satisfied in order for a surviving spouse to claim furniture and plenishings. In part these are broadly similar to those required for the dwelling-house right, although there are some important variations.

The first qualifying criterion is that the items in question must form part of the intestate estate. This may seem obvious, but it is an important condition when considering items that may have been in the possession of the deceased without being owned by him or her. Goods leased by the deceased are a common example, and clearly are to be excluded. Goods obtained under a hire-purchase agreement are also excluded, since ownership in them does not transfer to the buyer until the final payment is made.[45]

The second is that the items must be located in a dwelling-house in which the surviving spouse was ordinarily resident. The definitions of "dwelling-house" and "ordinarily resident" (such as can be established) are the same as those relating to the dwelling-house right, though it is important to note that the deceased *need not* have had an interest in the dwelling-house itself in order for the surviving spouse to claim its contents. As previously, if there are two or more qualifying dwelling-houses that contained furniture and plenishings owned by the deceased, the surviving spouse must, within six months of the intestate's death, elect only one to be the subject of the claim; he or she may not "pick and choose" from more than one dwelling-house.

The third is that the items must constitute "furniture and plenishings" as defined by the 1964 Act. According to this definition, furniture and plenishings "includes garden effects, domestic animals, plate, plated articles, linen, china, glass, books, pictures, prints, articles of household use and consumable stores".[46] This is an unusual definition in that certain items are specifically identified, whilst other elements are left unhelpfully vague. There can be no doubt as to whether something is "linen" or "a book", but "articles of household use"

4–17

4–18

---

[45] This can be contrasted with goods purchased under a credit sale agreement, in which ownership in passes to the buyer immediately. The amount outstanding constitutes a debt that can be claimed against the estate.

[46] Succession (Scotland) Act 1964 s.8(6)(b).

suggests an inclusiveness to the definition beyond that specifically identified; which may beg the question of why anything should be specified at all. Indeed, the very use of the term "includes" reinforces the idea that the list is not exhaustive. Specifically *excluded* are

> "any article or animal used at the date of death of the intestate for business purposes, or money or securities for money, or any heirloom".[47]

"Heirloom" is somewhat vaguely defined as

> "any article which has associations with the intestate's family of such nature and extent that it ought to pass to some member of that family other than the surviving spouse".[48]

It is not difficult to appreciate the motivation behind this exclusion, i.e. to ensure the passing of family heirlooms down a blood line, but no further guidance on the treatment of such heirlooms is provided by the Act, arguably leaving the job unfinished, as it were. This is especially apparent when legal rights are considered, which also allow a surviving spouse to claim items of moveable property, but under which there is no similar exclusion. Finally here, it is generally accepted that motors cars do *not* constitute furniture and plenishings, although the Act is silent on the matter and arguments for inclusion in exceptional circumstances have been put forward.[49]

Value of the furniture right

4–19 As with the dwelling-house right, the 1964 Act places an upper limit on the value that can be claimed by the surviving spouse in terms of furniture and plenishings. This upper limit has been increased incrementally since the creation of the right in 1964, and the current maximum value is £29,000.[50] It is interesting to note that this value has increased not nearly so steeply as that of the dwelling-house right, which is perhaps reflective of the dramatic changes that have been wrought in the Scottish housing market since the 1960s.

The practical effect of this right is that, where qualifying items have an aggregate value of not more than £29,000, the surviving spouse can claim the whole of them. Where the aggregate value exceeds this figure, the surviving spouse may choose items worth a total of £29,000, entirely at his or her own discretion.

Again as with the dwelling-house right, should there arise any question regarding the true value of an item to be claimed, this should be answered by a single arbiter at arbitration. The same rules apply regarding appointment of such an arbiter.[51]

---

[47] Succession (Scotland) Act 1964 s.8(6)(b).
[48] Succession (Scotland) Act 1964 s.8(6)(c).
[49] Meston M., *The Succession (Scotland) Act 1964*, 5th edn (Edinburgh: W. Green, 2002), p.44.
[50] Succession (Scotland) Act 1964 s.8(3)(a), set by the Prior Rights of Surviving Spouse and Civil Partner (Scotland) Order 2011.
[51] Succession (Scotland) Act 1964 s.8(5).

Furniture right example

Christine has died intestate, survived by her husband Daniel. Before Christine's   **4–20**
death the couple lived together in a privately rented house. Christine's share of
the furniture and plenishings has been valued at £32,000.

Daniel is entitled to exercise his right to furniture and plenishings, but only up
to a value of £29,000. He must choose which items he wishes to claim; the
remainder will pass according to the ordinary rules of intestate succession.

Right to financial provision

The third, and final, prior right entitles the surviving spouse to receive from the   **4–21**
intestate estate a financial sum, up to a certain value. This is regulated by s.9 of
the 1964 Act, and although such provision had been tentatively legislated on
previously, it was acknowledged that the rights were probably not adequate. The
purpose of the right is similar to that of the other prior rights, i.e. an attempt to
avoid the problem of a surviving spouse being left destitute upon the death of the
deceased. However, the right to financial provision differs from the previous two
rights in that, as will be seen, its terms seek to acknowledge certain other
competing rights to claim on the intestate estate.

Qualifying criteria

The right to financial provision is claimed from the "intestate estate",[52] which the   **4–22**
1964 Act clearly defines as the net remaining estate *after* satisfaction of the
dwelling-house and furniture rights.[53] So, it is important to note that the right to
financial provision is additional to the s.8 rights, but at the same time is
postponed to their favour.

Clearly, then, there must be remaining estate before the right to financial
provision can be claimed. If there are insufficient funds to allow the full relevant
value of the right to be claimed, then the right is satisfied by the transfer of the
entire remaining estate to the surviving spouse.[54] In such a case the surviving
spouse will also be entitled to be appointed executor.[55] In practice, it is actually
very common for the right to financial provision to exhaust the deceased's estate
in this manner.[56]

Of course, there is also the possibility that there will be more than enough
available estate to satisfy the right to financial provision in full. In this case, a
proportionate sum towards the full value of the right is payable respectively from
the available heritable and moveable portions of the estate.[57] To illustrate this
simply, if the available estate is composed of three-quarters heritable property

---

[52] Succession (Scotland) Act 1964 s.9(1).
[53] Succession (Scotland) Act 1964 s.9(6)(a).
[54] Succession (Scotland) Act 1964 s.9(2).
[55] Succession (Scotland) Act 1964 s.9(4). On executors see Ch.11.
[56] Scottish Law Commission, *Report on Succession* (Scot. Law Com. No.215), para.2.14.
[57] Succession (Scotland) Act 1964 s.9(3). See Ch.3 on the distinction between heritable and moveable
property.

and one-quarter moveable property, then three-quarters of the right to financial provision must be borne by the heritable estate, and one-quarter by the moveables.

The above rule serves two purposes. First, it increases the chances of the surviving spouse receiving the full value of the right to financial provision. If the right could be exercised over only one type of property or the other, then in mixed estates there is a chance the surviving spouse might receive less than the full value of the right, despite there being sufficient estate available. Secondly, it goes some way towards protecting the rights of subsequent claimants on the estate, in particular the legal rights of children or further issue, which can only be claimed against moveables.

There is a very important caveat to the above in that, in practice, the sums actually paid over to the surviving spouse need not, in fact, have been drawn proportionately from the respective parts of the estate. This seems contradictory, but to enforce such division in actual payment amounts might lead to inconvenient or undesirable outcomes, such as the forced sale of property. If it is more convenient, then the actual property made over to the surviving spouse can be heritable, moveable or indeed a mixture of the two. This will not be taken into account for the purposes of the calculation outlined above, and therefore makes no difference to the value of subsequent claims.

Value of the right to financial provision

4–23   As with the s.8 prior rights, there is an upper limit on the value that can be claimed by the surviving spouse in terms of financial provision. However, unlike the s.8 rights, the maximum value of this right depends on an as yet unconsidered factor; the presence or absence of issue of the deceased.

Where the deceased is survived by issue in addition to a surviving spouse, the maximum value of the right to financial provision is £50,000.[58] Where the deceased left no issue, the surviving spouse can claim up to £89,000.[59] The distinction is interesting because it demonstrates the balance that legislators attempted to strike between increasing the rights of the surviving spouse and acknowledging the fact that issue should also have a right to participate in the distribution of the deceased's estate. Of course, prior rights as a whole place the claims of issue very much as a secondary consideration, and critics would argue that this sole concession is insufficient.[60]

The definition of "issue"

4–24   Given that the presence or absence of issue of the deceased is so critical to the right to financial provision, it is important to define exactly what this means in this context.

---

[58] Succession (Scotland) Act 1964 s.9(1)(a), set by the Prior Rights of Surviving Spouse and Civil Partner (Scotland) Order 2011.
[59] Succession (Scotland) Act 1964 s.9(1)(b), set by the Prior Rights of Surviving Spouse and Civil Partner (Scotland) Order 2011.
[60] See the commentary on reform later in this chapter.

The first point to note is that only issue *of the deceased* need be taken into consideration. The presence or absence of issue of the claimant is not relevant. In many cases, of course, issue of the deceased will also be issue of the claimant, and it is likely that this was the expectation of the legislators. However, in modern times this is far from always the case, and so the distinction is important. The short point here is that "stepchildren" of the deceased do not constitute issue for purposes of the right to financial provision.

The second point is that "issue" has its ordinary meaning within the context of succession. Historically there has been significant development of this definition, but it is now well established that "issue" includes illegitimate as well as legitimate children,[61] and adopted as well as natural children.[62] These matters are further considered later in this chapter.

Right to financial provision example

Edward has died intestate, survived by his civil partner Frederick, and a son from a previous relationship. Edward's estate contains moveable property amounting to £100,000.

4–25

After any relevant dwelling-house and furniture rights, Frederick is entitled to claim £50,000 under his right to financial provision. Note that it is the lower of the two possible figures which applies here, since Edward was also survived by issue; whether or not Frederick himself has issue is not relevant.

Prior rights and partial intestacy

Where an estate is partially (as opposed to wholly) intestate, the surviving spouse still has prior rights.[63] However, certain of these rights are affected by legacies[64] that the surviving spouse might be entitled to under the terms of the will.

4–26

As a general rule, the s.8 rights (to a dwelling-house and furniture) are *not* affected by a legacy in a will. It has already been noted above that in order for a surviving spouse to claim either of the s.8 rights, the estate must include a qualifying dwelling-house or sum of furniture. It is perhaps self-evident, then, that the s.8 rights are defeated where such estate has been entirely disposed of by the provisions of a will. However, where a will disposes of only *some* qualifying property, s.8 rights can still be exercised against any that remains in the intestate estate. This is the case even if the surviving spouse is the beneficiary of the relevant legacy, meaning that there is nothing to stop a surviving spouse claiming *one* dwelling-house (with furniture) under the terms of a will, and *another* under s.8.

However, the same cannot be said for the s.9 right to financial provision. Here, the general rule is that the sum claimed under s.9 must be offset by the value of any legacy received by the surviving spouse.[65] The definition of "legacy" in this context is very broad, and includes "any payment or benefit to which a surviving

---

[61] Such a distinction in legal status essentially no longer exists.

[62] Succession (Scotland) Act 1964 s.23(1).

[63] Succession (Scotland) Act 1964 s.36(1).

[64] See Ch.6.

[65] Succession (Scotland) Act 1964 s.9(1) proviso.

spouse becomes entitled by virtue of any testamentary provision".[66] This covers a number of provisions that might not immediately be considered legacies in the traditional sense, such as special destinations and nominations under a life assurance policy.[67]

There is an important exception to the above, in that legacies to which s.8 would have applied (therefore, legacies of a dwelling-house and/or furniture) need *not* be deducted from the value of the right to financial provision.[68] This means that a surviving spouse can accept a legacy of a dwelling-house and furniture, and still claim the full value of the right to financial provision.

LEGAL RIGHTS

4–27 "Legal rights" is the term used to describe a range of entitlements claimable by certain family members against the estate of a deceased. They are based on the historical principle of a man's obligation to provide for his family, although today they are, as with prior rights, appropriately gender neutral. This shared motivation of protecting the interests of close relatives might lead to legal rights being confused with prior rights, but the two are very different in both origin and in application, and it is vital that they are not confused.

Also important to note is the fact that, although they are being considered here in the context of intestate succession, legal rights also apply in cases of testacy.[69] Claiming legal rights against an intestate estate does not involve any formality since it is a basic entitlement. In a testate estate, it does not constitute a challenge to the will. Nevertheless, oftentimes members of a family are reluctant to claim legal rights in the mistaken belief that it will require some kind of court action. There is much scope for misunderstanding in this area and it merely underlines how important it is for members of a family to seek competent advice on an individual basis.

General nature of legal rights

4–28 Legal rights are of ancient origin in Scots law. Although their exact source is a matter of academic dispute, rights of their kind can be traced to Roman law,[70] and the principles they enshrine can be found in the earliest surviving works documenting the law of Scotland.[71] In the words of Erskine:

> "Where a person has either wife or child, a certain portion of his moveable estate hath, since our earliest times, fallen upon his death to the widow, and a certain portion to the children."[72]

---

[66] Succession (Scotland) Act 1964 s.9(6)(b).

[67] See Ch.9.

[68] Succession (Scotland) Act 1964 s.9(1) proviso.

[69] The operation of legal rights in the latter context in considered in Ch.6.

[70] See, e.g. Watson J., *A Treatise on the Law of Scotland Respecting Succession* (Edinburgh: Bell & Bradfute, 1826), pp.278–283.

[71] See, e.g. commentary by Gardner, J.C., *The Origin and Nature of the Legal Rights of Spouses and Children in the Scottish Law of Succession* (Edinburgh: W. Green, 1928).

[72] Erskine, III, 9, 15.

Of course, legal rights have seen some development over time with the passing of relevant legislation,[73] but there has never been a statutory reworking, nor indeed even a comprehensive restatement, of the rights themselves. They remain deeply rooted in the common law tradition that the obligation to support one's family continues after death, and therefore that it should not be possible to entirely disinherit one's most closely connected relatives. The fact that legal rights can be claimed in cases of both intestacy and testacy further underline the importance placed on this principle.

It is therefore often said that, strictly speaking, legal rights are not so much rights of succession as debts due from the estate of the deceased; albeit debts that are postponed in favour of claims by other creditors. This, too, was long a matter of debate, but the prevailing view seems to be that expressed in *Naismith v Boyes*[74]:

> "In respect of their legal claims, the widow and children are heirs in competition with onerous creditors, and are creditors in competition with heirs."[75]

Indeed, there is an argument that the nature of legal rights means they do not, in fact, represent a limitation of the right to provide instructions regarding one's property after death, because in fact no such absolute right has ever existed.[76]

Property affected by legal rights

Legal rights can only be claimed against the moveable estate of the deceased. **4–29** There previously existed a common law right for a surviving spouse to make certain claims against a deceased's heritable property.[77] These (admittedly rather limited) rights were known as the widow's "terce" and the widower's "courtesy", and were claimable in addition to the legal rights applicable to moveables. Therefore, historically a surviving spouse had legal rights in respect of both funds of property, heritable and moveable.

However, terce and courtesy were abolished by the 1964 Act.[78] Despite much debate on the matter,[79] the decision was ultimately taken *not* to amass heritable and moveable property into one fund, or to extend the remaining rights, and so consequently no legal rights are claimable against a deceased's heritable estate.

Taking the above into account, and also their nature as postponed debts, it can be said that legal rights are claims made against the "net moveable estate" of the deceased. This means any moveable estate that is left after all debts, funeral expenses and administrative costs of winding up and dividing the estate have been met and prior rights (where appropriate) have also been satisfied.

---

[73] Not least their extension so as to apply equally to a woman's moveable estate, under the Married Women's Property (Scotland) Act 1881.

[74] *Naismith v Boyes* (1899) 1 F. (HL) 79.

[75] *Naismith v Boyes* (1899) 1 F. (HL) 79 at 81 per Lord Watson.

[76] Gardner, J.C., *The Origin and Nature of the Legal Rights of Spouses and Children in the Scottish Law of Succession* (Edinburgh: W Green, 1928), p.75.

[77] On the distinction between heritable and moveable property, see Ch.3.

[78] Succession (Scotland) Act 1964 s.10(1).

[79] Mackintosh Report, para.16.

Claims made under legal rights

4-30 There are two distinct legal rights in succession. To give them their ancient and traditional titles, they are the "relict's part", claimable by a surviving spouse (or civil partner) and "legitim", claimable by children or further direct descendants. Unlike prior rights, claims made under legal rights are not calculated according to set values. Instead, each comprises the right to claim a certain *portion* of the deceased's net moveable estate, depending on the presence or absence of other potential claimants.

To explain these rights in brief, where only *one* of the two legal rights is available to be claimed, it comprises a right to one half of the deceased's net moveable estate. Where *both* are available, each comprises a right to one third of the deceased's moveable estate. In either case, then, there will *always* be a portion of the estate unaffected by legal rights. This remaining portion is known as free estate or "dead's part", the former term being applied more commonly in intestate succession, and the latter where the deceased left a will.

Simple legal rights examples[80]

4-31 Harold has died intestate, survived by his wife, Wilma, and their daughter, Donna. His net moveable estate is valued at £60,000. Wilma is entitled to one third of the net moveable estate under her *jus relictae* right, and so can claim the sum of £20,000. Donna is also entitled to one third of the net moveable estate under her legitim right, and so can also claim £20,000. The remaining one third (which is also, of course, worth £20,000) is free estate. (See Figure 1.)

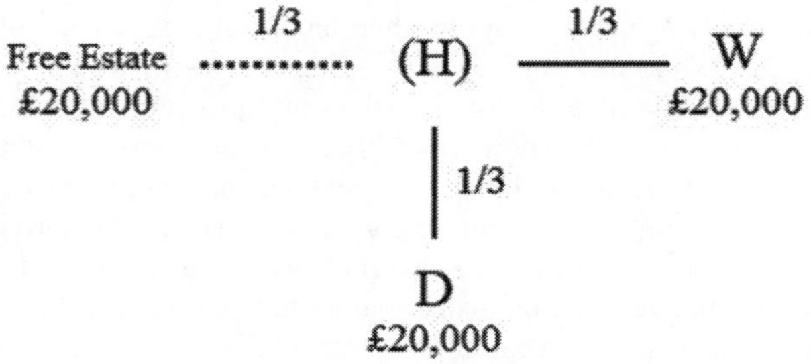

$$\text{Free Estate} \overset{1/3}{\cdots\cdots\cdots} \text{(H)} \overset{1/3}{\text{------}} \text{W}$$

$$\begin{array}{ccc} & 1/3 & \\ \text{Free Estate} & \cdots\cdots\cdots & \text{(H)} \quad\text{------}\quad \text{W} \\ £20,000 & & £20,000 \\ & | \; 1/3 & \\ & \text{D} & \\ & £20,000 & \end{array}$$

Figure 1

If, however, Harold were survived only by his wife Wilma, then she would be entitled to one half of the net moveable estate under her *jus relictae* right, allowing her to claim £30,000. The other half would be free estate. (See Figure 2.)

---

[80] Note that "free estate" has been included in these illustrative diagrams purely as a reminder that there will always be a portion of the estate unaffected by legal rights. Rights to inherit under the "free estate" are an entirely separate matter.

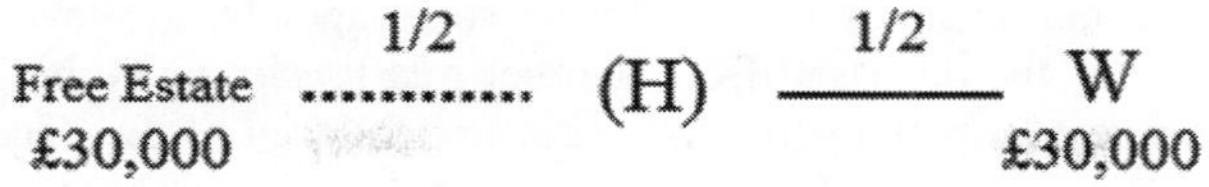

1/2   1/2

Free Estate   ....   **(H)** ———— **W**

£30,000   £30,000

Figure 2

Similarly, if Harold were survived only by his daughter Donna, then she would be entitled to one half of the net moveable estate under her legitim right, and the other half would be free estate. (See Figure 3.)

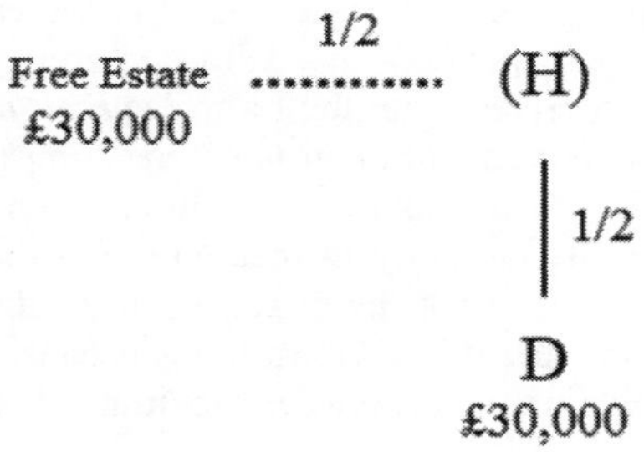

1/2

Free Estate   ....   **(H)**

£30,000

| 1/2

D

£30,000

Figure 3

The relict's part

"Relict" is an archaic term, derived from Latin and Old French, meaning "woman left behind" or simply "widow". This origin gave to Scots law the names by which a surviving spouse's legal right was traditionally known, being *jus relictae* (right of the widow) or *jus relicti* (right of the widower). The equivalent rights for surviving civil partners were established by statute rather than derived from common law, and consequently are known simply as "rights under section 131 of the Civil Partnership Act 2004".[81] Cohabitees do *not* have any rights in this context, although as mentioned earlier they do have certain other rights, which are discussed later in this chapter.

 Regardless of specific terminology, this right comprises a claim to one half of the deceased's net moveable estate, provided there are no surviving children or further direct descendants (known as "issue") of the deceased. If there are surviving children or further issue, the right comprises a claim to one third of the net moveable estate.[82]

4–32

---

[81] Succession (Scotland) Act 1964 s.36(1).
[82] Erskine, III, 9, 18.

It should be noted that only surviving issue *of the deceased* will have an effect on the relict's claim. Of course, in many cases, issue of the deceased will also be issue of the relict, but whether or not this is so is actually irrelevant.[83] As a consequence, issue of the deceased from another relationship must be taken into account, whilst issue of the claimant alone (i.e. stepchildren of the deceased) are not.

On the matter of stepchildren, it should also be noted that rights under the relict's part are only available to the surviving spouse or civil partner personally. Unlike legitim rights, there is no potential for "representation", i.e. the passing of rights to a descendant.[84] Any would-be relict's part rights extinguish upon death; to have it otherwise would essentially create a right by which stepchildren could claim against the deceased's estate, which would be contrary to the current spirit of the law.

Legitim

4–33 Legitim, or "bairn's part" to use its traditional name, is the right of surviving children (or further direct descendants) to claim a certain portion of the deceased's estate. The term is derived from the Latin *legitima portio*, meaning a rightful share, which itself is derived from *legitimus*, meaning lawful. The same root is shared by the term "legitimate" as it applies to children (i.e. born within lawful marriage), but despite the harmony in meaning, and the historical legal implications of such a status, that is not the direct origin of the term. Avoiding such confusion is especially important in modern times because, as will be seen, there is now virtually no distinction made between "legitimate" and "illegitimate" children.

The right to legitim comprises a claim to one half of the deceased's net moveable estate, provided there is no surviving spouse or civil partner of the deceased. If there is a surviving spouse or civil partner, the right comprises a claim to one third of the net moveable estate.[85]

Unlike the relict's part, it is, of course, possible for a legitim claim to be made by more than one individual. It is therefore important to note that the right is a collective one, and that the relevant portion must be shared between all claimants. For this reason, the relevant portion is often termed "the legitim fund", although this fund is essentially artificial as it exists only for the purpose of calculating entitlements, and might be subject to various theoretical additions or subtractions until the later stages of administration allow an accurate determination of rights. What is important, however, is that the legitim will ultimately be divided, according to a number of rules, between all qualifying claimants.

The definition of "children"

4–34 As in most matters of succession, the terms "child" and "children" are used here purely in terms of relationship to the deceased. It is common sense that most

---

[83] Erskine, III, 9, 17.

[84] This oversimplifies the concept of representation somewhat; it is considered more fully later in this chapter.

[85] Erskine, III, 9, 18.

claimants on a legitim fund will be far beyond the age at which they would be described as children in the general sense! "Children", then, includes all individuals so related to the deceased, be they legitimate or illegitimate, biological or adopted.

Historically, only children born within marriage could claim legitim.[86] A child born outwith marriage was regarded in the legal sense as a *filius nullius*, or "child of no one",[87] and had very limited legal rights at all. As regards succession, the situation was improved somewhat under statute in the early 20th century, to the extent that an illegitimate child could claim against his or her mother's estate, but only if there were no surviving legitimate issue.[88] The 1964 Act itself made no change to this position when enacted, but soon afterwards was amended so that illegitimate children were given an equal right to claim legitim against a parent's estate.[89] Subsequent legislation then established the principle that a person's legal rights ought not to be affected at all by the marital status of their parents,[90] subject to certain specialist exceptions regarding titles and coats-of-arms.[91] More recently, for all purposes other than those exceptions, the legal status of illegitimacy itself has been abolished.[92]

At common law, the position of an adopted child was somewhat complicated. Although it was far from uncommon for a child to be placed in the care of someone other than his or her parents, any would-be contract that purported to transfer custody permanently was not recognised.[93] The implication for succession was that an "adopted" child could have no claim against the estates of the "adoptive" parents, since such a legal status did not exist. The right to claim against the estates of *natural* parents remained, but this was often of little use since so many children surrendered into the care of another were illegitimate. Adoption as a legal process was, in time, established by statute,[94] although succession rights were expressly unaffected by it.[95] This was widely regarded as an undesirable position[96] and, accordingly, the 1964 Act placed adopted children in the same position as natural children regarding claims made on the estates of their adoptive parents. As a consequence, any rights in succession that adopted children have in respect of their natural parents are extinguished.[97]

Stepchildren are excluded from the definition, and have no lawful rights in succession in respect of a stepparent. It is acknowledged that this is not a simple issue, and that this exclusion might seem harsh in situations where a stepchild has been raised as part of the intestate's family. However, it must also be

---

[86] Erskine, I, 6, 51.

[87] *Clarke v Carfin Coal Co* (1891) 18 R. (HL) 63.

[88] Legitimacy Act 1926 s.9 (as enacted).

[89] Succession (Scotland) Act 1964 s.10A, inserted by the Law Reform (Miscellaneous Provisions) (Scotland) Act 1968 s.2 (as enacted).

[90] Law Reform (Parent and Child) (Scotland) Act 1986 s.1 (as enacted).

[91] Law Reform (Parent and Child) (Scotland) Act 1986 s.9.

[92] Law Reform (Parent and Child) (Scotland) Act 1986 s.1 (as amended by the Family Law (Scotland) Act 2006 s.21).

[93] *Kerrigan v Hall* (1901) 4 F. 10.

[94] Adoption of Children (Scotland) Act 1930; now regulated by the Adoption and Children (Scotland) Act 2007.

[95] Adoption of Children (Scotland) Act 1930 s.5(3) (as enacted).

[96] Mackintosh Report, para.24.

[97] Succession (Scotland) Act 1964 s.23(1).

acknowledged that the many and varied circumstances that might be encountered make it impractical to frame legislation that would be universally suitable. Consequently, anyone who wishes for stepchildren to be provided for after their death must take positive action do so, the obvious course being to make a will in their favour.[98]

"Representation"

4–35 Historically, only children who actually survived the deceased could have any claim against the legitim fund. This rule was logical in that it simply applied the basic principle of succession that only the living may inherit. However, there is an exception to this basic principle in the form of a concept known as "representation", whereby the issue of a predeceasing claimant may take a succession right to which the latter would have been entitled. This concept has long been recognised in succession, and indeed was crucial to the rules by which historically an "heir at law" was identified.

Nevertheless, for a long time representation did not apply to rights in legitim. The rule under common law was that there was no representation at all in rights relating to moveable property. Under statute, the concept *was* applied to moveable estate but, due to technical legislative wording, only to a limited extent which did not include legitim rights.[99] This position was viewed at best as an anomaly, and at worst as a grave injustice.[100]

This was remedied by the 1964 Act, which applies infinite representation to legitim rights.[101] So, not only grandchildren of the deceased, but any further issue can claim legitim rights in this manner.[102] At the time of enactment, only legitimate issue could represent (though, oddly, the child they were representing need not him or herself have been legitimate), but this was eventually addressed alongside the various other improvements made to the legal entitlements and status of children born outwith marriage.

Division of legitim

4–36 It is absolutely crucial to remember that legitim is claimed collectively by those entitled to it. Where there is only one legitim claimant this poses no problem, since the sole claimant takes the whole fund. However, where there are two or more claimants, it is necessary to calculate each's fair share; and "fair" does not necessarily mean "equal". Therefore to facilitate, rather, an equitable sharing of the legitim fund, a number of rules exist in relation to its division.

Where only immediate children of the deceased claim legitim, each receives an equal share of the fund. It does not matter whether these are natural or adopted children, nor whether the children themselves are related to each other by full blood, half-blood, or by adoption. It is the relationship to the deceased that creates the right, not the dynamics of the legitim fund claimants.

---

[98] For further discussion see Scottish Law Commission, *Report of Succession* (Scot. Law Com. No.215), paras 2.31–2.34.

[99] Intestate Moveable Succession (Scotland) Act 1855 s.9.

[100] Mackintosh Report, para.13.

[101] Succession (Scotland) Act 1964 s.11.

[102] *Turners Trustees v Turner* (1897) 24 R. 619.

These two concepts might, however, be connected where a predeceasing child is being represented by further issue of the deceased. The basic rule is that the claimant representing the predeceasing child is entitled to the latter's right.[103] This is a simple matter when there is only one representative claiming legitim, but when there are two or more, the situation becomes more complicated. In such a situation, division will be made either "*per stirpes*" (by branch, i.e. proportionately) or "per capita" (by head, i.e. equally), depending on the circumstances. To understand the difference between these two methods of division, it is useful to bear in mind that succession generally adheres to the principle of propinquity, i.e. that those who are closer in degree of relationship to the deceased tend to have greater rights than those who are farther.

Per stirpes division applies where the legitim claimants are of at least two different degrees of relationship to the deceased. Here, the legitim fund must be divided "by branch", i.e. equally at each degree of relationship, with any survivors in that degree taking their share, and any predeceased's share being further divided between representing claimants.[104] This is in line with the principle of propinquity because it tends to result in children receiving a greater share than grandchildren, who tend to receive a greater share than great-grandchildren, and so on.[105]

Per capita division applies where the legitim claimants are all of the same degree of relationship to the deceased. Here, the legitim fund is simply divided "by head", i.e. equally among all claimants, ignoring all interim degrees of relationship.[106] This is also in line with the principle of propinquity because it ensures that where only grandchildren are claiming they will all receive the same, where only great-grandchildren are claiming they will all receive the same, and so on.

Examples of legitim division

Winifred, a widow, has died intestate with a net moveable estate of £40,000. **4–37** Winifred had two children, Simon and Doris, and a total of five grandchildren, two from Simon and three from Doris. Since there is no surviving spouse or civil partner, the only legal right to be claimed is legitim, which will comprise one half of the net moveable estate, giving a total legitim fund of £20,000. This sum would then be divided among the legitim claimants, depending upon who survives Winifred. In all circumstances, the other half of the net moveable estate will be free estate.

If Winifred were survived by both her children, each would be entitled to an equal share of one half of the net moveable estate, i.e. one quarter each. This would be an example of per capita division, with each child receiving £10,000. The grandchildren would have no claim. (See Figure 4.)

If, however, one child had predeceased Winifred (say, Simon) then the grandchildren of that predeceasing child would be entitled to claim as

---

[103] Succession (Scotland) Act 1964 s.11(1).
[104] Succession (Scotland) Act 1964 s.11(2)(b).
[105] It should be noted that this is not an absolute; actual division will always depend on the variety of claimants and their respective degree of relationship to the deceased.
[106] Succession (Scotland) Act 1964 s.11(2)(a).

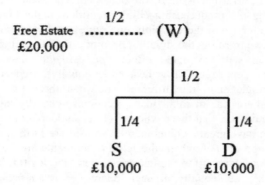

Figure 4

representatives. This would mean that Simon's one quarter share would be divided among his two representatives, giving each a one eighth share, or £5,000. The £10,000 claimed by Doris would not change. This would be an example of *per stirpes* division. (See Figure 5.)

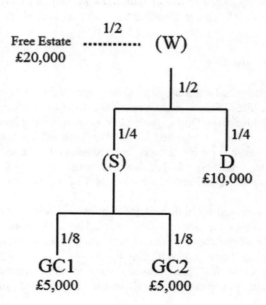

Figure 5

A final relevant consideration would be the situation where both of Winifred's children have predeceased, meaning she is survived by only by her five grandchildren, two from Simon and three from Doris. If *per stirpes* division were applied here, then Doris's three representatives would ultimately receive less by way of legitim than Simon's two. This is deemed unfair, since all are in the same degree of relationship to the deceased, and so should be treated equally. Therefore, per capita division would apply, and each grandchild would take an equal share of the fund, i.e. £4,000 each. The "branches" connecting the children of the deceased to the grandchildren are ignored. (See Figure 6.)

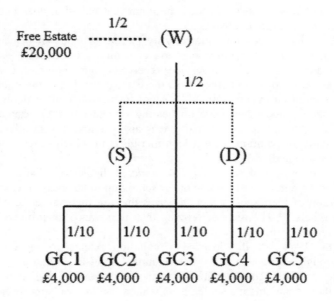

Figure 6

Collation inter liberos

This is a principle, derived from common law but expressly retained by the 1964 Act,[107] which seeks to facilitate equitable treatment in the division of the legitim fund.[108] It applies where a potential legitim claimant has received, during the lifetime of the deceased, a substantial advance of funds that was not similarly enjoyed by other legitim claimants. In such a situation, the claimant having received the advance can be compelled by the other claimants to "collate" (add back) the amount of the advance to the legitim fund. The total fund is then divided *inter liberos* ("among the children") in the normal way. This is, in fact, a   **4–38**

---

[107] Succession (Scotland) Act 1964 s.11(3).
[108] Erskine, III, 9, 24.

paper exercise since money is not literally paid back into the fund; it is merely taken into account for purposes of calculating each claimant's rights.

It should be noted that collation is only required where legitim is actually claimed. A would-be claimant who has received such a substantial advance so as to be financially worse off by collating can simply choose *not* to claim legitim, and instead retain the benefit of the advance.[109] The choice is entirely theirs in this matter. In *Coats' Trustees v Coats*,[110] each of five siblings had received cash advances from their father before his death, but one daughter had received significantly less. This daughter wished to claim legitim and was willing to collate, but her siblings, who were satisfied with their advances, did not want to do this. She raised an action attempting to compel her siblings to do so, but was unsuccessful. This case also affirmed the point that collation does not apply if there is only one legitim claimant.

Not all advances need be collated. Any payments made in discharge of a parent's general duty of maintenance and education are excluded, as are any payments made in satisfaction of services received under a contract. Loans made to a child are not subject to collation, as these are debts due to the estate and so will be accounted for as such instead.[111] Any advance made of heritable property is also excluded, since they have no bearing on the moveable estate, against which legal rights are claimed. Finally, it is also possible for an advance to be made explicitly in addition to any legitim rights, in which case it would not require to be collated.[112]

Common examples of advances that *would* be liable to collation are funds provided for the purchase of a home or for setting up in business, payments made in anticipation of marriage, or any advances that are made so as to enrich one child over others.[113] The onus of proving that an advance must be collated lies with the executor.

Under the 1964 Act, the doctrine of collation extends to anyone claiming legitim through representation. Such claimants must collate a "proportion appropriate ... of any advances made" to the predeceased being represented.[114] However, there is no guidance given as to what a "proportion appropriate" might be, leading to difficulties of interpretation, and much academic debate on the issue.[115]

Example of collation

4–39   To return to the same characters from previous examples, Winifred, a widow, has died with a net moveable estate of £40,000, leaving two children, Simon and Doris, both of whom are entitled to claim £10,000 each by way of their legitim right. However, imagine that Simon had received an advance of £8,000 from his mother during her lifetime, which can be proven and established as liable to

---

[109] This involves the "renunciation" of legitim rights, discussed later in this chapter.

[110] *Coats' Trustees v Coats*, 1914 S.C. 744.

[111] Erskine, III, 9, 24.

[112] Erskine, III, 9, 25.

[113] *Duncan v Crichton's Trustees*, 1917 S.C. 728.

[114] Succession (Scotland) Act 1964 s.11(3).

[115] See, e.g. Meston M., *Collation of Advances to Ancestors*, 1967 S.L.T. (News) 195, and related correspondence in 1967 S.L.T. (News) 224 and 247.

collation. If he wished to claim his legal rights, he would be required to "repay" the advance back into the legitim fund, increasing it to £28,000. This is then divided as normal, giving each claimant £14,000. Simon would be advised to do this since, even deducting the £8,000 that he is required to "repay", he is still better off by £6,000 than if he had not claimed his legal rights. On the other hand, if the advance received by Simon was significantly greater, say £22,000, then repaying it would increase the fund to £42,000, giving each child £21,000; in this case Simon would be better off *not* collating, and simply keeping his advance instead.

Extinction of legal rights

Throughout the long history of legal rights, they have been designed to be indefeasible. However, that same history has provided a range of circumstances whereby legal rights will not be enjoyed by those entitled to them. One relatively straightforward example is that legal rights are subject to rules of "prescription", meaning that they will lapse if not claimed within 20 years of becoming enforceable.[116] More contentious, however, is the deliberate exclusion of legal rights, known as "discharge". Two possible circumstances will be considered here; discharge by someone other than the would-be claimant, and discharge by the claimant personally. The latter is also referred to as "renunciation".

4-40

Discharge by someone other than the claimant

Historically, it was possible for parents to discharge their children's legal rights by way of an antenuptial marriage contract, often referred to as a prenuptial agreement.[117] It was at one time common for such agreements to make provision for any children that would be born of the marriage, and as a consequence legitim rights were expressly excluded. This was deemed to be an effective discharge,[118] but the practice became notorious for its potentially inequitable results.

4-41

For example, in *Galloway's Trustees v Galloway*,[119] a marriage contract made provision for "children", but the father later directed that the whole of this fund should be paid over to his eldest son only. His other two children failed in a claim for legitim, since their rights had been discharged by the marriage contract. Similarly, in *Callander v Callander's Executor*,[120] a marriage contract established a trust fund, the income from which would be received by the children in lieu of legitim. The father later terminated the trust, and bequeathed his whole estate to one of his two sons. The disinherited son failed in a legitim claim, the court holding that the termination of the trust did not revive his legal rights.

Under the 1964 Act, however, it is no longer possible to exclude the legitim rights of a child or further issue by way of an ante-nuptial marriage contract.[121]

[116] Prescription and Limitation (Scotland) Act 1973 s.7 and Sch.1, para.2(f).
[117] Despite there being varied opinion regarding the moral and ethical aspects of such agreements, these are, and long have been, generally enforceable in Scotland; see, e.g. Clive E.M., *The Law of Husband and Wife in Scotland*, 4th edn (Edinburgh: W. Green, 1997).
[118] Erskine, III, 9, 23.
[119] *Galloway's Trustees v Galloway*, 1943 S.C. 339.
[120] *Callander v Callander's Executor*, 1972 S.C. (HL) 70.
[121] Succession (Scotland) Act 1964 s.12.

This has always been the case for *jus relictae* and *jus relicti* rights,[122] which cannot be discharged by someone other than the claimant. It is therefore now the case that *all* legal rights can only be discharged voluntary by the person entitled to them.

Discharge by the claimant: "renunciation"

4–42   It has always been open to any person entitled to claim legal rights to give up or "renounce" this claim. There are a number of possible motivations behind this, such as breakdown of a relationship between the relevant parties, or where a would-be claimant elects to take an alternative benefit to their legal rights.[123] Regardless of the reason, such a renunciation can have a profound effect on the estate as a whole, and therefore make a considerable difference to the rights enjoyed by other beneficiaries. The most important factor influencing these effects is whether the renunciation takes place before or after the death of the person upon whose estate the rights are exigible.

If the discharge or renunciation takes place before the death of the "deceased", that claimant is deemed, for this purpose only, to have predeceased and to have left no issue. As a result, the amount available to other claimants is increased, either by altering the value of the relevant portion comprising the remaining right, or by decreasing the number of claimants to the legitim fund. In *Hog v Hog*,[124] a father had made during his lifetime provisions for all but one of his six children, who in turn had renounced their legal rights. The sixth child, a daughter, had offended him by entering into a marriage he disapproved of, and although he did ultimately intend for her to inherit an equal portion of his estate, this was not arranged during his lifetime and therefore her legal rights were never discharged. Upon her father's death, the daughter was able to claim a full one-half of his moveable estate as legitim.[125]

However, if (as is more common) the discharge takes place after death, the effect is quite different. As legal rights are fixed at the moment of death, nothing which takes place *after* the death can affect the amount designated for each claimant. As a result, the value of any legal right which has been so renounced falls into the free estate.[126] In short, it has no effect on the amounts received by other claimants. In *Fisher v Dixon*,[127] a father had made testamentary provision for his children, but upon his death one of his daughters wished to reject her legacy and claim legitim. The court held that acceptance of their legacies by the other siblings did *not* amount to renunciation during the deceased's lifetime, and therefore that the daughter's share would not be increased.

It is worth noting that the courts may reject a renunciation of legal rights if, for example, it appears that the individual is doing so only to unfairly manipulate the rules. In *Obers v Paton's Trustees*,[128] a son who had been declared bankrupt renounced his claim to legitim shortly before his father's death. This served to

---

[122] *Keith's Trustees v Keith* (1857) 19 D. 1040.
[123] The latter is more an issue of testate succession, on which see Ch.6.
[124] *Hog v Hog* (1791) Mor. 8193.
[125] A similar decision was reached in the later case of *Baron Panmure v Crokat* (1856) 18 D. 703.
[126] Or residue if the estate is testate, again on which see Ch.6.
[127] *Fisher v Dixon* (1840) 2 D. 1121.
[128] *Obers v Paton's Trustees* (1897) 24 R. 719.

deny his creditors access to his would-be share, which instead went to his siblings. This was undoubtedly an astute move, but the court declared the discharge void as it was a "gratuitous alienation" made to the prejudice of his creditors.

Example of renunciation

Again returning to the same fictitious family, Winifred has died leaving two children, Simon and Doris, who are entitled to legitim of £10,000. Imagine, however, that Simon renounced his legal rights before Winifred's death; he would be treated as having predeceaced Winifred *and*, importantly, would be deemed to have left no issue. Therefore Simon would be discounted as far as the calculation of legal rights is concerned and the entire legitim fund of £20,000 would go to Doris. On the other hand, if Simon renounces his legal rights after Winifred's death, the outcome would be different. Because legal rights are fixed at the moment of death, Doris's share of the legitim fund cannot be increased and she will only receive her own portion of the fund (£10,000), just as if Simon had accepted his share. The £10,000 which Simon has rejected will fall into the free estate or residue.

4–43

THE FREE ESTATE

"Free estate" is the name given to the whole of a deceased's property that is subject to the ordinary rules of succession, rather than being subject to specific legal claims. This fund is also referred to as the "dead's part", since it is the estate over which the deceased was, in his lifetime, entitled to make testamentary provisions. In the context of intestate succession, the term refers to any balance that remains after the satisfaction of both prior rights and legal rights. From what has already been demonstrated in this current chapter, it stands to reason that if someone dies intestate, with no surviving spouse, civil partner or children, his entire estate constitutes free estate, subject to certain specialist exceptions.

4–44

General approach

Under common law, different mechanisms applied in respect of succession to heritable and moveable property. Part 1 of the 1964 Act introduced a new regime for intestacy whereby heritable and moveable property are combined into one single estate, and disposed of according to a scheme similar (but not identical) to the common law rules regarding moveable property.

In establishing this scheme, s.2 of the 1964 Act outlines a list of specified relations to the deceased, in the order in which they are entitled to succeed. It must be read in conjunction with s.5, which provides for representation, and s.6, which outlines rules for division where two or more people have an equal right to succeed. The approach of s.2 is to give a right of succession to the relative or relatives identified in each paragraph, with all except the first class being subject to exclusion by "prior relatives", i.e. those identified in earlier paragraphs. The wording of this section (and indeed the foregoing explanation!) may seem

4–45

complicated, but its operation is actually very simple. The "highest-ranking" relative identified by the order inherits the whole estate, or shares it with other members of exactly the same rank. The rights of relatives who rank any lower in the order are then irrelevant, having been excluded by those who will actually inherit.

The order of succession

4–46   Under s.2(1) of the 1964 Act, the order of succession to the free estate is as follows:

(a)   children;
(b)   parents *and* siblings, where there is at least one of each surviving;
(c)   siblings, where there are no surviving parents;
(d)   parents, where there are no surviving siblings;
(e)   spouse or civil partner;
(f)   uncles and aunts;
(g)   grandparents;
(h)   great-uncles and great-aunts; and
(i)   remoter ancestors.

Where no surviving relative of the deceased can be identified, the historical common law right of the Crown to succeed to the estate as *ultimus haeres* is explicitly retained by the 1964 Act.[129]

Representation within the order

4–47   Representation applies in respect of the rights outlined by s.2(1) for most, but not all, of the relatives identified.[130] This means that certain relatives need not be specifically identified within the order. So, for example, s.2(1)(a) provides for the succession rights of "children" of the deceased, but these rights extend to further issue by virtue of s.5, thereby providing for the succession rights of grandchildren, great-grandchildren and so on. Similarly, s.2(1)(c) provides for the succession rights of "siblings" of the deceased, but these rights also extend to nieces and nephews. In cases of representation, the rules of division applied are very similar to those directing division of the legitim fund in legal rights. In short, division among the entitled persons will be per capita where all are in the same degree of relationship to the deceased, and *per stirpes* in any other case.[131]

There are two important exceptions to the above, in that neither parents nor a spouse of the deceased can be represented. The exclusion of parents in this regard is fairly logical, since any potential representative of a predeceasing parent would also be a sibling of the deceased.[132] The exception preventing spouses and civil partners from being represented serves to exclude stepchildren of the deceased

---

[129] Succession (Scotland) Act 1964 s.7.
[130] Succession (Scotland) Act 1964 s.5.
[131] Succession (Scotland) Act 1964 s.6.
[132] Although note that there are certain rules regarding half-blood siblings, discussed later in this chapter.

from succession. This is similar to the position regarding legal rights of a surviving spouse, and is in keeping with the current spirit of the law.

Children and further descendants

Section 2(1)(a) provides that any children of the deceased have the right to inherit   **4–48**
the whole intestate free estate. Much of the rules regarding the claiming of legitim apply equally here, such as the definition of "children" and the correct manner of division in cases of representation. In fact, it is worth noting that where a deceased dies intestate and is survived by both a spouse and children, the calculation of legitim will be identical to the calculation of rights to the moveable free estate. In such cases, legitim is for practical purposes a notional right, since all property net of prior rights will be divided among the children or further issue.

Parents and siblings

If no descendant of the deceased can be identified, then under s.2(1)(b) there is a   **4–49**
shared right of succession given to parents and siblings. Provided there is at least one of each class of relative (or, where siblings are concerned, a representative), then each class is entitled to one-half of the free estate. Where there is more than one person in a class entitled to inherit, the one-half share is divided according to s.6, i.e. following the rules of per capita or *per stirpes* division as appropriate.

Also relevant here are s.2(2) and s.3, which provide for relatives of the half-blood. Section 2(2) establishes a right of half-blood siblings to succeed to the free estate, but under s.3 (which uses the term "collaterals" for siblings), half-blood collaterals are excluded in favour of full blood collaterals *and* their representatives. Where half-blood collaterals do inherit, it makes no difference whether they are related to the deceased through the mother or the father. In addition to immediate siblings, these same principles extend to all such relatives of the intestate's ascending lines.

Sections 2(1)(c) and 2(1)(d) then establish the rights of siblings and parents respectively to succeed where there are survivors from only one of those two classes. In terms of siblings, no preference is given according to sex or order of birth. Parents rank equally with each other and share any estate per capita, with no distinction made between the rights of a mother and a father, or between the rights of an adoptive parent and a natural parent.[133]

Spouse or civil partner

The 1964 Act's inclusion of a spouse in the list of those entitled to succeed to the   **4–50**
free estate was a major departure from the common law position. Previous to the Act, a surviving spouse was entitled to legal rights and certain statutory preferences, but was never the deceased's heir and had no right to share in the free estate. In *Brown's Trustees v Brown*,[134] a Scots woman died in Australia,

---

[133] Succession (Scotland) Act 1964 s.23.
[134] *Brown's Trustees v Brown* (1890) 17 R. 1174.

survived by her husband and two siblings. A claim by her husband to her estate failed, on the grounds that he was not her heir, by either the law of Scotland or of Australia.

Section 2(1)(e) establishes that the spouse (and now civil partner) is one of the ordinary heirs in succession in addition to enjoying prior and legal rights. In the absence of direct descendants, siblings (or their representatives) or parents of the deceased, the spouse shall therefore be entitled to the whole free estate. In practice, of course, this means that the spouse shall inherit the entire intestate estate, albeit via a number of different claims.

It is worth reiterating the point that there is no right of representation in respect of a predeceasing spouse, which excludes stepchildren from claiming against the free estate.

Uncles and aunts

4–51   Section 2(1)(f) provides that, in the absence of prior relatives, surviving uncles and aunts of the deceased are entitled to share the whole free estate. "Uncles" and "aunts" are defined as "brothers or sisters of either parent of the intestate", a definition that has two implications.

The first is that only relations by blood or adoption are entitled to succeed under this subsection. No matter how affectionately someone who has married into the family might be regarded, an "uncle" or "aunt" related to the deceased by affinity takes no place in the order of succession. Half-blood uncles and aunts are entitled to succeed by virtue of s.2(2), but are excluded in favour of full blood under s.3.

The second noteworthy point is the opening of succession to the intestate's maternal relations as well as paternal. This was another radical change from the common law position, and effectively doubled the range of relatives potentially entitled to succeed. No distinction is made between relatives through each parent, and division among them all is per capita.

Representation applies to this class, with division being either per capita or *per stirpes*, as appropriate.

Grandparents and remoter ancestors

4–52   In the absence of any prior relatives, succession to the free estate opens up to grandparents of the deceased under s.2(1)(g). No distinction is made between the paternal and maternal lines, and surviving grandparents share the free estate per capita. Representation is irrelevant to this class, since any surviving issue of grandparents to the deceased would be uncles or aunts of either full blood or half-blood, and therefore rank as prior relatives.

Siblings of grandparents (i.e. "great-uncles" or "great-aunts") then enter the order by virtue of s.2(1)(h), again with no distinction made between paternal and maternal relations. Representation also applies, as do the rules regarding full and half-blood.

Section 2(1)(i) then continues this pattern, opening the succession to ancestors of the intestate remoter than grandparents, then the siblings of such ancestors, or the representatives of those siblings, and so on.

There is no limit placed on the remoteness of relative who can succeed to the free estate. The matter was considered by the Mackintosh Committee, who in their report stated that they were "much attracted to the view that among collateral relatives succession should not extend further than to uncles and aunts and the issue of these".[135] However, respondents to the Committee's enquiries were "uncompromisingly against" such a proposal, so no recommendation to that end was made. The matter continued to be discussed throughout the Bill's progress through Parliament, and at one point it was proposed that relatives no more remote than lineal grandparents should be included in the order.[136] Ultimately, no limitation was placed, and the principle of infinite succession was embedded in the provisions as enacted.

The Crown

Given the vastly increased pool of potential heirs to the free estate under the provisions of the 1964 Act, the possibility of the deceased having no qualifying relative at all is a remote one. However, it is acknowledged that the tracing of very remote ancestors, and their surviving issue who might actually be in a position to inherit, can give rise to significant practical problems. So, in the case where a surviving relative of the deceased genuinely cannot be found, the right of the Crown to succeed as *ultimus haeres* is retained by s.7.

4–53

The executor (or other relevant person) is obliged to transfer the deceased's estate to the Queen's and Lord Treasurer's Remembrancer, who will administer it on behalf of the Crown. Advertisements will normally be placed to the effect that the estate has fallen to the Crown, inviting any would-be heirs not identified by the executor to come forward and stake their claim. In the absence of such, the Crown continues its practice of making grants from the estate to persons who can establish a "moral claim", for example someone who had rendered services to the deceased without payment, or someone for whom the deceased might reasonably have been expected to make provision. Information on the making of such claims, and on the *ultimus haeres* function generally, can be found on the Queen's and Lord Treasurer's Remembrancer website.[137]

EXAMPLES OF DIVISION OF INTESTATE ESTATES

Example 1

A husband dies leaving a widow, one son and one daughter. His net estate is £220,100 made up of dwelling-house (£160,000), furniture (£4,100) and investments of £56,000. (Note that figures in brackets indicate deductions from the estate, and "NME" refers to "net moveable estate".)

4–54

---

[135] Mackintosh Report, para.26.
[136] Hansard, HL Deb 23 March 1964, Vol.256, cc.1062–1121.
[137] Queen's and Lord Treasurer's Remembrancer. *Ultimate Haeres*, available at *http://www.qltr.gov.uk/content/ultimus-haeres* [Accessed 31 March 2017].

	Heritable	Moveable
Estate		
Dwelling-house	160,000	
Furniture		4,100
Investments		56,000
Balances	*160,000*	*60,100*
Deduct prior rights		
Dwelling-house	(160,000)	
Furniture		(4,100)
Financial provisions		(50,000)
Balances	*Nil*	*6,000*
Deduct legal rights		
Relict's part 1/3 NME		(2,000)
Legitim 1/3 NME		(2,000)
Balances	*Nil*	*2,000*
Deduct dead's part		
To children		(2,000)
Balances	*Nil*	*Nil*

The final distribution would be:

Widow	
Prior rights	£214,100
Relict's part	£2,000
Total	*£216,100*
Son	
1/2 legitim	£1,000
1/2 dead's part	£1,000
Total	*£2,000*
Daughter	
1/2 legitim	£1,000
1/2 dead's part	£1,000
Total	*£2,000*

The above example is one of classic simplicity. Notice that even in this case, where there are sufficient funds to make a legitim payment, the lion's share of the estate passes to the widow.

Example 2

In this second example, the family circumstances are the same, as is the total **4–55** amount of moveable estate, but there is a second heritable property (a holiday home), which increases the total net estate to £304,100. The holiday home complicates things regarding calculation of the financial provision, and so this is explained in detail following the distribution table.

	Heritable	**Moveable**
Estate		
Dwelling-house	160,000	
Furniture		4,100
Holiday home	84,000	
Investments		56,000
Balances	*244,000*	*60,100*
Deduct prior rights		
Dwelling-house	(160,000)	
Furniture		(4,100)
Financial provisions	(30,000)	(20,000)
Balances	*54,000*	*36,000*
Deduct legal rights		
Relict's part 1/3 NME		(12,000)
Legitim 1/3 NME		(12,000)
Balances	*54,000*	*12,000*
Deduct dead's part		
To children	(54,000)	(12,000)
Balances	*Nil*	*Nil*

The final distribution would be:

Widow	
Prior rights	£214,100
Relict's part	£12,000
Total	*£226,100*
Son	
1/2 legitim	£6,000
1/2 dead's part (her)	£27,000
1/2 dead's part (mov)	£6,000
Total	*£39,000*

Daughter

1/2 legitim	£6,000
1/2 dead's part (her)	£27,000
1/2 dead's part (mov)	£6,000
Total	*£39,000*

The fact that there is a mixture of heritable and moveable property left after the dwelling-house and furniture rights have been satisfied means that the financial provision has to be met proportionately out of the balances, i.e. in a ratio of £84,000/£56,000 which, expressed as a percentage, is 60/40 per cent. Thus 60 per cent of £50,000 is taken from the heritable estate and 40 per cent from the moveable: £30,000 and £20,000 respectively. The fact that the dead's part also contains a heritable and moveable balance does not create any problem, at least on paper, as the value of each will simply be halved between the two children.

COHABITING COUPLES

4-56   There is nothing new about couples cohabiting. However, relationships between couples have become more complex over the last 50 years or so. Subject to the exception of irregular marriage, it was normally clear whether couples were married or not. If they were married, there were rights of succession, but not otherwise. To all intents and purposes, same-sex couples who have entered into a civil partnership are in a virtually identical position to married couples when it comes to succession; and of course same-sex couples are now free to marry as well.[138]

However, there is no legal form of partnership available for members of the opposite sex who cohabit but are not legally married, or for members of the same sex who live together as partners, but have not married or entered into a civil partnership. There was previously a form of "irregular marriage" that could be constituted between cohabiting couples, but this was abolished by the Family Law (Scotland) Act 2006 (the 2006 Act), which also made a range of considerable changes relevant to this area.

Cohabitation prior to the Family Law (Scotland) Act 2006

4-57   So-called "irregular marriage" has long been recognised in Scots law; indeed historically only very basic formalities were required in Scotland to constitute a marriage at all.[139] Although the Marriage (Scotland) Act 1977 outlines the modern requirements for a formal or "regular" marriage, the possibility of constituting such a relationship by other means endured for some time; and indeed still does, although to an ever-decreasing extent.

---

[138] Under the Marriage and Civil Partnership (Scotland) Act 2014 which, among other things, amended the Marriage (Scotland) Act 1977 to accommodate this change.
[139] See, e.g. Clive E.M., *The Law of Husband and Wife in Scotland*, 4th edn (Edinburgh: W. Green, 1997).

The last surviving form of irregular marriage was marriage by "cohabitation with habit and repute". The principle of this is that, if a couple can be shown to have cohabited with each other as husband and wife, with the general reputation of being so, the court can on application grant a declarator confirming constitution of their marriage. The relevance for succession is obvious; successful application would grant a cohabitant the equivalent status of a surviving spouse, allowing claims to be made in respect of prior rights, legal rights, and rights to the free estate.

Each application would be judged on its own merits, taking into account a number of factors. The length of the relationship and duration of cohabitation was relevant but not conclusive.[140] The couple's own view of their relationship, where this could be evidenced, was often crucial,[141] as was the way in which the relationship was viewed by others.[142] A relatively recent case example is *Sheikh v Sheikh*,[143] which, although brought to court due to separation of the parties rather than death, still provides a useful illustration of the relevant issues. Here, the couple had been cohabiting for a period of 13 years, during which the claimant had used her partner's surname. They had two sons together, who also bore their father's surname and were seemingly shocked to discover that their parents were not, in fact, married. The family of the claimant's partner also believed the couple to be married. In opposing the action, the defender averred that the claimant had rejected several marriage proposals from him, and that he only acquiesced in their reputation as husband and wife because he did not want his sons to be considered illegitimate among his wider family. The court held that sufficient evidence had been led by the claimant to justify granting the decree.

Many cohabiting couples in recent times make it publicly known that they are not married; irregular marriage had no relevance for them. Equally, it had no relevance to people of the same sex who cohabited since, at the time, marriage could only be constituted between members of the opposite sex.

Irregular marriage has virtually been abolished by the 2006 Act,[144] subject to the exception that any period of cohabitation which began before its provisions came into force[145] can still be taken into account in a claim to be irregularly married, even when the period ends or continues after the date of commencement.[146] There is also provision to recognise as valid a marriage entered into abroad where, unknown to the parties, the marriage was invalid under the law of that country.[147] Despite the statutory terminology, it is perhaps fairer to say that marriage by cohabitation with habit and repute is being phased out rather than abolished, at least in terms of its most common purposes.

It is also worth noting that there is really no such thing as a "common law spouse" under Scots law, and the expression is best avoided. The same applies to the curious term "significant other person" so beloved of officialdom.

---

[140] *Kamperman v MacIver*, 1994 S.C. 230.
[141] *Shaw v Henderson*, 1982 S.L.T. 211.
[142] *Mackenzie v Scott*, 1980 S.L.T. (Notes) 9.
[143] *Sheikh v Sheikh*, 2005 Fam. L.R. 7.
[144] Family Law (Scotland) Act 2006 s.3(1).
[145] On 4 May 2006.
[146] Family Law (Scotland) Act 2006 s.3(2).
[147] Family Law (Scotland) Act 2006 s.3(3) and 3(4).

Rights of cohabitants under the Family Law (Scotland) Act 2006

4–58   The 2006 Act gave groundbreaking rights to cohabiting couples. These are distinct from the previous regime of rights acquired through constitution of irregular marriage, although it is probably fair to say that their purpose is, in many ways, similar. It is vitally important to understand that these rights are *not* automatic; a successful application must be made to the court. Equally it is also important to note that, in succession, the rights of a surviving cohabitee are not equivalent to those of a surviving spouse or civil partner, even if the eventual result achieved by their application might be very similar.

For the purposes of succession and certain other rights of property, then, a cohabitant is defined as either party to a relationship in which a man and a woman are or were living together as if they were husband and wife, or two persons of the same sex who are or were living together as if they were civil partners.[148] The 2006 Act outlines a number of factors that the court should have regard to, namely: the length of the period during which the two persons lived together; the nature of their relationship during that period; and the nature and extent of any financial arrangements subsisting, or which subsisted, during that period.[149]

A person who is deemed to be a cohabitant can make a claim on their partner's estate if their partner died without leaving a valid will.[150] If the deceased cohabitant *has* left a valid will, then the law is unchanged and a cohabitant would not be entitled to claim any financial provision from the deceased's estate, other than any legacy in the will. It is important to note, therefore, that these provisions apply only on intestacy.

In such a circumstance, then, an application may be made to the court by the surviving cohabitant for an award to be made. The deceased must have been domiciled in Scotland and the claimant must have been cohabiting with him or her immediately prior to death.[151] The award may take the form of a capital sum or property transfer order, or any appropriate interim order,[152] and is made entirely at the discretion of the court. A range of relevant circumstances will be taken into account, such as the size of the estate, other benefits received (for example the proceeds of a life assurance policy) and other claims on the estate.[153] Any capital payment will be made as specified by the court, and may be made by instalments.[154]

Significantly, the surviving cohabitee is not entitled to a larger amount than he or she would have been entitled to if the parties had been married or in a civil partnership.[155] Furthermore, any payments must be made from the deceased's net intestate estate, i.e. after payment of inheritance tax, debts and satisfaction of any prior or legal rights claims of a surviving spouse or civil partner.[156] The wording

---

[148] Family Law (Scotland) Act 2006 s.25(1).
[149] Family Law (Scotland) Act 2006 s.25(2).
[150] Family Law (Scotland) Act 2006 s.29.
[151] Family Law (Scotland) Act 2006 s.29(1).
[152] Family Law (Scotland) Act 2006 s.29(2).
[153] Family Law (Scotland) Act 2006 s.29(3).
[154] Family Law (Scotland) Act 2006 s.29(6).
[155] Family Law (Scotland) Act 2006 s.29(4).
[156] Family Law (Scotland) Act 2006 s.29(10).

of this section seems to provide that whilst claims by a cohabitant are postponed in favour of all claims made by a spouse or civil partner, they rank before legitim claims made by children. The balance of interests as between a cohabitant and children of the deceased was considered by the court in *Windram, Applicant*,[157] where a substantial capital payment was made to the applicant, who had cohabited with the deceased for a period of 24 years.

It is also important to note that there is a six month time limit from the death of the intestate partner to raise these claims.[158] There is no judicial discretion to extend this period, except in the very narrow circumstance of a cross-border mediation.[159] That said, it has recently been held that an action raised within the required time limit, but raised in incorrect form, was still competent even if amended outwith the time limit.[160]

Indeed, although the law in this area is still relatively new, and therefore subject to development, a number of cases have been reported interpreting the relevant provisions. Issues including the required length of cohabitation and of the deceased's domicile were considered in *Chebotareva v Khandro*.[161] Here, the deceased had been born in England, where he owned property and claimed benefits, and where he had also died. It was demonstrated that he and the claimant had been in a committed relationship for a substantial period of time, and had lived together in England for a period of at least a year. The deceased also owned property in Scotland, which he had visited with the claimant several times in the period leading up to his death. It was claimed that the couple's ultimate intention had been to reside in Scotland permanently, and that they had begun to habitually reside there. The court held that whilst a period of living together that exceeded a year, as part of a committed relationship, was sufficient to establish cohabition, there was insufficient evidence to establish that the deceased had been domiciled and habitually resident in Scotland. Accordingly, the claim failed.

The meaning of the deceased's "net intestate estate" was considered in *Kerr v Mangan*,[162] in which the deceased owned property in both Scotland and Ireland. It was held that a cohabitant could only claim against property which would devolve according to Scots law, taking into account exclusions under Scots private international law. Since heritable property in Ireland would be so excluded, it did not form part of the deceased's "net intestate estate" for the purposes of the claim. The related issue of factors affecting the potential extent of a cohabitant's claim was relevant in *Savage v Purches*,[163] where the claimant's action failed on the basis that he had already received a substantial lump sum from the death benefit payout of the deceased's pension scheme.

---

[157] *Windram, Applicant*, 2009 Fam. L.R. 157.
[158] Family Law (Scotland) Act 2006 s.29(6).
[159] Family Law (Scotland) Act 2006 s.29A, inserted by the Cross Border Mediation (Scotland) Regulations 2011. A cross-border mediation is essentially a method of resolving a dispute that involves parties who are domiciled in different Member States of the European Union.
[160] *X v A (No.1)*, 2016 S.L.T. (Sh Ct) 404.
[161] *Chebotareva v Khandro*, 2008 Fam. L.R. 66.
[162] *Kerr v Mangan* [2014] CSIH 69.
[163] *Savage v Purches*, 2009 S.L.T. (Sh Ct) 36.

The Scottish Law Commission recommended in its 2009 report that the rights of cohabitees in succession should be further reformed by a new statutory regime, which would extend also to claims made against a testate estate.[164] As yet no such change has been implemented.

THE FUTURE OF INTESTATE SUCCESSION

4–59 It has been mentioned at various points throughout this chapter that the current rules regarding division of an intestate estate may have lost some of their significance. The potential for even harsher criticism has also been alluded to. It cannot be argued that the rules are, by legal standards, somewhat old; having been established in the 1960s, they have remained largely unchanged for over half a century. What is more open to debate is whether they remain appropriate given the changing nature of Scotland's family demographics.

Critics observe that in some cases there is potential for the current scheme of intestate succession to cause more harm than good. The classic problem is that which arises due to "second families". It can occur, for example, where spouses divorce but have children together; should either remarry, the second spouse could, on intestacy, claim the bulk or even the entirety of the deceased's estate to the exclusion of his children. Worse, if the second spouse has children of her own, they will upon her death inherit to the exclusion of the (first) deceased's children. The same situation applies where a death has occurred and a surviving spouse remarries, but here the problem is actually exacerbated because the aggregate of *both* "first" spouses' estates can effectively be passed to an entirely separate family line. There is a strong argument to be made that this is undesirable, although of course counter-arguments can also be put forward.[165]

In the above situation it is the effect of prior rights in particular that causes consternation. Should there be estate left after satisfaction of these, the disappointed heirs would still have had a claim under their legal rights upon their father's passing. Of course, preventing disinheritance is the primary purpose of legal rights, since they can be claimed even where there is a will. However, the rigid application of legal rights as part of either scheme of division in succession does not escape criticism either.[166]

The Scottish Law Commission have recommended that the current system of rules regulating division of an intestate estate be simplified. In essence, their suggested scheme would involve a spouse or civil partner inheriting the entire estate where the deceased left no issue, or issue inheriting the whole intestate estate where there is no surviving spouse or civil partner. Where there is a surviving spouse or civil partner *and* surviving issue, the spouse or civil partner would claim the estate up to a certain value (the "threshold sum"), and any surplus over the threshold sum would be divided equally between the spouse or civil partner and the issue of the deceased.[167] Whilst this would certainly be a more straightforward system, it would not address the "second family" problem;

---

[164] Scottish Law Commission, *Report on Succession* (Scot. Law Com. No.215), Pt 4.

[165] See, e.g. McK Norrie K., "Reforming Succession Law: Intestate Succession" (2008) 12 Edinburgh Law Review 77.

[166] See, e.g. Cusine D., "Legal Rights: a Little Discretion Required?" (2014) S.L.T. 13.

[167] Scottish Law Commission, *Report on Succession* (Scot. Law Com. No.215), Pt 2.

the Commission acknowledges in its considerations the difficulties of regulating these situations, but does not make any firm recommendations regarding them.

As stated in Ch.1, 2016 saw the introduction of a new Succession (Scotland) Act, which had very little impact on intestate succession. It was also observed in Ch.1, however, that further statutory reforms have been hinted at and it is the possibility that these might finally overhaul the rules of intestacy that whets the collective appetites of many in the legal community. It will be very interesting to see the shape any such reforms take and, in particular, the extent to which it has been possible to accommodate the various competing arguments that surround this issue.

CHAPTER 5

Testamentary Documents

INTRODUCTION

Testate succession describes the situation where a deceased's property is disposed of by way of a will, or other equivalent testamentary writing. In a broader sense, the term can also be used to encompass the various rules and principles surrounding the making of such expressions of one's wishes. Someone who has made such expressions is called the "testator" or, if female, the "testatrix".[1]

The average lay person might perceive that there will be fewer complications in the event of someone dying testate rather than intestate. This has an element of truth in it, but it is not the whole truth. Certainly, testate succession offers the obvious advantage of people knowing where they stand, and the great majority of wills present no problems in execution and indeed prevent certain other problems from arising. However, the contents of a will might not be palatable to the survivors of the deceased, or there might a legal impediment preventing their implementation. There is also the possibility of problems surrounding the nature and circumstances of the will's drafting. These benefits and potential complications must be weighed against those inherent to intestate succession, which offers greater certainty but lacks any flexibility in application. On balance, the prevailing view among legal professionals is that having in place a comprehensive and well-drafted will is preferable to surrendering one's estate to the dispassionate rules of intestacy. Indeed, this is underlined by the increasing tendency for solicitors in Scotland to participate in "free wills" events.[2]

5–01

TYPES OF TESTAMENTARY WRITING

To "test" means to witness or verify, especially in the context of making a will.[3] Most people are very familiar with the general concept of a will, but actually the term itself has no precise meaning in Scots law, and there has never been a single prescribed form that such a document must take.[4] There are, in fact, a number of methods by which an individual can leave instructions regarding the distribution of his property upon death.

5–02

---

[1] The male form is used for sake of brevity throughout this text.
[2] See, e.g. Law Society of Scotland, *Making a Will* (online document, undated). Available at *http://www.lawscot.org.uk/for-the-public/what-solicitors-can-do-for-you/making-a-will/* [Accessed 8 May 2017].
[3] From the Latin *testor*.
[4] McLaren, 508.

Having said that, in general parlance the term "will" tends to be used in a narrow sense, i.e. a written declaration clearly expressing what the testator wishes to be done with his estate after death. This can be contrasted with certain other documents that may also have a testamentary effect, such as marriage contracts that contain provisions regarding disposal of assets upon death, though it is fair to say that these are less common nowadays than historically. Also common were informal documents, such as letters, written by the deceased during his lifetime in which bequests of property were promised. Perhaps of more modern-day relevance is the often-employed device of a "codicil", which is a secondary (but separate) document that makes amendments, or additional testamentary provisions, to an earlier will.

In correct drafting, it is common for the testator to explicitly revoke earlier wills; this is logical since a testator is, of course, entitled to change his mind, and so it is important that only the most recent expression of his wishes is valid and will be given effect. There is a potential pitfall in the use of the narrow term "wills" in such revocations rather than the broader "testamentary writings". In *Clark's Executor v Clark*,[5] a testator had written a letter three years before his death to an old friend, in which he bequeathed said friend his stamp collection. In a will made two years later, the testator left his entire estate (barring certain exceptions) to a charitable cause. The will contained the clause "I cancel all wills previously executed by me". It was held that this did *not* serve to revoke the promise of the stamp collection.

It is also appropriate to distinguish between a simple will (i.e. in the sense as used above) and a "trust disposition and settlement". Under the former, the testator's estate is placed in the possession of an executor for distribution directly to the relevant beneficiaries. Under the latter, the estate (or at least part of it) is retained in the hands of testamentary trustees and administered for a continuing purpose, such as a liferent or for a charitable benefit.

Although they differ in terminology and, to some extent, in exact purpose, the documents mentioned above share many similarities from a legal standpoint. They are all forms of testamentary writing, and common rules apply regarding their validity and application. Anything in the text that is said to apply to a "will" can also be applied to any of these documents, unless the contrary is stated.

There are also a number of documents that serve the same ultimate purpose as a testamentary writing, i.e. the transfer of property upon death, but do so by different mechanisms. These are subject to their own specialist rules, and a selection of these is considered in Ch.9.

ESSENTIAL VALIDITY

5–03   As mentioned above, most people understand the basic purpose of a will, and indeed it is in essence a fairly straightforward concept. However, as with any legal act, a testator must understand the entire nature and true consequences of what he is consenting to. It must also be clear that he did indeed intend to make a definite testamentary instruction, rather than something more vague regarding

---

[5] *Clark's Executor v Clark*, 1943 S.C. 216.

future possibilities. In legal terminology, he must have had both testamentary capacity and concluded a testamentary intent.

Capacity to make a will

The testator must have the necessary capacity in law to test, i.e. he must have the legally-recognised capability of expressing what he wishes to be done with his property after death, and of understanding the nature and consequences of such an expression. Testamentary capacity can be affected by a number of issues, some far more complex than others; the approach taken by the law to tackling these is, understandably, similarly complex.

Age

The testator's age is a relatively straightforward matter when considering testamentary capacity, although the historical legal position was slightly less so. Under the old common law, boys having reached the age of 14 years and girls having reached 12 were classed as "minors", and as such had capacity to test, but over moveable property only.[6] Below these ages, children were classed as "pupils" and were regarded as not having the sufficient use of reason to make a will. This position was altered by statute to include capacity to test over heritables.[7]

The current law is contained within the Age of Legal Capacity (Scotland) Act 1991, a wide-ranging statute which replaced the previous distinctions regarding young people with a somewhat simpler system. This Act sets a "general" age of legal capacity of 16,[8] but includes a number of diverse exceptions to this. The rule relevant to succession is that the age of testamentary capacity is fixed at 12 years, for both boys and girls.[9] This is effective only in regards to wills executed on or after the date of the Act coming into force, namely 25 September 1991; the previous position is retained the respect of documents executed prior to this.

The age of testamentary capacity is surprisingly low to some, but it is likely to be of little relevance in practice. Most individuals will not hold significant property, or have family obligations, until they reach the age of 16 and can enter fully into employment and get married (or enter into a civil partnership). Even where an individual between the ages of 12 and 16 *would* benefit from the capacity to test, it is likely that the rules of intestate succession would provide adequate provision. That said, the law favours freedom in most matters, and testamentary capacity is an important legal right, so the issue should not be ignored entirely.

There is no "upper age" at which someone would lose testamentary capacity, however, it is logical that in advancing age it becomes more likely that someone's mental faculties might be affected to the extent that their capacity is compromised.

5–04

5–05

---

[6] McLaren, 490.
[7] Succession (Scotland) Act 1964 s.28 (now repealed).
[8] Age of Legal Capacity (Scotland) Act 1991 s.1.
[9] Age of Legal Capacity (Scotland) Act 1991 s.2(2).

Mental incapacity

5–06   Illness and other factors affecting a person's decisions, particularly decisions that have a legal consequence, is a matter of the utmost delicacy. The term "insane" has long been used in cases and legal texts to describe someone not in control of their faculties, but this is a blunt term with somewhat negative connotations and its use is perhaps on the wane. "*Incapax*" is a commonly-encountered Latin term meaning "incapable", which in this context can be used to describe someone who lacks the necessary mental capacity to make a will. "Soundness of mind" is another phrase seemingly inextricably linked with the making of wills.

Regardless of terminology, the problem of determining whether or not someone has made a decision whilst in full appreciation of its nature and consequences is an issue of great complexity. Indeed, it has long been recognised as such, leading to several attempts at judicial clarification as to how the issue ought to be approached. The leading case is *Morrison v Maclean's Trustees*,[10] where an eccentric testator's will was held to be valid, despite the fact that much of his everyday speech had been of an obscene and bizarre nature, and that he claimed to have been fed from an eagle's nest when young. The court was very clear on the point that just because a will's terms are objectionable to the testator's family, this is not sufficient in itself to render the will invalid.

It is important first to note that there is a general presumption in favour of sufficient mental capacity. The onus is on the person seeking to challenge a will to prove that such capacity was absent at the time of its making. Where the testator was under medical supervision for a condition likely to impair his mental capabilities, this might give rise to a contrary presumption, but this can be rebutted and the question is always one of fact. In *Nisbet's Trustees v Nisbet*,[11] a testator made a will whilst under long-term residential psychiatric care. When he died two months later, members of his family challenged the will's validity on grounds of lack of mental capacity. On the evidence presented, the court was satisfied that, despite the general condition of the testator, he had possessed sufficient reason at the time the will was executed; therefore it was valid. It was noted in this case that the rationality of the document itself was an important consideration when considering whether a testator had capacity at the relevant time.

The issue of "partial unsoundness of mind" was also considered in the *Nisbet* case, although a conclusion was not reached on how exactly it should affect testamentary capacity. The concept was later developed in *Sivewright v Sivewright's Trustees*,[12] which involved a challenge raised against the will of a testator who was described generally as "a sane man". However, his widow alleged that he was under a delusion regarding how he had been treated by her and her sister, and this so aggrieved him that he had treated her unfavourably under his will. The court rejected the widow's claims and the will was held to be valid.

There were (at least) two important points to emerge from the *Sivewright* case. First, a basic test for mental testamentary capacity was outlined, whereby

---

[10] *Morrison v Maclean's Trustees* (1862) 24 D. 625.
[11] *Nisbet's Trustees v Nisbet* (1871) 9 M. 937.
[12] *Sivewright v Sivewright's Trustees*, 1920 S.C. (HL) 63.

"a testator must be able to exercise a rational appreciation of what he is doing. He must understand the nature of his act".[13]

Secondly, in considering the effects of a temporary delusion, it was stated that

"the will must be shown to have been the outcome of the special delusion … [it] must be shown to have been an actual and compelling influence".[14]

A modern application of these rules can be found in *Stewart v Franks*,[15] in which the children of a testator sought to challenge his will on the grounds of his long-standing paranoid personality disorder. An extensive account of the testator's abusive behaviour towards various family members was presented, and was accepted by the court to be generally accurate. However, the court held that whilst this behaviour reflected poorly on the testator's moral character, it was not sufficient to establish a lack of testamentary capacity. This case serves as a reminder that the courts will not lightly strike down a will on grounds of mental incapacity.

Finally here, it should also be noted that a person's testamentary capacity can be affected by short-term impairment such as intoxication by alcohol or drugs. This is particularly relevant where someone is receiving medical treatment for a severe or terminal illness, although the same principles are likely to apply to voluntary intoxication. In the oft-cited *Laidlaw v Laidlaw*,[16] it was accepted that a strong dose of opiates given to the testator to relieve the pain of his disease had rendered him incapable of understanding the meaning and effect of the will he had executed whilst under such influence; the will was therefore invalid. There is more recent authority which, although English, suggests that the relevant considerations in such situations has not changed in modern times.[17]

Influence of others

In addition to having the requisite understanding of a will and its effect, it is also important that a testator is providing instructions genuinely of his own free will. In some situations there is a possibility that a testator might have been positively influenced by someone seeking to direct his testamentary instructions, and this too can affect a will's validity.

5–07

Facility and circumvention

A person who is old or infirm might suffer a degree of mental deterioration which, without removing mental capacity entirely, leaves him vulnerable to manipulation by others. Someone may, for any number of reasons, take advantage of this by persuading him to execute a will in certain terms. This is the essence of facility and circumvention.

5–08

---

[13] *Sivewright v Sivewright's Trustees*, 1920 S.C. (HL) 63 at 64, per Viscount Haldane.
[14] *Sivewright v Sivewright's Trustees*, 1920 S.C. (HL) 63 at 64, per Viscount Haldane.
[15] *Stewart v Franks* [2013] CSOH 63.
[16] *Laidlaw v Laidlaw* (1870) 8 M. 882.
[17] *Sharp v Adam* [2006] EWCA Civ 449.

Three elements are necessary for a will to be successfully challenged on such grounds. There must be "facility" on the part of the testator, "circumvention" of his normal defences by another, and "lesion" done to his interests. These elements are interrelated, and will be considered by the court as a whole, with the effect that where there is greater facility established, less evidence of circumvention is required, and vice versa. In *Munro v Strain*,[18] a testator who was generally of sound mind was persuaded to change his will by a clergyman following the death of his son. The court held that facility need only be shown in relation to the circumvention used; "facility may be inferred from, or may consist in, circumstances giving to one man an unusual power and influence over another".[19]

"Facility" is a concept which is easier to appreciate than to precisely define. In the leading case of *Gibson's Executor v Anderson*,[20] it was described as

> "something other than weakness of mind … It means that a person is in such a mental state that he is unable to resist pressure, and that someone else can mould and fashion his conduct as he pleases".[21]

It is very much a matter of scale, with mere suggestibility at one end and a mental state falling just short of incapacity at the other; indeed, facility and circumvention is often pled as an alternative to incapacity.[22] As observed in the *Morrison* case, "a man may be weak and facile from want of judgement or reason … [or] from mere nervousness and incapacity to resist solicitation".[23]

Facility can take a number of forms, and can have been brought on or exacerbated by various factors such as bereavement,[24] alcoholism,[25] or the general onset of dementia.[26] The vital element is susceptibility to persuasion; this should not be confused with a lack of intellect or general difficulties of comprehension. It must be shown that the testator was particularly liable to influence or intimidation.[27]

"Circumvention" is similarly nebulous, but encompasses any conduct designed to steer the testator's will. It was defined in the *Morrison* case as "improper practices and solicitation by interested parties".[28] This can take any number of forms, ranging from general intimidation,[29] to the making of positive threats,[30] to physically taking the testator to a solicitor's office and presenting him with a document to sign.[31] Depending on the circumstances it might not be possible to establish exactly what form the circumvention took, but this is

---

[18] *Munro v Strain* (1874) 1 R. 1039.
[19] *Munro v Strain* (1874) 1 R. 1039 at 1043–1044, per Lord Justice-Clerk Moncreiff.
[20] *Gibson's Executor v Anderson*,1925 S.C. 774.
[21] *Gibson's Executor v Anderson*, 1925 S.C. 774 at 790, per Lord Justice-Clerk Alness.
[22] This was the case in *Morrison v Maclean's Trustees*, considered above.
[23] *Morrison v Maclean's Trustees* (1862) 24 D. 625 at 635, per Lord Justice-Clerk Inglis.
[24] As in *Munro v Strain* (1874) 1 R. 1039.
[25] *Pascoe-Watson v Brock's Executer*, 1998 S.L.T. 40.
[26] *Horsburgh v Thomson's Trustees*, 1912 1 S.L.T. 73.
[27] *Cairns v Marianski* (1850) 12 D. 1286.
[28] *Morrison v Maclean's Trustees* (1862) 24 D. 625 at 628 per Lord Justice-Clerk Inglis.
[29] *Horsburgh v Thomson's Trustees*, 1912 1 S.L.T. 73; *Cairns v Marianski* (1850) 12 D. 1286.
[30] *Love v Marshall* (1870) 9 M. 291.
[31] *Wheelans v Wheelans*, 1986 S.L.T. 164.

acknowledged by the court; it was observed in *Clunie v Stirling*[32] that "the actual mode or particular acts of circumvention may not be discoverable or easily proved".[33] If strong evidence of facility is presented, then circumvention can be inferred from the surrounding facts.[34]

A relatively modern case example, and one which involves circumstances very familiar to this area, is *Horne v Whyte*.[35] Here, a mentally and physically impaired widower executed a codicil that greatly reduced the legacies left to his family members. This was done to the benefit of his housekeeper, who had taken control of the testator's finances, and upon whom he had become heavily dependent. It was held that his general medical condition, coupled with his dependence on his housekeeper, was sufficient to establish his facility, and that circumvention could be inferred due to the control she was able to exert, and the benefit she had received under the altered will.

"Lesion" essentially means harm, the point being that the testator's interests must be adversely affected as a result of the circumvention. The mere fact that the testator himself has been moved to take action he otherwise would not have is sufficient, since his true and natural intentions have been interfered with.[36] That said, the majority of challenges arise from family members who would otherwise have benefitted from the testator's uncompromised wishes, or even where they would benefit more from intestacy than from the terms of the will in question. It is important to restate the point in *Morrison*, however, that facility and circumvention is not just a mechanism by which disgruntled family members can seek to increase their benefit; all three factors must be present for a challenge to succeed.

Undue influence

Someone exerting undue influence on the testator is a different concept to facility **5–09** and circumvention, but the distinction is sometimes very fine. Perhaps the primary difference between them is that there is no need to show that the testator was facile to any great degree, although in practice there is often at least an element of facility and this makes a challenge much more likely to succeed. What must be demonstrated is that there was a relationship of trust and confidence between the testator and the beneficiary, of which the latter has taken advantage. This is the essence of undue influence.

Perhaps the classic example is the relationship between a solicitor and his client. In *Ross v Gosselin's Executors*,[37] a 90 year-old testatrix left a substantial part of her estate to her nephew, who had also acted as her solicitor. It was alleged by another family member that this nephew had manipulated the testatrix and induced her to give him large gifts, whilst also encouraging her to disinherit her other relatives to his benefit. Facility and circumvention could not be proven, but the court accepted the alternative pleading of undue influence.

---

[32] *Clunie v Stirling* (1854) 17 D. 15.
[33] *Clunie v Stirling* (1854) 17 D. 15 at 17–18, per Lord Justice-Clerk Hope.
[34] *West's Trustees v West*, 1980 S.L.T. 6.
[35] *Horne v Whyte* [2005] CSOH 115.
[36] *Williams v Philip* (1907) 15 S.L.T. 396.
[37] *Gosselin's Executors*, 1926 S.C. 325.

There is no "closed list" of relevant relationships, but there must be an element of dependency present. This often exists where the person allegedly exerting the influence has a professional association with the testator, or where the two are in a so-called "fiduciary or quasi-fiduciary relationship".[38] In *Honeyman's Executor v Sharp*,[39] it was stated that such a relationship arises

"where a person, in pursuance of his profession or calling, undertakes the giving of advice to another and where, as a result, there develops a relationship between the adviser and the advised in which ... the latter places trust and confidence in the former".[40]

The *Honeyman* case was perhaps unusual in that it involved a fine art dealer influencing a customer; previous examples have involved persons in somewhat more "official" positions such as clergymen[41] and doctors.[42] Close family members are also commonly accepted as being in a position to exert undue influence,[43] but friends are less likely to be so.[44]

The mere existence of a relationship likely to allow influence over the testator is not enough. There must be have been some conduct or behaviour whereby that influence has in fact been exerted. In *Forrest v Lowe's Trustees*,[45] the advice given by a solicitor to his client was called into question. It was held that undue influence could only be established if some misrepresentation had been made, or some coercion effected. The onus is on the person alleging undue influence to prove that it occurred. In *Tiarks v Paterson*,[46] a relative of the testator had prepared a codicil in her own favour, but it was not proven that she had exerted undue influence. In particularly suspicious circumstances it is possible for undue influence to be inferred from the surrounding facts; this requires the trusted person to provide an innocent explanation for what has occurred.[47]

Intention to test

5–10 No specific form of words is required in order to establish that a document is to have testamentary effect. Many wills from the world of fiction begin with the words "I, being of sound mind and body ... " but it is highly unlikely that this would actually be encountered in practice. What *must* be clear is that the wording used, whatever it may be, demonstrates testamentary intent on the part of the testator. A document that shows mere deliberations on the part of the deceased, or an intention to make a will in the future, will not be sufficient.

Sometimes, it is clear that a document is still in the stages of drafting. In *Sprot's Trustees v Sprot*,[48] a purported will headed with "rough" was held to be

[38] Considered at length in *Forbes v Forbes' Trustees*, 1957 S.C. 325.
[39] *Honeyman's Executor v Sharp*, 1978 S.C. 223.
[40] *Honeyman's Executor v Sharp*, 1978 S.C. 223 at 228, per Lord Maxwell.
[41] *Allcard v Skinner* (1887) 36 Ch. D 145.
[42] *Radcliffe v Price* (1902) 18 T.L.R. 466.
[43] *Weir v Grace* (1899) 2 F. (HL) 30.
[44] *McKechnie v McKechnie's Trustees*, 1908 S.C. 93.
[45] *Forrest v Lowe's Trustees*, 1907 S.C. 1240.
[46] *Tiarks v Paterson*, 1992 G.W.D. 23-1328.
[47] *Read v Cattanach*, 1990 G.W.D. 31-1839.
[48] *Sprot's Trustees v Sprot*, 1909 S.C. 272.

ineffective. More often, the circumstances are more ambiguous, and each case is decided on its own merits. Generally a mere list of names or items will fail, even if the word "will" is used; this was the case in *Colvin v Hutchison*,[49] where a list of apparent legacies had been signed by the deceased, but overall the document was inaccurate and barely comprehensible, and was held to be invalid. On the other hand, in *Ayrshire Hospice, Petitioners*,[50] a lady had written a three page document in her own handwriting. It contained a list of legacies to relatives, prefixed by the word "To", and the final page referred to "remainder" and gave a list of charities. The document was found in an envelope on which were printed the words "Will of …….. " but nothing else. The same was repeated on the head of the document. In context, this was held to be a valid will.

A document that appears to express future testamentary intention, or that gives instructions to a person other than a law agent, is much more likely to be accepted as a will than a document that gives instructions to a solicitor. In *Rhodes v Peterson*,[51] a woman wrote to her daughter, informing her that she intended to make a will in which the daughter would be left her house and its contents. It was held that the letter was a valid will itself, rather than an indication of future intention. Conversely, in the old case of *Munro v Coutts*,[52] a testator sent a letter to his law agent enclosing a provision with instructions to include it as a codicil in his will. This was held to be no more than an instruction and not a testamentary document in itself.

A related problem is encountered when, within a document that is intended to be testamentary, it is unclear whether certain provisions constitute an instruction or are merely expressing a wish. These are sometimes referred to as "precatory bequests", from the Latin *precari* (to pray). Unsurprisingly, the problem might arise most frequently in a homemade will, where a testator is more likely to use phrases such as "I would like" or "I would prefer" rather than more assertive verbs such as "instruct" or "direct" found more commonly in professionally drafted wills. The obvious question is whether or not such a precatory provision is binding in law, apart from any possible moral obligation. The rough rule of thumb seems to be that if a wish is expressed to an executor or testamentary trustee, it is more likely to be taken as an instruction than if it is expressed to a beneficiary. Thus in *Barclay's Executor v McLeod*,[53] a desire expressed to an inheriting spouse that she should make testamentary provisions for other relatives was not legally binding. On the other hand in *Reid's Trustees v Dawson*,[54] where a testator "preferred" his trustees to pay a capital sum to a beneficiary, this was held to be an instruction and thus a valid bequest. There may also be cases where a request or instruction to an executor cannot be carried out. In *Milne v Smith*,[55] the testator provided a legacy to his son in the hope that the partnership, of which the father had been part, would be continued by the son. This was beyond the powers of the executor to fulfil and the legacy was paid without being subject to conditions.

---

[49] *Colvin v Hutchison* (1885) 12 R. 947.
[50] *Ayrshire Hospice, Petitioners*, 1993 S.L.T. (Sh Ct) 75.
[51] *Rhodes v Peterson*, 1971 S.C. 56.
[52] *Munro v Coutts* (1813) 1 Dow 437.
[53] *Barclay's Executor v McLeod* (1880) 7 R. 477.
[54] *Reid's Trustees v Dawson*, 1915 S.C. (HL) 47.
[55] *Milne v Smith*, 1982 S.L.T. 129.

Errors

5–11   In theory a will, like various other documents of a legal nature, can be deemed invalid on the basis that an error has been made. At one extreme, is it possible that someone could be duped into executing a testamentary document in the belief that they are doing something else entirely. At the other, there might be a simple clerical error made that could potentially completely undermine the purpose of the will. Whilst the former example has more in keeping with matters such as facility and circumvention already discussed, and the latter perhaps relates more to matters of formal validity discussed below, this area does straddle the two somewhat and so is deserving of separate treatment.

The case of *Munro v Strain*,[56] considered above, provides an example whereby a will could have been struck down on the basis of essential error, in addition to the arguments made regarding facility and circumvention. The particular issue in this case was an alteration made to the testator's will that an orphanage, which had long been intended to be set up using funds from the testator's estate, should be for the exclusive benefit of Catholic children. This was a condition that the testator had previously, and in strenuous terms, refused to apply. However, the alteration was affected, at the behest of the interested clergyman and by a solicitor other than testator's usual law agent. The circumstances were dubious at best, and whilst the court accepted that facility and circumvention applied, essential error could have been argued as an alternative.

Where an error has been made in drafting, and the testator has omitted to check over the prepared document or, having checked, failed to detect the error, it is possible that it does not reflect his true intentions. Worse, it is possible that the error is more fundamental, such as being someone else's will entirely. (This is not as far-fetched as it may seem, as will be shown.)

Historically, in such cases the will could fail on grounds of essential error,[57] although on occasion the courts have corrected minor mistakes where they were obviously mere errors.[58] The limitations on the courts' power in this area were highlighted by the recent decision of *Marley v Rawlings*[59] that, though English, did raise the question of how a similar situation might be dealt with in Scotland. In this case, a husband and wife instructed their solicitor to draft wills in near-identical terms, whereby each spouse left their entire estate to the other or, in the event that their spouse predeceased, to their adoptive son. As a result of a mistake made by the solicitor, husband and wife were given the wrong will to sign, an error that was not detected until after both had died. After a lengthy legal campaign and appealing to the Supreme Court, the adopted son was successful in his claim that this error could be rectified.

Following this case there is modern statutory authority under the 2016 Act. Tacitly affirming the approach taken in *Marley*, the court is explicitly granted extensive powers to "rectify" a document where it does not reflect the instructions of the testator.[60] There are conditions attached, the most significant being that the will must have been prepared on the testator's behalf, and not by

---

[56] *Munro v Strain* (1874) 1 R. 1039.
[57] *Yeatman v Proctors* (1877) 5 R. 179.
[58] *Reid's Trustees v Butcher*, 1929 S.C. 615.
[59] *Marley v Rawlings* [2015] A.C. 129.
[60] Succession (Scotland) Act 2016 s.3.

the testator himself. This perhaps serves as a warning against homemade wills and "will kits" that, alongside other matters, are considered below.

FORMAL VALIDITY

It has already been stated that there is no set wording required to demonstrate testamentary intention. Similarly, there is no set form a will need take in order to be valid. There are, however, a number of basic requirements to which a will, or any testamentary document, must conform. An obvious problem when these two facts are considered together is that no two wills are ever identical, even if they are very similar, and it is possible that even a well-drafted (and appropriately-intentioned) document will fail on technical grounds. This is unlikely to be the case with a professionally drafted will (although legal practitioners are not immune from making mistakes, as demonstrated below), but it can be an issue with less formal wills; even those prepared using "will kits" that, whilst not to be derided, certainly require to be approached with caution. Indeed, one of the most common failings in homemade wills is that often they import half-understood jargon from books, novels and films. In practice, it is much safer to refer to "children" than "issue", because issue means not only children but also all further direct descendants. Yet, to some people, "issue" sounds more impressive. The other main failing concerns the formal validity of the document.

5–12

The vast majority of legal systems require some formalities to be complied with in the drafting and execution of a testamentary document. The reasons for this are obvious; they help to guard against fraud, and to assist in determining the genuine intent of the testator. It is, of course, possible that a testator could be coerced, as demonstrated previously in this chapter, but formal requirements at least make the task of achieving such misdeeds that much more difficult.

There is a balance to be struck between respecting the need for formalities, and giving effect to the clearly expressed intentions of a testator. Scots law has traditionally taken a somewhat liberal view of formalities, in least in comparison to other jurisdictions. Few countries allow oral (or "nuncupative") wills, since there is far too great a potential for contradictory claims and the inevitable evidentiary problems they would give rise to. That said, it was formerly the case in Scotland that an oral legacy for a very small amount was valid, but this is an old law that has no modern relevance.

The crucial point, then, is that a will requires to be in some form of writing. (It is, incidentally, perfectly true that a will can competently be written on the back of a cigarette packet, although this is hardly the most respectful way of treating potential beneficiaries.) Even if someone, on his death bed, states that he is changing his will, this is of no significance unless the new provision is put into writing and properly signed as explained below. It is not possible (at least yet) to execute a valid will by means of recording other than writing, such as by way of video or electronic communication.

Provided there is a written testamentary document in place, the most relevant factor as regards formality is whether it was signed before 1 August 1995, or on or after this date. This is due to statutory changes that were introduced at this time. In either case, there are two main issues to consider. The first is legal validity of the document, i.e. whether or not it conforms to the minimum formal requirements. The second is proof of the document's veracity, i.e. whether or not it requires further supporting evidence to be led before it will be given effect.

Wills executed before 1 August 1995

5–13   There are likely still a considerable number of wills executed before the above date by people who are still alive. This means that the "old law" in this area continues to be relevant, although of course as time passes it will gradually be applied less often. Moreover, in order to fully understand the changes implemented in 1995, it is necessary to appreciate something of the regime they replaced.

Pre-1995 practice was governed partly by common law and partly by ancient statute. The statutory provisions were found in a venerable collection of Acts of the Scots Parliament, interpreted over the years by the courts and partly modernised by 19th and 20th century legislation, known by the august collective title of the "Authentication Statutes".

For wills executed under the old law, the two issues of validity and proof are very much linked. In terms of validity, any method of writing is acceptable, be it typed or handwritten. Even writing in pencil is acceptable,[61] although there are obvious risks associated with this, not least that pencil alterations on a document otherwise completed in ink will not necessarily be deemed to show conclusive testamentary intent.[62] The type of writing is directly related to the issue of whether further supporting evidence is required.

There are, broadly, three distinct forms of valid document. An "attested" will is one that has been executed before witnesses. A "holograph" will is one that has been drafted in the testator's own handwriting, and signed by him. A will that is "adopted as holograph" is a document, howsoever prepared, that the testator has written those words upon to indicate that they constitute his will. In addition, any formally valid will may incorporate less formal documents, such as letters, provided they demonstrate sufficient testamentary intent.

An attested will is said to be self-proving or "probative". This means that the court will presume it has been validly executed and that it is authentic, with no requirement for supporting evidence. Wills that are holograph or adopted as holograph are not probative but "privileged", which means that while they are formally valid, evidence is required to confirm that the handwriting and signature are genuinely that of the testator. This having been done, the distinction disappears and holograph wills then become probative.

Challenging the validity of a probative document is possible, by raising an action in the Court of Session. However, very strong evidence is required, and cases rarely succeed. In *McArthur v McArthur's Trustees*,[63] a challenge was made on the grounds that a will had not been properly witnessed, but failed because the supporting evidence offered was insufficient to rebut the presumption of validity. Similarly, in *McLure v McLure's Executrix*,[64] the pursuer intentionally delayed

---

[61] *Tait's Trustees v Chiene*, 1911 S.C. 743.
[62] *Munro's Executors v Munro* (1890) 18 R. 122.
[63] *McArthur v McArthur's Trustees*, 1931 S.L.T. 463.
[64] *McLure v McLure's Executrix*, 1997 S.L.T. 127.

his action in an attempt to avoid paying debts due to the estate. The court held that it was no longer open to him to challenge the will, and his action failed.

Attested wills

The requirements for attestation were developed by several of the Authentication Statutes, particularly the Subscription of Deeds Act 1681 and the Deeds Act 1696. An attested will is one that has been signed (or "subscribed") on every page by the testator, with the signature on the last page witnessed by two individuals, who confirm their witnessing by adding signatures of their own. As stated above, an attested will is both valid and probative, and essentially constitutes the "best practice" under the old law.

5–14

The witnesses must both be at least 16 years old,[65] must have the required mental capacity, and in theory must be "independent" and must "know" the testator. However, in practice the application of these tests was very flexible. A family member is acceptable, even one who stands to benefit under the will,[66] but of course there is then a risk that undue influence might later be alleged. At the other extreme, someone who has just been introduced to the testator is also acceptable. Witnesses should add their signatures as quickly as possible, not necessarily at the same time but certainly before the testator dies. In *Walker v Whitwell*,[67] the testatrix dictated her will to her son, who saw her sign but did not do so himself until after she had died six days later. Although the Court of Session had held this to be acceptable, the House of Lords disagreed, stating that signatures are essential formalities, and that witnesses sign only with the testator's consent, which lapses upon death.

The *Walker* case illustrates an example of a "fatal" flaw in formal validity. If there is a less-serious informality of execution, such as a testator omitting to sign one of the pages, this would not necessarily be fatal to the validity of the will. It is possible to ask the court for such an informality to be cured, under the provisions of the Conveyancing (Scotland) Act 1874 s.39. This is generally known as "section 39 procedure"; what the title lacks in originality it more than compensates for in clarity. An informality of execution renders a will improbative, so the person seeking to rely on it has the onus of proving that it was in fact subscribed by the testator and attested by the witnesses.

Whether or not section 39 procedure would cure a defect is very much a matter of degree. In the case of *Williamson v Williamson*,[68] Mrs Williamson had signed her will in 1988. The two witnesses were a Mr Wilson and his wife. In a fit of absent-mindedness and in the heat of the moment, Mr Wilson accidentally signed his surname as "Williamson"; his wife managed to sign her name properly. After Mrs Williamson's death, a member of her family noticed this obvious inconsistency and challenged the validity of the will. Eventually, the will was declared to be invalid, as one of the witness' signatures was fatally flawed. This was deemed to be more than mere informality of execution and so was not

---

[65] Age of Legal Capacity (Scotland) Act 1991 s.9(g). The minimum age prior to this Act's passing was 14.
[66] *Simsons v Simsons* (1883) 10 R. 1247.
[67] *Walker v Whitwell*, 1916 S.C. (HL) 75.
[68] *Williamson v Williamson*, 1997 S.L.T. 1044.

curable under section 39 procedure. Mrs Williamson's estate fell into intestate succession. If the witness had signed his correct name but had been wrongly designed in the testing clause, this would have been curable under section 39 procedure. This is illustrated by *Braithwaite v Bank of Scotland*,[69] where a witness to a pre-1995 Act document, as a joke in poor taste, described himself falsely as a "consultant gynaecologist". Although, in context, the document did not require to be probative, the judge expressed the view that this defect could probably have been curable by section 39 procedure. Sometimes, section 39 procedure is deemed not to even be necessary at all, such as in *Grieve's Trustees v Japp's Trustees*,[70] where a witness included her maiden name as part of her signature.

Holograph wills

5–15   The term "holograph" simply means handwritten, and at Scottish common law a will was regarded as valid if it was handwritten in all essential parts and signed by the testator.[71] No witnesses are necessary. A document that has been typed by the testator, or prepared in any form by another person, can be "adopted as holograph" by the testator signing and writing those words (or similar) at the end. Again, no witnesses are required.

In rare cases it has been decided that a document entirely typed save for the signature is valid, though the required circumstances are understandably very narrow. In *McBeath's Trustees v McBeath*,[72] the testator typed a will, including in it a statement that he had typed it and the words "adopted as holograph" above his handwritten signature. Evidence showed that due to illness, typing was the testator's invariable method of preparing documents. By a narrow majority the Court of Session held that the will was valid. By contrast, in *Chisholm v Chisholm*,[73] the facts were similar but there was no statement that the testator had typed the will, or an adoption as holograph. The will was held to be invalid.

As stated above, a holograph will is valid but not probative. Anyone seeking to rely on it must lead evidence that the handwriting and signature are genuinely that of the testator. The required proof is by way of affidavits from at least two people.[74] In essence, once the holograph will is supported by these two affidavits it is, for all intents and purposes, probative.[75]

It has been stated that the requirement for a signature is absolute and inflexible.[76] That said, in practice the courts have accepted some very informal testamentary writings and, in context, even signatures in "pet" names have been deemed valid. The nickname "Connie" was accepted in *Draper v Thomason*,[77] as

---

[69] *Braithwaite v Bank of Scotland*, 1997 G.W.D. 40-2037.
[70] *Grieve's Trustees v Japp's Trustees*, 1917 1 S.L.T. 70.
[71] Erskine, III 2 22.
[72] *McBeath's Trustees v McBeath*, 1935 S.C. 471.
[73] *Chisholm v Chisholm*, 1949 S.C. 434.
[74] Succession (Scotland) Act 1964 s.21.
[75] Succession (Scotland) Act 1964 s.32. This oversimplifies the matter somewhat; see also Ch.11 on Executry Practice.
[76] See, e.g. *Foley v Costello*, 1904 6 F. 365.
[77] *Draper v Thomason*, 1954 S.C. 136.

was simply "Mum" in *Rhodes v Peterson*.[78] Such signatures would not be acceptable in an attested will. In rare cases a signature might, strictly speaking, even be absent as regards the actual document; this is not necessarily fatal. In the relatively recent case of *Davidson v Convy*,[79] a document expressing clear testamentary intent and straightforward in its terms was written entirely in the hand of the testatrix, but it was unsigned. However, it was found within an envelope on which "my will" had been handwritten by the testatrix, under which was one version of her signature. It was held that this constituted a valid will.

It is possible to buy or download "will forms" with certain words already pre-printed. The testator fills in the blanks in relation to legacies, appointment of executor and suchlike. Whilst these do have their uses, not least because they encourage testators to consider matters they otherwise might neglect, they do pose potential issues. One of the most common problems, particularly under the old law, was that many of these forms were designed for English law rather than Scottish; although there are Scottish versions available, not everyone appreciates the considerable differences between the two jurisdictions. As alluded to above, they may also encourage the use of little-understood terminology, which can have serious implications for the unwary.

If, under the old law, such a form was properly signed and witnessed, then the fact that it is partly written and partly printed does not create any problem in itself. The real problem arises where a will form, whilst signed under the old law, is neither attested nor adopted as holograph. It *is* possible to regard the parts written in the testator's own handwriting as a holograph will in and of themselves provided, when read separately, the words make testamentary sense. The approach of the courts in this area has evolved from one of severe strictness to one of far greater flexibility. In the old case of *Macdonald v Cuthbertson*,[80] a testator made an unwitnessed will on a printed will form. Reading the printed and handwritten parts together, the will made perfect sense; but there was no way in which the handwritten parts on their own made any sense, testamentary or otherwise. The will was invalid. In the later case of *Carmichael's Executors v Carmichael*,[81] all the vital words were holograph and it was possible to deduce intelligible intentions from them, even whilst disregarding the printed words. The will was held to be valid. In the still later case of *Bridgeford's Executor v Bridgeford*,[82] it was held that it was sufficient for the holograph parts to identify the testator, the legatee and the executor; the document ought to be read as a whole and, provided the printed parts do not add to or contradict the holograph parts, the will is valid and will be given effect. However, the approach is still not to allow complete flexibility, as demonstrated by *Tucker v Canch's Trustees*.[83] Here, there was a holograph clause revoking previous wills, but there were no holograph legacies; the will could not stand.

---

[78] *Rhodes v Peterson*, 1972 S.L.T. 98.
[79] *Davidson v Convy*, 2003 S.C. 420.
[80] *Macdonald v Cuthbertson* (1890) 18 R. 101.
[81] *Carmichael's Executors v Carmichael*, 1909 S.C. 1387.
[82] *Bridgeford's Executor v Bridgeford*, 1948 S.C. 416.
[83] *Tucker v Canch's Trustees*, 1953 S.C. 270.

Wills executed on or after 1 August 1995

5–16   The Requirements of Writing (Scotland) Act 1995 (the 1995 Act) came into force on 1 August 1995, but only affects documents or deeds executed after it came into force. If a document is dated, this is presumed to be accurate,[84] and where a document is undated, it is treated as having been executed under the new law.[85] The changes as they affect the execution of a will are not particularly radical, although the law has been simplified somewhat. As mentioned above, verbal nuncupative legacies of moveables not exceeding £8.33 (£100 Scots) were formally abolished although, in practice, they had long since fallen out of use. The privileged status of a holograph will also disappeared under the 1995 Act; as explained below, there is no longer any reason for retaining this status.

Basic formalities

5–17   The 1995 Act stipulates that testamentary documents, including any will, testamentary trust disposition and settlement, or codicil, must be constituted by way of a written document.[86] It must be subscribed by the granter,[87] i.e. signed by the testator. Subscription must be effected at the end of the final page of the document,[88] but requirements regarding the signature itself remain somewhat flexible. Ideally, this should be the testator's full name or at least his surname and initial(s), but another name, initial or mark is acceptable for purposes of validity.[89] However, in the latter case such a signature would require to be fortified by evidence that it was the granter's usual manner of signing or that it was intended, in context, as a signature.

Thus, it does not now matter whether a will is handwritten, typed, printed, word processed or a mixture of the above: provided the will is signed at the end, it is formally valid. Signing on all pages, or witnessing, it no longer required for formal validity. This liberalisation of the rules, and the fail-safe provisions they provide, are greatly welcomed. It still must be clear, of course, the document demonstrates sufficient testamentary intent, but that is a separate issue.

Presumption of validity

5–18   However, there is still a further hurdle which must be overcome; that of proving authenticity of the will. If it is to be given effect, the will requires to be self-proving, which is more or less the equivalent of being probative under the old law. In other words, if there is any challenge based on the execution of the document, the court will presume it to be genuine until the opposite is proved. For a will to have this status under the new law, certain extra formalities are required.[90]

---

[84] Requirements of Writing (Scotland) Act 1995 s.3(10).
[85] Requirements of Writing (Scotland) Act 1995 s.14(6).
[86] Requirements of Writing (Scotland) Act 1995 s.1(2)(c).
[87] Requirements of Writing (Scotland) Act 1995 s.2(1).
[88] Requirements of Writing (Scotland) Act 1995 s.7(1).
[89] Requirements of Writing (Scotland) Act 1995 s.7(2).
[90] Requirements of Writing (Scotland) Act 1995 s.3.

First, it must have been signed by the testator on every separate sheet which, in practice, is taken to mean every page; although there is the possibility of a single sheet of paper having been folded to create several "pages", which strictly speaking would only require the one signature.[91] Secondly, although witnesses are no longer required for basic formal validity, attestation of the testator's signature by one witness is required for a will to be self-proving. The requirements regarding this are broadly the same as under the old law; the witness must be at least 16 years of age, have the required mental capacity, and must know the testator. The witness must be identified by name and, ideally, address, although certain details may be added later if necessary. The testator must sign in the presence of the witness, or acknowledge his signature, and the witness must then sign in a continuous process; i.e. it is not sufficient for a witness's signature to be added at a later date.

If a will does not conform to the requirements for self-proving status, but it is otherwise formally valid, an action can be raised to prove its authenticity[92]; alternatively, as is often the case in practice, this can be done as part of related proceedings. Affidavit evidence of one witness requires to be led that the testator's subscription is genuine.[93] In effect, this process is analogous to the procedure for proving authenticity of a holograph will under the old law.

To contrast the two regimes, if the *Williamson* will, referred to above, had been executed under the new law, it would have fared much better. Even if an attestation is botched, the will can still stand as formally valid. It can then be given self-proving status, after the necessary proof.

Vicarious subscription

There may be occasions when someone wishes to sign a will, but for some reason is unable to write. This might be due to blindness or physical incapacity, either temporary or permanent. In such cases, someone else is required to subscribe vicariously. There are obvious dangers inherent to such a process, so the law in this area is understandably strict. As with wills signed by the testator himself, there are certain differences between the rules applicable prior to and since the commencement of the 1995 Act.   5–19

It is important to note that, under either regime, vicarious subscription is purely voluntary. There is nothing to stop a blind testator from executing a will himself,[94] although doing so of course runs a grave risk of fraudulence by interested parties.

Notarial execution

A "notary" is, in modern parlance, a solicitor, and a "notary public" is a solicitor who has been empowered to administer oaths for affidavits. This is useful where sworn legal statements are required, but it is convenient for these to be made   5–20

---

[91] See, e.g. *Ferguson, Petitioner*, 1959 S.C. 56 which, although decided under the old law, demonstrates this in practice, including a number of potential problems.

[92] Requirements of Writing (Scotland) Act 1995 s.4.

[93] Act of Sederunt (Requirements of Writing) 1996 (SI 1996/1534).

[94] *Duff v Earl of Fife* (1823) 1 Sh. App 498.

outwith a courtroom. Any solicitor in Scotland can apply to be appointed a notary public, and in practice the vast majority do.

Under the "old law", a document could be signed on a testator's behalf under a procedure known as notarial execution. Despite its name, notarial execution could be by a solicitor, a notary public, or a minister of the Church of Scotland or his assistant in his own parish. It was essential that the notary was absolutely independent; any personal interest in the will could render his subscription, and thus the entire will, invalid.[95] This rule would be applied strictly where the notary received a direct benefit, such as a legacy or being appointed executor or trustee, but where the interest was indirect, he would be disqualified only where there was a connection sufficient to give him a likely benefit. So, for example, it was generally acceptable for a solicitor to notarise where his employer was trustee,[96] but if the will allowed the trustee to appoint his own firm as solicitors to the trust, then the notary might receive a benefit in fees, and would be disqualified.[97]

The procedure required to effect notarial execution was laid down in statute, and had to be meticulously observed.[98] Testator, notary and two witnesses had to be gathered, and the will was read to the testator. The testator would state that he was blind or otherwise unable to sign by himself, and that he gave authority for the notary to do so. This was recorded by the notary in a "docquet" (i.e. a written endorsement) added to the will, and the notary would sign, stating his capacity. The witnesses would then sign opposite his signature.

The above procedure had to be completed as one continuous act. Any break in the process, such as the docquet being completed later, was fatal and the will would fail; it could not be cured by section 39 procedure.[99]

Procedure under Requirements of Writing (Scotland) Act 1995

5–21   Under the new law, vicarious subscription is made somewhat more user-friendly. The rules are outlined in s.9 of the 1995 Act. Under these, a "relevant person" may undertake the vicarious subscription, i.e. a practising solicitor, advocate, justice of the peace or sheriff clerk. Church of Scotland parish ministers, and their assistants, have been excluded from the list.

The basic procedure is the same, although only one witness requires to be present; of course the testator and the notary are still also required. The document should be read over to the testator by the notary. If the testator wishes to waive the reading he can do so, but this fact should be explicitly declared and recorded. The testator must give authority to the notary to subscribe, which the notary then does. There is no separate handwritten docquet as there was with notarial execution. If the document is a will and it is wished (as it will be) to make it self-proving, it should be vicariously subscribed on every page.

The "relevant person" should have no interest in the deed. However, such an interest is no longer fatal to the whole document. If it confers a money benefit

---

[95] *Ferrie v Ferrie's Trustees* (1863) 1 M. 291.
[96] *Hynd's Trustee v Hynd's Trustees*, 1955 S.C. (HL) 1; though in this case subscription was invalid for other reasons, as discussed below.
[97] *Finlay v Finlay's Trustees*, 1948 S.C. 16.
[98] Conveyancing (Scotland) Act 1924 s.18 and Sch.1.
[99] *Hynd's Trustee v Hynd's Trustees*, 1955 S.C. (HL) 1.

directly or indirectly on the relevant person, or on his immediate family, then that particular benefit is invalid, but the remainder of the document is preserved.

CHAPTER 6

Testamentary Provisions

INTRODUCTION

In the making of a will, the law generally presumes in favour of a testator's   **6–01**
freedom. Even in today's complex and highly regulated society, people may
generally do as they please with their own property when alive. Similarly, they
can, broadly speaking, decide how to dispose of it after death.

Once a potential testator has decided in principle what he wishes to be done
with his estate after death, the obvious next step should be to consult with a
solicitor so that an appropriate will can be drawn up and signed, according to the
rules of formal validity outlined in Ch.5. It is not surprising that some parts of a
professionally drafted will are in formal legal jargon but most simple modern
wills are perfectly easy for a lay person to understand. The language of a will is
intended to avoid confusion, not to create it.

There are a number of very commonly encountered testamentary provisions
that will comprise the majority of most wills, particularly those that have been
drafted under professional legal supervision. There are also some more unusual
provisions found in the world of testate succession, a number of which the law
will not tolerate. It is also necessary to consider certain other restrictions on
testamentary freedom, not least of which is the potential for legal rights to be
claimed by family members.

COMMON WILL PROVISIONS

Most testators are not too concerned about what they cannot do by will. They   **6–02**
want to achieve something much more positive, and to provide a fair and just
settlement of their affairs after their death.

In practice, many testators make quite simple wills, perhaps leaving all their
property to a spouse or civil partner, or dividing their property between a spouse
or civil partner and children. Other close relatives might also benefit, or property
might even be left to a favourite charity. In other cases, the testator may wish to
make more detailed instructions, perhaps involving a more complex scheme of
distribution, or even longer term benefits.

In any case, there are generally three main types of commonly encountered
testamentary provisions. These are legacies, annuities and liferents, and will now
be examined in turn.

Legacies

6–03   By far the most common testamentary provision, a "legacy" is a simple bequest of property. The "subject" of the legacy is the property to be bequeathed, and the "object" is the recipient, also known as the "legatee". Both the subject and object must be suitably identified in order for a legacy to be given effect. This is normally straightforward, but lack of clarity can give rise to difficulties. A question as to subject arose in *Dunsmure v Dunsmure*,[1] were a testator made a legacy of "any money I am entitled to under my father's will". The testator was also due money under his parents' marriage contract. The court held that these funds should also be included under the legacy. The issue of uncertainty, along with other matters related to interpretation, is considered in Ch.8.

Legacies can be divided into three main categories: special, general or residuary. These categories are not merely artificial. The executor must pay the legacies in the order of special first, followed secondly by general and lastly residuary.

A special (also known as a specific) legacy is, as the name would suggest, a bequest of a specific item such as a house, a grandfather clock or "my shares in Black & White Plc". Special legacies present the lowest potential for problems of uncertainty, but they are not immune entirely as will be demonstrated.

A general legacy is one in which the subject matter of the item has no distinct individual character of its own to distinguish it from others of the same kind. This somewhat complicated definition actually translates to something very simple in practice; the easiest and most common example is a sum of money, e.g. "the sum of £5,000". It could also be a quantity of goods coming under a generic or general description.

A residuary legacy, also known simply as the residue of the estate, is a legacy of whatever is left after the special and general legacies are paid in full. Obviously, the amount of residue will vary greatly, depending on what is included in the estate. A residuary legatee could receive nothing or next to nothing, or could receive a very large amount. In many cases, it falls somewhere in between.

Legacies example

6–04   Peggy Sue, a widow with no children, has died. In her will, which has been validly executed, she makes the following provisions:

1.   Her house and all furniture therein is to go to her brother, Bill.
2.   Her wedding ring is to go to her niece, Maggie.
3.   Her car is to go to her nephew, Jimmy.
4.   £10,000 in cash is to go to Bill.
5.   £5,000 in cash is to go to Maggie.
6.   £5,000 in cash is to go to Jimmy.
7.   £1,000 in cash is to go to the local cat and dog home.
8.   Any remainder is to be donated to the local church fund.

---

[1] *Dunsmure v Dunsmure* (1879) 7 R. 261.

Peggy Sue's net estate is £216,000, comprising her house (£175,000), furniture (£8,500) wedding ring (£1,000), car (£1,500), and other moveable property amounting to £30,000. It can be seen that in her will she makes three special legacies, four general legacies, and one residual legacy. These would be dealt with in order as outlined in the table below. (Figures in brackets indicate deductions from the estate.)

	Heritable	Moveable	6–05
Estate			
House	175,000		
Furniture		8,500	
Wedding ring		1,000	
Car		1,500	
Other moveable estate		30,000	
Balances	*175,000*	*41,000*	
Deduct special legacies			
House	(175,000)		
Furniture		(8,500)	
Wedding ring		(1,000)	
Car		(1,500)	
Balances	*Nil*	*30,000*	
Deduct general legacies			
£8,000 to Bill		(10,000)	
£5,000 to Maggie		(5,000)	
£5,000 to Jimmy		(5,000)	
£1,000 to cat and dog home		(1,000)	
Balances	*Nil*	*9,000*	
Deduct residue			
Reside to church fund		(9,000)	
Balances	*Nil*	*Nil*	

The final distribution would be:

Bill

Special legacy	£183,500
General legacy	£10,000
Total	*£193,500*

Maggie

Special legacy	£1,000
General legacy	£5,000
Total	*£6,000*

Jimmy

Special legacy	£1,500
General legacy	£5,000
Total	*£6,500*

Cat and dog home

General legacy	£1,000

Church fund

Reside	£9,000

6–06   In this example, the residuary legatee has been left with a substantial amount; a sum greater, in fact, than most of the other legatees. However, this should not suggest that the residual legatee will always be in such a favourable position. In fact, in theory at least, the opposite is true, since the residuary legatee will only inherit if there is property left over to allow this. Since the residuary legatee is paid last, it is very possible that special and general legacies will exhaust the estate, therefore leaving the residuary legatee with nothing at all.

Indeed, there are also a number of situations in which the estate falls short in some other way, e.g. because there are insufficient funds to satisfy every legacy, or if a special legacy attempts to bequeath an item no longer belonging to the testator. These issues are remedied by two mechanisms known as "abatement" and "ademption".

Abatement

6–07   A problem can arise when, even though the estate is solvent (i.e. all debts can be paid), there is not enough left to pay every beneficiary named in the will. This problem is dealt with by bringing in certain presumptions (unless the will expressly provides otherwise) and these presumptions are known as the rules on "abatement", or "cutting back".

Special legacies must be paid first and in full, even if there is not sufficient to pay general legatees in full. Thus a special legatee, in many ways, is in the best position.

General legacies are paid next. If there are not sufficient monies to pay them in full, general legacies are "abated pari passu" (cut back in equal proportion). To achieve this, the shortfall of the estate must be calculated as a percentage, and this percentage is then applied to each general legacy. For example, if the estate is short by 20 per cent, each general legacy is cut back by 20 per cent, thus ensuring that every general legatee is treated fairly.

Lastly, the residue is due to be paid over. Of course, if general legacies have had to be abated, then there will be nothing left for the residuary legatee, who therefore gets nothing. To put this another way, the residue is the first class of legacies to be abated, even although in practice it is last to be paid.

Continuing the practical example from above might help to illustrate the principle of abatement, which admittedly appears complicated at first, but is actually relatively straightforward in practice.

Staying with Peggy Sue, then, say the facts of the situation are exactly as before, but instead of Peggy Sue's estate including £30,000 of moveable estate, it includes only £15,750. Special legacies are unaffected by this change, so they are paid out exactly as before; Bill takes the house and furniture, Maggie takes the wedding ring and Jimmy takes the car. However, there is a problem with the general legacies, which (according to Peggy Sue's will) should total £21,000. As there is only £15,750 of moveable estate available to pay these general legacies, there is a shortfall of £5,250, or 25 per cent. Therefore, each general legacy will be abated by 25 per cent; Bill will receive £7,500 of his general legacy, Maggie and Jimmy will each receive £3,750, and the cat and dog home will receive £750. The church fund, as residuary legatee, gets nothing at all, since its legacy is abated first and in full.[2]

Ademption of special legacies

Where a testator provides for a special legacy and, at the date of his death, the subject of the legacy no longer forms part of his estate, the legacy is said to be "adeemed" (the noun is ademption) and nothing is due to the legatee. The motives of the testator in disposing of the item are irrelevant. Thus, if Peggy Sue leaves her car to her nephew Jimmy, but at the date of her death no longer owns that car, Jimmy's legacy lapses and nothing is due to him under this heading.

6–08

Occasionally, a testator may leave something in his will that never belonged to him (as distinct from an article which did once belong to him but of which he has disposed). This is obviously different from ademption and is known as *legatum rei alienae* (legacy of a thing belonging to someone else). The normal presumption is that the testator made a mistake and, accordingly, the legacy fails. However, if it can be proved that the testator knew that the property was not his, then the legacy can be interpreted as an instruction to buy the item from its owner or, if it cannot be bought, to hand over the value to the legatee. Fairly obviously, it may be difficult, if not impossible, to prove what the testator knew.

Annuities

An annuity is the right to a periodical fixed payment of a sum of money from the revenue of the estate. It can also be used to signify an arrangement with a financial institution in which, in return for a capital sum, an income is paid, usually for the remainder of a person's life. At this stage, we are confining ourselves to the first alternative. An annuity may be created in favour of any person either inter vivos (taking effect during the lifetime of the granter) or mortis causa (by will after death). The annuity may be for any sum that the granter wishes and may continue as long as he desires. The most common practice is to provide an annuity for a beneficiary for their lifetime but it should be noted that

6–09

---

[2] Residual legacies are considered in more detail later in this chapter.

the granter may fix the period for a shorter time. There may even be a provision that the annuity will terminate should some particular event take place, such as the remarriage of the beneficiary. On the other hand, an annuity, unlike a liferent (below), need not be limited to the lifetime of a human being. It could be granted for a longer period or it could even be perpetual, such as the endowment of a prize fund. Nowadays, such an endowment would more likely be provided by an initial capital sum which trustees would invest and use the fluctuating interest to fund the particular purpose.

Assuming that the annuity is granted mortis causa the testator can fix the method by which it is to be paid. However, if he directs that an annuity is to be bought for the beneficiary by way of a lump sum payment to an insurance company, with the result that the beneficiary could sell the annuity in return for a capital sum, this could be an example of a repugnant condition (explained later in this chapter). Normally, the testator will provide that the annuitant is entitled to an annuity of £[*number*] per annum out of the free annual income of the estate. This means that the payment of the annuity is made without diminishing the capital of the estate. However, if, in the future, the income of the trust funds is not sufficient to pay the annuity in full, the trustees must make up the full amount of the annuity by encroaching on the capital (unless the trust deed prohibits this, in which case the annuity would have to be reduced).

Although traditionally an annuity was for a fixed sum, the value of such an income is bound to be eroded by inflation. It is perfectly in order for an annuity provision to be inflation-proofed in some way, but this has to be provided for expressly, not merely by implication.

Liferent and fee

6–10   It is necessary to distinguish a liferent from an annuity. It has just been demonstrated that, unless provided to the contrary, trustees may encroach on capital (if need be) to pay an annuity in full. The opposite rule applies to a liferent, as (unless the will provides otherwise) no encroachment on capital is permitted. Although liferent can be provided inter vivos it is more commonly provided mortis causa. A key element of liferent is that there must always be a right of fee, i.e. a full and unencumbered right of property, at the end of the liferent period. So, a common enough provision would be " ... to my wife Doris in liferent and my son John in fee". If what purports to be a liferent does not have a right of fee at its conclusion, whatever else it may be, it is not a liferent.

The liferenter has the right to use the property and enjoy the income and fruits from it *salva substantia* (without destruction of the substance). It is sometimes necessary to make a fine distinction between income and capital. In the case of an estate of timber, the rule appears to be that the liferenter is entitled to ordinary windfalls, to copse wood cut in normal course and to wood cut for estate purposes such as fencing. The fiar (person entitled to the fee) is entitled to final mature trees and to trees blown down by extraordinary storms. The liferenter is entitled to royalties from mineral workings let or worked during the lifetime of the testator. Royalties from minerals let or worked after the testator's death normally fall into capital. The liferenter is entitled to dividends from shares and to other cash payments made by the company out of profits. Bonus shares are classed as capital unless they are issued in lieu of a cash dividend. Most liferents set up by a will are said to be "beneficiary" (sometimes called "improper"), which means that the property is held by trustees during the liferent period. At the end of the liferent, the trustees "denude" (make a final and total distribution of the trust estate) in favour of the fiar.

The Apportionment Act 1870 provides that all rents, regular annual receipts, dividends and interest are to be considered as accruing from day to day. This means in practice that the liferenter is only entitled to income on the trust investments which actually accrue during the liferent period. So, income accrued before the commencement of the liferent period (usually the date of the testator's death) falls ("effeirs") to capital, as does income accrued after its termination. If shares are bought during the liferent, the liferenter receives only the proportion of dividend accrued after purchase. Similarly, if shares are sold, the liferenter only receives the proportion of income accrued up to date of sale. Clearly, this is all rather complicated. It is perfectly competent, and common professional practice, to disapply the provisions of the Act in the testamentary deed.

The crucial concept to grasp is that the fiar actually owns the property but cannot enjoy the fee absolute (ownership *and* possession) until the burden of the liferent comes to an end.

Traditionally, liferents tended to affect heritable property but, with the passage **6–11** of time, liferents of both heritable and moveable property have become more common. A classic situation would be where a testator directs that his house is to be held by his trustees in liferent to his widow until her death or remarriage and then to the child(ren) in fee. The effect of this provision is that the widow may continue to live in the house without it ever becoming her property.

One obvious good reason for such a provision is to prevent the house going out of the family, should the liferenter remarry. Although a fiar does acquire a vested right in the property at the time of the testator's death (*a morte testatoris*), actual possession of the subjects is not given until the termination of the liferent. To put it another way, the widow's liferent is a burden on the fiar's right to the property so that although the fiar could sell the property during the subsistence of the liferent, he cannot give a higher or better right than he himself possesses. Thus, any purchaser or secured creditor can only take the property subject to the rights of the liferenter.

There is no reason for a liferent to be gender specific although, traditionally, more liferents have been enjoyed by women than men.

As indicated above, liferent includes the rights to enjoy the fruits or income from property without diminishing the capital. So if (as is often the case) the liferented property is a house, the liferenter (to use the example quoted above) would bear the expense of the upkeep of the property, plus the usual burdens such as local taxes, insurance and normal maintenance (an elusive concept at the best of times) of the property. The liferenter would also pay any interest on a heritable security, but would not be liable to repay any of the capital of an outstanding mortgage. Larger repairs or more fundamental alterations or renovations would probably be the responsibility of the fiar but each instance would have to be considered on its merits. In practice, parties may come to their own arrangements about who pays for what.

If the liferenter were to leave the property for good, it would revert to the fiar in fee absolute.

Alimentary liferents

6–12   Sometimes a liferent is declared in the will to be alimentary, with the intention of providing for the maintenance of the liferenter. Traditionally, a liferent was declared to be alimentary in order to provide the liferenter with some safeguard against personal rashness and to give some protection against hard times. It would be of most relevance where the property includes more than a dwelling house, such as an element of income.

There are two main features of an alimentary liferent. First, it may not be assigned, e.g. by sale, gift or security, to a third party. The alimentary liferent is entirely personal to the liferenter. Once it has been accepted, it cannot be assigned or renounced. Secondly, it is not liable to the diligence of creditors, which means that it cannot be forcibly seized and used to repay debts. This is clearly of great advantage to the liferenter, but it should, however, be noted that the protection only applies to the extent that the income payable to the liferenter is reasonable, bearing in mind the liferenter's own personal circumstances and position in life. Any excess over such a reasonable amount will be liable to diligence. What is reasonable is always a matter of fact. (And of course, not everyone who receives an alimentary liferent is foolish or wayward in financial matters!)

There are cases where a beneficiary has wished to assign or renounce the liferent. At common law, an alimentary liferent cannot be revoked once it has become operational. It can, however, be revoked *before* it becomes operational.[3] Under s.1 of the Trusts (Scotland) Act 1961, the court may allow an arrangement to vary or revoke an alimentary liferent provided it is satisfied that such an arrangement is reasonable in the circumstances, e.g. that there is sufficient income from other sources for the maintenance of the liferenter. Normally an alimentary liferent is expressly declared by the testator to be alimentary, but this is not actually essential. Provided the testator makes it clear in some other words that the liferent is of an alimentary nature, this is sufficient in law to give it that status.

Right of occupancy

6–13   It is necessary to distinguish a right of liferent from a right of occupancy of a dwelling-house. The latter is a lesser right than that of liferent; it merely confers a personal right to occupy the subjects stated for a specific period, as directed. An occupant would be liable for local taxes, but not for the type of repairs normally carried out by a landlord nor for interest on a heritable security. Sometimes there may be a problem in deciding whether the testator has, in fact, granted a right of occupancy or a liferent. In the case of *Cathcart's Trustees v Allardice*,[4] it was held that even though the word "liferent" had been used in a will, only a right to occupy had been intended.

---

[3] *Douglas-Hamilton v Duke and Duchess of Hamilton's Trustees*, 1961 S.C. 205.
[4] *Cathcart's Trustees v Allardice* (1899) 2 F. 326.

RESIDUARY AND SUBSTITUTIONARY PROVISIONS

In the course of human history, many people have claimed to be able to see into   **6–14**
the future. Readers can make their own assessments of such claims. In dealing
with succession, while it is not necessary to attempt to foretell the future, it is
necessary to consider at least a range of viable possibilities as to what
eventualities could take place in the future. It is important, when making a will,
that testators make provision for uncertainties, even those that may be unpleasant.
For example, parents do not normally expect to outlive their children, but there is
no guarantee in life how events will unfold. It may be painful to consider a child
or other younger beneficiary predeceasing, but it is always a possibility.
Traditionally, the average married man assumes that he will die before his wife,
and whilst this might be borne out by general statistics and life expectancy,
people do not always die in what might be seen as the "natural order".

There are, therefore, a number of provisions that can be made in order to
accommodate unexpected events, and maximise the potential for a will
comprehensively dealing with the testator's estate.

The residue clause

It is fair to assume that if a person makes a will, the intention is that this   **6–15**
document will deal with the whole of his estate. It would be both perverse and
unwise to want to leave a will which only disposes of part of the estate and leaves
the rest to intestate succession. There are a number of situations in which partial
intestacy might arise,[5] but few people, if any, would purposely set out to achieve
such an inconvenient mess being made of their affairs after their death.

Very few people know exactly how much they are worth in purely financial
terms. There is an uncomfortable ring of truth in the cynical saying that most
people are, financially, "better off dead". Even if a person knows roughly what
his house and furniture is worth and how much he has in the bank or building
society, it is unlikely that he will be able to take account of every last penny
which will be credited to his estate.

One of the many problems of the homemade will is that, surprisingly often, a
testator will forget altogether about the residue of his estate. He will make
bequests of his house and valuables and general legacies to a number of people,
but forget about all that is left over. If there has been a long interval between
making the will and his actual death, that residue could have increased very
substantially. Equally, it could also have diminished, if the testator was living on
capital.

A typical example of a residue clause would be "I leave the rest, residue and
remainder of my means and estate to . . . ". It is common enough, and perfectly in
order, for a residuary legatee to be given a special or general legacy in addition to
this, e.g. he may receive the grandfather clock and the residue. In the "Peggy
Sue" example given earlier, the residuary legatee was a charity, but this is not by
any means the only option; it is just as common for family members to receive
the residue of an estate. It should also be borne in mind, however, that as

---

[5] See, e.g. the issue of uncertainty mentioned earlier, and discussed more fully in Ch.8.

demonstrated the residuary legatee in the weakest position if it transpires that the estate does not contain sufficient funds to provide for all legacies.

The destination-over

6–16   A major purpose of a residue clause is to prevent any part of the estate falling into intestacy. Of course, a problem could arise if the residuary legatee were to die before the testator. The general rule, already explored, is that no one can benefit under a will unless he survives the testator. This might seem almost painfully obvious, since how can anyone benefit if he is dead? That is fair comment, but the question does not so much concern a benefit the predeceasing legatee did not have the opportunity to enjoy; the real question is, did he, at the time of his death, have what is called a vested right? If he did, that vested right can pass on to his heirs. It is crucially important to understand that a potential beneficiary cannot have a vested right if he dies before the testator. (The wider issue of vesting is explored in Ch.10.)

One way of avoiding the residue (or indeed any kind of legacy) failing altogether, is by nominating at least one alternative legatee. This can be achieved by a "destination-over", a device also known as a "whom failing" provision. Under such a clause the legacy goes, for example, " . . . to John, whom failing Betty". Destinations-over are simple to insert and very common in practice. The effect is that if John dies before the testator, he has no vested right and the legacy will pass to Betty (assuming, of course, that she does survive the testator).

However, there is another potential problem. Suppose that at the time of the testator's death, John is alive. Obviously, the legacy vests in him. So, where does that leave Betty? Does she have any hope of eventually succeeding to that same legacy when John dies? The simple answer is usually not, but the matter requires further exploration. Unfortunately, it is necessary to look at some technical jargon at this point.

In the destination-over, John is the institute, i.e. the main legatee. Betty, on the other hand, is either the conditional institute or the substitute. If she is the conditional institute, the position is clear. When John inherits the legacy, Betty's right is said to "fly off". This is a curiously colloquial expression but abundantly clear in its meaning. If, however, Betty is the substitute there is just a possibility that she could still inherit after John's death. It all depends on what John does during the time of his ownership. If he alienates the legacy by sale or gift or if he leaves it in his will to someone other than Betty, any right she might have had in it is effectively defeated. But if he does not take any such steps, she could claim it on his death.

Obviously, the crucial opening question is whether Betty is a conditional institute or a substitute. The first place to look is the actual will itself in the hope that the testator's intentions are clear. If the will is unclear, or is silent, certain legal presumptions will be invoked. Prior to the passing of the 2016 Act, a distinction was made between heritable and moveable property in this regard.

Under the previous position, if the subject of the legacy is heritable, Betty would be a substitute. If it is moveable, she would be merely a conditional institute. In *Crumpton's JF v Barnardo's Homes*,[6] money was left to certain

---

[6] *Crumpton's JF v Barnardo's Homes*, 1917 S.C. 713.

charities in case the original legatee (institute) were to die without issue. In fact, the institute did die without leaving issue but, because the will was silent on the matter and because the legacy was of moveables, the charities were deemed to be conditional institutes. As a consequence, their potential right had flown off when the institute inherited. By contrast, in *Watson v Giffen*,[7] a lady bequeathed heritable property (a half-share of the family home) to her son, whom failing her brother. The son inherited the half-share but died intestate and still in ownership of it. Because heritable property was involved and the will was silent, the brother was deemed to be the substitute and inherited. Significantly, he did not inherit moveable property passing under the same will on similar terms. This illustrates how strong the legal presumptions were in this area.

However, the law has now been harmonised as between the two types of property. Under the 2016 Act, the presumption is always that the secondary legatee is a conditional institute.[8] This means that where property has vested in the main legatee, the secondary legatee loses all rights in that property. This is, however, still only a presumption, which can be defeated if the deed states otherwise, or if the intention of the granter can clearly be inferred. Whilst this harmonisation certainly simplifies matters, the best approach for anyone drawing up a will containing a destination-over is still to ensure that it does actually contain the full wishes of the deceased.

RESTRAINTS ON TESTAMENTARY FREEDOM

It was stated earlier that, generally, a testator can do as he pleases in his will, subject of course to legal rights. Whilst this is broadly true, there can be cases where the provisions of a will shall not be given effect. Sometimes, a legacy suffers from a fundamental flaw and so will fail entirely; it is also possible that the conditions *attached to* a legacy are flawed, in which the legacy might stand but without the conditions being enforceable. There are also rules designed to deal with contradictory provisions, and to place certain other limitations on a testator exerting an undesirable degree of influence long after his death.

6–17

Void provisions

A legacy, or more commonly a condition attached to a legacy, may be void if it is impossible, illegal, immoral or "contrary to public policy". The first two of these are relatively straightforward, since it is usually clear if something is impossible or illegal; although admittedly there might be degrees of interpretation in certain areas of legality. The second two, on the other hand, are very much subjective, since opinions regarding morality vary widely, and a precise definition of "public policy" is notoriously elusive. The best that can be offered is a selection of examples from case law, in order that a picture can be formed of how these issues are dealt with in practice.

6–18

---

[7] *Watson v Giffen* (1884) 11 R. 444.
[8] Succession (Scotland) Act 2016 s.8.

Void legacies

6–19   In terms of legacies themselves being void, the most common reason is where the testator directs a certain use for his estate, but in a manner that is excessively self-glorifying and whereby there is no identifiable beneficiary. This is often deemed "contrary to public policy" on the grounds that it is an abuse of testamentary power, with the result that the legacy falls. In *Mackintosh's JF v Lord Advocate*,[9] a lady who was illegitimate by birth directed that her entire estate was to be spent on erecting a mausoleum in which her remains were to be interred, along with those of two predeceasing friends whom she called "uncle" and "aunt", but were unrelated to her. The remains of these friends would first have had to be exhumed. Whilst there was divided opinion regarding the erection of the mausoleum, and indeed there is of course no general objection to providing a reasonable memorial for oneself, the provision regarding the exhumation was deemed to be beyond the entitlements of the testatrix. As stated by Lord President Clyde,

> "if a testator's directions reach a certain pitch of grotesqueness, of extravagance, of wastefulness, or of futility, then the testator's act may be regarded as going beyond the right of *testamenti factio*".[10]

It might possibly have been different if the two friends had been close members of her family. There is a sad element in this case; perhaps the testator was trying to create a proper family for herself after her death at a time when popular views on illegitimacy were different from the present day.

Some eccentric testators have attempted to do some rather remarkable things. One oft-cited series of cases involves the famous "folly" overlooking Oban. In *McCaig v University of Glasgow*,[11] Mr McCaig, who originally built the folly, directed his testamentary trustees to erect artistic towers and statues of himself and his family on his estate. His sister challenged the legacy and the court struck it down as being of no benefit to anyone,

> "if it is not unlawful, it ought to be unlawful, to dedicate ... the whole income of a large estate to objects of no utility... which benefit nobody".[12]

Then, some years later, in a twist of irony that surely could not have been lost on those concerned, the same sister attempted to do something similar in her will, which included erecting statues of the McCaig family on top of the folly. This was challenged in *McCaig's Trustees v Lismore United Free Kirk Session*,[13] with the result that the provisions were struck down and, as there was no beneficiary, the legacy could not be paid.

Later cases have been decided on grounds that are perhaps more directly related to public policy. In *Aitken's Trustees v Aitken*,[14] a Musselburgh butcher

---

[9] *Mackintosh's JF v Lord Advocate*, 1935 S.C. 406.
[10] *Mackintosh's JF v Lord Advocate*, 1935 S.C. 406 at 410 per Lord President Clyde.
[11] *McCaig v University of Glasgow*, 1907 S.C. 231.
[12] *McCaig v University of Glasgow*, 1907 S.C. 231 at 242 per Lord Kyllachy.
[13] *McCaig's Trustees v Lismore United Free Kirk Session*, 1915 S.C. 426.
[14] *Aitken's Trustees v Aitken*, 1927 S.C. 374.

directed that his shop was to be demolished and, on its site, was to be erected a massive bronze equestrian statue of himself in his uniform of Champion of the Riding of the Marches. The court held that whilst the object of the legacy, i.e. remembrance of the testator, was reasonable, the method, which would of course involve demolition of part of the High Street, was "irrational, futile and self-destructive".[15] Again, this legacy was struck down. Similarly in *Sutherland's Trustee v Verschoyle*,[16] a lady made provision in her will to preserve and display her art collection. In fact, the collection was not of outstanding value and was, in any case, somewhat of a mixture. The court took the view that to provide for the display of such an unimportant collection would be so wasteful as to be contrary to public policy.

Void conditions

In terms of conditions attached to a legacy being void, again "contrary to public policy" is perhaps the most often cited, although the others have been employed. "Impossibility" is strictly defined, and must mean more than improbability. In *Barker v Watson's Trustees*,[17] the testator attached a condition to a legacy in favour of his daughter's children that she must have reconciled with her husband by the date of his (the testator's) death. He explicitly stated that "reconciliation" meant living together as husband and wife. The daughter had been undergoing treatment for drug addiction, which had severely harmed her relationship with husband, and at the time of her father's death was residing in a rehabilitation clinic. The court rejected the claim that the condition of the two reconciling was "impossible".

    Regardless of the specific reason, where a condition is deemed void it is said to be treated *pro non scripto* (as not having been written). The actual legacy therefore does not fall, merely the objectionable condition. In *Fraser v Rose*,[18] a daughter was left a legacy by her father on condition that she did not live with her mother (the deceased's widow) who was to be thrown out of the house. The court set aside the condition and the daughter received the legacy unconditionally. Similarly, in the English case of *Re Johnson's Will Trusts*,[19] a condition attached to a legacy that could be seen as an encouragement to a wife to leave her spouse was declared to be ineffectual. On the other hand, in *Earl of Caithness v Sinclair*,[20] it was not contrary to public policy to make a legacy conditional on the beneficiary not succeeding to a peerage. Neither was it contrary to public policy that a legatee would be required to cease association with an orphan of whom the testator disapproved.[21]

6–20

[15] *Aitken's Trustees v Aitken*, 1927 S.C. 374 at 383 per Lord Sands.
[16] *Sutherland's Trustee v Verschoyle*, 1968 S.L.T. 43.
[17] *Barker v Watson's Trustees*, 1919 S.C. 109.
[18] *Fraser v Rose* (1849) 11 D. 1466.
[19] *Re Johnson's Will Trusts* [1967] 1 All E.R. 553.
[20] *Earl of Caithness v Sinclair*, 1912 S.C. 79.
[21] *Balfour's Trustees v Johnston*, 1936 S.C. 137.

Repugnancy

6–21   A legacy is said to have a repugnant condition if that condition is inconsistent with the main tenor of the legacy itself. One example would be where a legacy appears to be given absolutely and without restriction, but trustees are then directed to hold the capital and pay only the revenue to the beneficiary. In such a case, the direction to the trustees to hold the capital would be repugnant and the beneficiary would receive payment of the capital of his legacy. Another possible example would be where a testator directs that an annuity be purchased for the legatee, as in *Dow v Kilgour's Trustees*,[22] but the legatee could immediately sell the annuity for a lump sum. In such a case, the beneficiary would be entitled to payment of the lump sum which would have been used to buy the annuity. In *Miller's Trustees v Miller*,[23] a father left property in trust for his son. The trustees of the estate were directed to administer the property until he attained the age of 25, or on his earlier marriage, at which date he would attain a full vested right. The son married before the age of 25 but his father's trustees refused to denude in his favour. It was held that where an absolute right of property is given to a beneficiary of full age, he can require the trustees to denude in his favour, even if the original will had directed retention for a longer period. If there had been other trust purposes still to be carried out, or if the trustees had been given some element of discretion, the son would not have been able to make the trustees denude until he attained the age of 25.

Accumulations of income

6–22   It is not always the case that a beneficiary under a testamentary provision will immediately receive their benefit. If he so desires, a testator may set up a testamentary trust, which will administer his estate after his death for the purposes outlined in his will. The income derived from the investment or other operation of the estate held in trust can be "accumulated" with the capital sum over time, and directed to some future purpose. A common example would be where property is to be held in trust for the benefit of children, who will inherit when they reach adulthood.

There is nothing wrong in essence with this type of trust provision, and provided the purposes are sufficiently certain and not contrary to public policy, they are perfectly valid. It is not uncommon for trusts to be administered for charitable purposes such as to benefit hospitals, orphanages, and so on. However, such a device also has the potential to be used for far less laudable purposes, such as disinheriting one's children. There are, therefore, certain limits placed on the duration of such accumulations.

Although now contained in later statute, the law in this area originated in the Accumulations Act 1800 (the 1800 Act), better known as the Thelluson Act after the case which inspired it. In *Thelluson v Woodford*,[24] a very wealthy English merchant directed that his entire estate was to be invested in land and the income accumulated. His estate was only to be shared out among members of his family

---

[22] *Dow v Kilgour's Trustees* (1877) 4 R. 403.
[23] *Miller's Trustees v Miller* (1890) 18 R. 301.
[24] *Thelluson v Woodford* (1799) 4 Ves. 227; (1805) 11 Ves. 112; (1817) 34 E.R. 864.

when the last of the class of his children and/or grandchildren died. In other words, he was effectively attempting to disinherit two generations. In Scotland, his children could at least have claimed legal rights but not so south of the border. When the case came to the House of Lords, it was decided, with reluctance, that the provisions of the will were valid. The 1800 Act was passed as something of a knee-jerk reaction to ensure that history did not repeat itself. Its purpose, along with that of subsequent legislation, is to limit the potential of applying excessive periods of accumulation to the detriment of immediate descendants, for the benefit of a future generation.[25]

The current law is found in the Trusts (Scotland) Act 1961 and the Law Reform (Miscellaneous Provisions) (Scotland) Act 1966, although they are still referred to as the Thelluson Act provisions. It is not possible to contract out of these statutory provisions.[26]

There are actually six possible maximum periods of accumulation, affecting both lifetime and testamentary trusts. The trust provisions must fall within one of them, and whilst there might be some overlap between the periods it is not possible to add one period to another in order to increase the maximum permitted. The exact intention of the grantor (i.e. for succession purposes, the testator) is irrelevant; the rules apply, of course, where accumulation is expressly directed, but also in any case where accumulation results from the trust's terms. If it is not clear which period should apply, the court will decide which is most appropriate in the circumstances of the case.[27]

As far as testamentary trustees are concerned, the simple rule of thumb is that income cannot be accumulated for more than 21 years from the death of the testator.[28] However, it is possible for this period to be slightly longer in practice. To explain, it is common to direct that income be accumulated until someone (usually, but not necessarily, the beneficiary) reaches the age of "majority", which in this context is deemed to be 21 years of age.[29] The person identified need not have been born at the date of the testator's death, but must have been *in utero* (in the womb); therefore, the actual maximum period is 21 years and about nine months following the testator's death.[30]

6–23

Income directed to be accumulated contrary to the statutory provisions goes to those who would have otherwise been entitled to it, i.e. as if accumulation had not been directed in the first place.[31] It is perfectly legal to accumulate for up to 21 years, and whatever fund is thus "in the bag" is perfectly legitimate, but after the 21 years have passed, the surplus income must be distributed even if the original will or trust disposition and settlement provides otherwise. What this means in practice depends very much on the circumstances and the exact terms of the will or trust deed; the income may go to a beneficiary, it may be considered residue, or it may fall into intestacy if the deed has made no other applicable provisions.

---

[25] As summarised in *Re Berkeley, deceased* [1968] Ch. 744.
[26] *Maxwell's Trustees v Maxwell* (1877) 5 R. 248.
[27] *Carey's Trustees v Rose*, 1957 S.C. 252.
[28] Trusts (Scotland) Act 1961 s.5(2)(b).
[29] Trusts (Scotland) Act 1961 s.5(6).
[30] Trusts (Scotland) Act 1961 s.5(2)(c).
[31] Trusts (Scotland) Act 1961 s.5(3).

One leading case is *Elder's Trustees v Free Church of Scotland*.[32] Mr Elder provided in his will for an adequate annuity for his widow, but the whole residue of his estate was to be held by trustees until her death. On Mrs Elder's death, the trustees were to set aside certain legacies to provide a chair in one of the Free Church Colleges, to erect and endow a new Free Church, with a manse, and to apply any remaining estate to schemes of the Free Church to be selected by his trustees. The income from the estate more than covered Mrs Elder's annuity and surplus income was accumulated. She survived her husband by more than 21 years, so further accumulation thereafter was void. The question arose as to who was entitled to this surplus revenue. Not surprisingly, the Free Church of Scotland claimed to be the residuary legatee and thus entitled to the revenue. However, the church was not the residuary legatee. The residue was to be paid to schemes of the church to be selected by the trustees and this selection could only take place after Mrs Elder died. So, until Mrs Elder died, there could be no residuary legatee. Accordingly, the surplus revenue fell into intestate succession.

Beneficiaries entitled to inherit on intestacy are ascertained as at the testator's death. This can obviously be a complex matter when the rules are being applied many years later. A specific issue of relevance is whether or not legal rights can be claimed when accumulated income falls into intestacy.[33] The case law is inconsistent in supplying an answer; legal rights were deemed to be claimable in *Moon's Trustees v Moon*,[34] but not so in *Lindsay's Trustees v Lindsay*.[35] In the latter case, it was held that it was not possible for legal rights to be claimed out of such revenue as it has come into the estate only after the death of the testator. In the absence of modern authority it seems likely that this is the more reliable interpretation.

Creation of successive liferents

6–24   The common testamentary device of "liferent and fee" has been discussed previously in this chapter. In brief, it allows one party (the liferenter) to enjoy the use of property for his lifetime, and upon his death that property reverts in full ownership to another party (the fiar). Historically, a specific type of liferent over land, called an *entail* or *tailzie*, was used by titled persons to ensure that a family estate would be kept intact and would pass only to subsequent lineal descendants. To achieve this, the estate was placed in trust whereby it would pass to the owner's heir, subject to the condition that he maintained it and in turn passed it to his heir with the same conditions. This ensured that each generation would be bound by the same terms as the previous, and that the family would hold the estate in perpetuity.

In more modern times, such restrictions on freedom of commerce became increasingly unpopular, leading to statutory reform in this area. The Entail Amendment Act 1848 allowed applications to be made to the Court of Session to disentail land,[36] and prohibited the creation of successive liferents over heritable

---

[32] *Elder's Trustees v Free Church of Scotland* (1892) 20 R. 2.
[33] See Ch.4 for a full discussion of legal rights in intestate succession, and below for consideration of how they operate in testate estates.
[34] *Moon's Trustees v Moon* (1900) 2 F. 201.
[35] *Lindsay's Trustees v Lindsay*, 1931 S.C. 586.
[36] Entail Amendment Act 1848 s.3.

property,[37] which achieved the same result as an entail. The creation of new entails was later prohibited by the Entail (Scotland) Act 1914, and similar restrictions regarding successive liferents over moveable property were introduced by the Trusts (Scotland) Act 1921. These statutory provisions still regulate deeds executed up until 1968, at which point further statutory reforms were implemented.

These came as part of the Law Reform (Miscellaneous Provisions) (Scotland) Act 1968. Section 18 states that it is not possible to create a liferent in favour of someone who is not alive or *in utero* at the date of the creator's death. This applies to both heritable and moveable property. If someone tries to do this, the effect is that the liferent property belongs absolutely to the beneficiary at the date when he becomes entitled to the liferent, provided he is at least 18 years of age or, if younger, when he attains the age of 18.[38]

TESTAMENTARY PROVISIONS AND LEGAL RIGHTS

It has been remarked several times that legal rights cannot be defeated by a will. This is because the law imposes certain responsibilities to provide for one's immediate family. In life, these responsibilities are reflected by the obligation to financially support one's spouse (or civil partner) and children. In death, they are reflected by legal rights. A spouse or civil partner, alongside children or further issue of the deceased, is entitled to claim a certain portion of the deceased's moveable estate, regardless of a will's contents.[39]   **6–25**

Legal rights, therefore, operate as a control on testation. The theory is simple enough; any person entitled to claim legal rights can do so, if they are dissatisfied with the provisions of a will. They, of course, simply accept their benefit under the will, and not claim legal rights.

It is important to note that claiming legal rights in cases of testacy is *not* a challenge to the validity of the will itself. The will remains valid in as much as it can be given effect, but any legacies will require to be cut back proportionately to account for the deduction in value; this operates in exactly the same way as "abatement", discussed earlier in this chapter. The other effect is that the person claiming legal rights forfeits all benefits under the will.

Evasion of legal rights

Whilst legal rights cannot be defeated by the terms of a will, it is possible for a determined testator to employ strategies which will evade, or at least minimise, the claiming of legal rights by persons so entitled.   **6–26**

The first such strategy is to maximise the amount of heritable property in one's estate. This reduces the amount of estate liable to legal rights, since claims are only made on *moveable* property. The most reliable is simply to buy heritable property and make provision for its disposal in one's will, but there is also the

---

[37] Entail Amendment Act 1848 s.48.
[38] Age of Majority (Scotland) Act 1969, unaffected by the Age of Legal Capacity (Scotland) Act 1991.
[39] See Ch.4 for an outline of these claims, and how they are calculated.

option of directing executors to purchase heritable property with moveable assets (i.e. cash), thus "constructively converting" the moveable estate to heritage. In practice, both of these are actually quite difficult to achieve, due to the relative complexity of purchasing heritable property, and the significant amounts of capital usually required. The latter option is particularly unreliable since there is a potential claim of "reconversion" from heritable to moveable.

The second method, which is easier and perhaps more likely to succeed, is to dispose of one's moveable property during one's lifetime, by way of an inter vivos deed. In the very old case of *Agnew v Agnew*,[40] a father assigned his estate to his elder son, retaining a liferent over it for himself. The deed also expressly excluded his younger son's right to claim legitim. The court held that as the unlimited proprietor of his estate, the father could dispose of it as he wished. Similarly, in *Hutton's Trustees v Hutton's Trustees*,[41] it was held that substantial lifetime gifts made by a testator to his wife did not require to be taken into account for purposes of calculating legitim claims by his children.

Thirdly, in a similar (but distinct) manner to the above, one can exclude certain moveable assets from one's estate, without disposing of them inter vivos. This can be achieved with certain assets by directing that they are to be placed in trust for the benefit of a nominated person. The proceeds of a pension or life assurance policy are particularly relevant here as they will often form a significant part of the estate. If these are payable to the deceased or his executors, they form part of the estate and are therefore liable to legal rights claims. However, if they are payable to another person, they do not form part of the estate at all, and are therefore free from legal rights claims.[42]

Finally, it might be possible to evade the legal rights claims of children or further issue by dying intestate. This is only relevant if the value of one's estate is below the various thresholds relevant to the claiming of prior rights by a surviving spouse or civil partner (or, in limited circumstances, a cohabiting partner).[43] The principle here is that legitim claims are not defeated per se but, because prior rights are paid before legal rights, there will be nothing against which to claim legal rights, rendering them worthless.

This final method is, admittedly, very narrow in scope, and is rather too passive to be described as a positive strategy on the part of a deceased. However, it does raise a relevant point, not least because it provides a mechanism whereby a potential claimant of prior rights (which are available only on intestacy) can defeat the legal rights of legitim claimants even where there is a will. In the case of *Kerr, Petitioner*,[44] a widow was left all of her husband's relatively modest estate. There were no other bequests under the will. The children of the marriage wished to claim their legal rights. If they were to succeed, obviously less of the estate would be available to the widow. If the husband had died intestate, the widow's prior rights would have exhausted the entire estate. The widow decided to disclaim her benefit under the will and, as her legacy was the only provision, the estate fell into intestacy. She then claimed her prior rights and received the

---

[40] *Agnew v Agnew* (1775) Mor. 8210.
[41] *Hutton's Trustees v Hutton's Trustees*, 1916 S.C. 860.
[42] For a judicial consideration of the relevant legal principles see *Beveridge v Beveridge's Executrix*, 1938 S.C. 160.
[43] See Ch.4 for a full explanation of prior rights.
[44] *Kerr, Petitioner*, 1968 S.L.T. (Sh. Ct) 61.

entire estate. The children could still, as a matter of law, claim legal rights, but as there were no remaining funds to meet them, these rights were worth precisely nothing. The case is undoubtedly an unusual one, but it does not necessarily undermine the general advice that it is normally prudent to leave a will rather than rely on intestacy. Nevertheless, in *Kerr* the result of putting the estate into intestacy certainly had the effect of carrying out the testator's real wishes. It should be noted, however, that the device only worked because there was no other provision in the will. If the will had left everything to the wife, whom failing the children (which would in practice be more usual), the wife's renunciation of the legacy would not have pushed the estate into intestacy. Her options then would have been to surrender her benefit under the will and claim legal rights alongside her children, or accept the remaining estate after their portion was deducted.

Approbate and reprobate

Also relevant in the *Kerr* case above was the principle of "approbate and reprobate". The meaning of this complex sounding phrase is actually quite simple; whilst certain family members cannot be deprived of their legal rights by a testamentary document, they may be required to choose (or, in the perhaps simpler English terminology "elect") between such rights and a legacy to their benefit in the will. In essence, the principle states that it is not possible for someone to both accept and reject the same document. Put more colloquially, a claimant cannot "have his cake and eat it too".

6–27

It does not matter whether the legacy provision is of heritable or moveable property or both, nor whether the provision is more or less generous than the legal rights that might be claimable by the beneficiary; the same principle applies. In effect, accepting a legacy provision, by statutory implication, serves as a renunciation of legal rights after the death of the parent. Thus, if there are two children and each is left property in the parent's will, but one elects to claim legal rights, he receives only one half of the notional legitim fund. It is possible for a will to provide that a beneficiary will not lose his right to claim legal rights by accepting a legacy but such a provision is uncommon; this is explored further below.

This principle extends beyond just legal rights, and in fact prevents in any circumstance the acceptance on one hand of a document, and simultaneous rejection (expressly or impliedly) on the other. In *Crum Ewing's Trustees v Bayly's Trustees*,[45] a testator instructed that part of his estate should be held in trust for his daughter in liferent and grandchildren in fee, the proportions of the latter to be directed by his daughter. These proportions were duly decided and accepted by the grandchildren, who then sought to challenge the daughter's appointment in making the directions. It was held that they could not challenge her appointment whilst at the same time accepting the benefits conferred upon them.

---

[45] *Crum Ewing's Trustees v Bayly's Trustees*, 1911 S.C. (HL) 18.

There are four conditions to be met in order that a valid election can be made. The first is simple, and perhaps self-evident; the will itself must be valid and enforceable. If it is not, it is challengeable on other grounds, which might serve the interested persons better.

Presuming the document is valid, the election must be the result of a free and fully informed choice. If made in ignorance of alternative courses of action, the election may be later set aside by the court. In *Walker v Orr's Trustees*,[46] the electing children were not fully aware of the material facts, and in particular were not shown the will or informed as to the value of the estate. They were able, 13 years later, to revoke their election. Also in this case the children were not encouraged to seek independent legal advice; this is not absolutely essential, but is considered to be a duty of the executor,[47] and is now standard practice within the legal profession when a solicitor is acting in the capacity of executor.

6–28
Further, the elector must have sufficient capacity to make the election. A child under 16 cannot make a binding election,[48] and whilst a person aged 16 or 17 can, this is subject to potential revocation later if they can show they were unfairly prejudiced in doing so.[49] Someone who lacks the requisite mental capacity may not be able to make an election, and an application to the court will be necessary in order for an election to be made on his behalf.[50]

Finally, the legatee must be able to give effect to the legacy in making his election. In the case of *Brown's Trustees v Gregson*,[51] the creation of a trust for property situated in Argentina had been deemed unlawful under Argentine law. One beneficiary had claimed legitim rather than accepting her benefit under the trust, and an application was later made that the other beneficiaries ought to be required to make a similar election between the testamentary provisions in their favour, and the share of the property in Argentina they had acquired directly as a result of the trust being rendered invalid. The court rejected this application, as it was not possible for the legacies to be given effect.

An election may be made by a number of methods. Explicit election in writing in obviously the best method, and safest for the executor. Mere silence or lengthy delay might ultimately be classed as an election, as in *Pringles' Executrixs*,[52] where a widow died not having made an election regarding rights to her husband's estate after 10 years, and was deemed to have accepted the provisions made for her in his will. It must be said that such circumstances are rare and, in any case, that legal rights prescribe after 20 years,[53] so eventually the point will become moot.

Where election is to be implied, there must be conduct which is clearly consistent with acceptance or rejection of the legacy. Accepting the office of executor under the will does not in itself constitute acceptance of the will's

---

[46] *Walker v Orr's Trustees*, 1958 S.L.T. 220.
[47] See, e.g. *Donaldson v Tainsh's Trustees* (1886) 13 R. 967.
[48] Age of Legal Capacity (Scotland) Act 1991 s.1.
[49] Age of Legal Capacity (Scotland) Act 1991 s.3.
[50] *Allan's Executors v Allan's Trustees*, 1975 S.L.T. 227.
[51] *Brown's Trustees v Gregson*, 1920 S.C. (HL) 87.
[52] *Pringles' Executrixs* (1870) 8 M. 622.
[53] Prescription and Limitation (Scotland) Act 1973 s.7 and Sch.1 para.2(f).

provisions, but to do so and then claim legal rights in contradiction of the provisions creates a conflict of interest which is, of course, best avoided.[54]

The distinction between express and implied election is important in terms of the effect that such election has. Express renunciation of legal rights is deemed to apply to the whole estate, testate or intestate, unless the elector specifically reserves the right to claim against assets which fall into intestacy.[55] Implied renunciation extends only as far as the will and legal rights conflict, leaving the possibility that legal rights can still be claimed against any intestate estate.[56] In practice, this question is often avoided by the inclusion of a "forfeiture" clause, or similarly a clause stating that provisions made under a will are in "full satisfaction" or "full and final settlement" of legal rights. Some of the issues involved here are complex, and therefore are worthy of further consideration.

Forfeiture, "full satisfaction" and equitable compensation

It has long been common practice to include either a forfeiture or a "full satisfaction" clause in a will. Although distinct in wording, the effect is the same in either case[57]; it removes the possibility of a beneficiary attempting to subvert the general rules of approbate and reprobate. Prior to the passing of the 1964 Act, such a clause meant that acceptance of a legacy would constitute forfeiture of any and all claims to legal rights, and claiming legal rights would constitute forfeiture of any benefit under the will.[58] In the absence of such a clause, it was in theory possible to accept a legacy in respect of one part of the estate, and claim legal rights in respect of another.[59]

6–29

What exactly happens to a forfeited legacy depends on the wording of the will. If a destination-over clause is in place, as discussed earlier in this chapter, it can be given effect and the legacy redirected to the secondary legatee. It may go to the residue of the estate and therefore be claimed by a residuary legatee. It may even fall into intestacy, in which case there is a strong possibility that it will be claimable by the person who rejected it! In *Tindall's Trustees v Tindall*,[60] a testator granted a liferent of the income from the residue of his estate to his wife, and thereafter his only son, with the fee to be held for the lawful children of his son. The liferent was stated to be in full satisfaction of their legal rights, but was rejected by the wife and son who claimed the latter instead. The court held that the son's forfeiture also constituted the forfeiture of his children's rights, with the effect that the fee fell into intestacy. It therefore passed to the son as heir-at-law of the testator.[61] However, the courts have not always been amenable to such a result. In the later case of *Macnaughton v Macnaughton's Trustees*,[62] which had similar facts, a testator granted a liferent to his children and the fee to his

---

[54] *Smart v Smart*, 1926 S.C. 392.
[55] *Petrie's Trustees v Mander's Trustees*, 1954 S.C. 430.
[56] *Campbell's Trustees v Campbell's Trustees*, 1950 S.C. 48.
[57] *Rose's Trustees v Rose*, 1916 S.C. 827.
[58] *Naysmith v Boyes* (1899) 1 F. (HL) 79.
[59] *White v Finlay* (1861) 24 D. 38.
[60] *Tindall's Trustees v Tindall*, 1933 S.C. 419.
[61] Note that this case was decided prior to the 1964 Act, which would have more likely benefitted the testator's wife on intestacy instead; the point illustrated remains the same.
[62] *Macnaughton v Macnaughton's Trustees*, 1954 S.C. 312.

children's issue. All the children decided to forfeit the liferent and claim legitim, expecting that the relevant estate would fall into intestacy. The court rejected this, and held that the residue after payment of the legitim claims should be held in trust for the benefit of the children's issue, as clearly intended by the testator.

These cases also allude to a particularly thorny problem that can arise where a will provides a liferent income, which the legatee wishes to renounce and in preference to which claim legal rights. The amount claimable is due as a capital sum, in contrast of course to the legacy benefit which would be enjoyed over time. This means that the estate is burdened by an increased immediate debt, which will likely necessitate other legatees suffering a pro rata reduction of their benefits. This shortfall is addressed by the operation of a principle known as "equitable compensation", whereby income from the capital value of the estate is accumulated and, in time, used to compensate those who have been disadvantaged by the legal rights claim.

6–30 Whilst this seems perfectly logical and fair (indeed, "equitable"!) the doctrine was previously susceptible to a curious quirk whereby, in the absence of a "full satisfaction" clause (or equivalent), once the other beneficiaries had been compensated for their loss, any subsequent income would again become payable to the legal rights claimant who had, of course, renounced his rights under the will. In *Macfarlane's Trustees v Macfarlane*,[63] a testator granted alimentary liferents to his two children, a son and a daughter. The daughter elected to reject her benefit and claim legitim. After the son had been duly compensated through accumulation of income from the remaining estate, the daughter sought to revive her claim on the liferent income. The case was considered by the whole court of the First Division of the Court of Session, who held by majority that she should succeed; all that was required was complete compensation to those who had suffered as a result of her claiming legitim. This was, in effect, an exception to the normal rules of approbate and reprobate and, whilst the principle had its merits in theory, was widely criticised due to its complexity in application.[64]

The 1964 Act went some way to simplifying the situation. It states that in every will or testamentary document executed since its coming into force, it shall be implied, unless stated otherwise, that any provision is made in full and final satisfaction of legal rights.[65] Wills executed under the previous legal position are unaffected, although of course over time these will dwindle in number.

This did not, however, abolish equitable compensation; it merely mitigated one of its less favourable aspects. The principle can still have occasion to be applied, as demonstrated in *Munro's Trustees v Munro*.[66] Here, a testatrix executed a post-1964 Act will, in which she granted to her husband and two sons a liferent, and to her grandson the fee. The husband and sons preferred to claim legal rights, and thereby forfeited the liferent. The court held that equitable compensation fell to be made to the grandson.

There remains a lack of clarity regarding how the doctrine of equitable compensation ought to be applied in any given case and, significantly, there is no general formula by which rights may be calculated. It seems the approach

---

[63] *Macfarlane's Trustees v Macfarlane* (1882) 9 R. 1138.
[64] Mackintosh Report, para.19.
[65] Succession (Scotland) Act 1964 s.13.
[66] *Munro's Trustees v Munro*, 1971 S.C. 827.

continues to be the historic standard of whatever is reasonable in any given case.[67] However, the continued recommendations made by the Scottish Law Commission[68] for further statutory reform in this area have resulted in the passing of statutory provisions that should simplify matters somewhat, at least as regards renunciation of a liferent. This particular issue is considered in Ch.10.

Legal rights in testate succession example

Phil E. Buster, a retired politician, has died. He is survived by his wife Bertha, and two children, Billy and Brenda. Phil's net estate is £369,500, comprising the family home (worth £320,000), an antique sceptre (£16,000), a portrait of Phil's favourite former prime minister (£500) and other moveable property valued at £33,000. In his will, Phil has directed that his entire estate be given over to a fund that supports retired parliamentarians, which his family are very unhappy about. Having been advised that Phil's will is valid, and that there was no question regarding his mental capacity at the time of drafting, the family's only option is to claim legal rights.   **6–31**

If they do so, the net moveable estate must be calculated and divided as it would upon intestacy. The sceptre, portrait and other moveables together are worth £49,500 (the house, which is heritable, is not counted). Bertha can claim one third of this amount, so she will receive £16,500. Billy and Brenda will share another one third between them, and will receive £8,250 each. The remaining one third of the moveable estate, plus the house, will be distributed according to the terms of the will; therefore the retired parliamentarians' fund will receive £16,500 moveables plus the £320,000 of heritables, for a total of £336,500.

It is not difficult to see that the family of a testator who left such a will might feel aggrieved at how they had been treated. Whilst these feelings might be justified from a moral perspective, from a legal point of view the position is clear and there is little (if anything) else that the family could do. Perhaps the best advice would be to ensure that family relations are kept so amicable as to prevent a testator wishing to disinherit his family in the first place!

---

[67] *Russel's Trustees v Gardiner* (1886) 13 R. 989.
[68] Scottish Law Commission, *Report on Succession* (Scot. Law Com. No.215), paras 6.44–6.47.

CHAPTER 7

Revocation

INTRODUCTION

It should be clear that one of the primary purposes of leaving a will is to ensure   **7–01**
that one's wishes are known regarding the distribution of property upon death.
Once a will has been executed, then subject to any matters of interpretation this
purpose has been achieved. However, it is very important to appreciate that one's
wishes might alter over time. This can be influenced by any number of factors,
including variations in the makeup of family relationships, changes in financial
circumstance, or simply a shift in one's personal priorities or whims. It is very
important, therefore, to ensure that a will reflects one's *current* wishes and, if it
does not, to take the steps necessary in amending it. Where the desired changes
are relatively minor, it may be possible to alter or add to an existing document.
Where changes are more extensive it might be better to execute an entirely new
document. In either case, it is important to make clear that the provisions or
documents previously in place are no longer effective; in short that they have
been "revoked".

ADDITIONS AND ALTERATIONS

After someone has made a will, it is common (and sensible) for him to leave it   **7–02**
with his solicitor for safekeeping, although of course this practice is not always
followed. A law agent who deals regularly with a client will advise that
opportunities should be taken, at appropriate times, to update and review the
settlement. This need not involve vast amounts of legal work (or the
accompanying fees), but it is surprising that so many testators consider the "job
done" having left a will, and are reluctant to revisit the exercise. As more time
passes, it is less likely that the will is genuinely reflective of what the testator
would currently want. Nevertheless, in absence of any positive evidence to the
contrary, the general presumption is that a will remains valid until the testator's
death, irrespective of the passage of time or the changing of circumstance. If
nothing else, then, it is wise for a testator to make alterations or additions to his
settlement as required.

Codicils

7–03   Codicils were already mentioned in Ch.5 in the context of testamentary documents. Put simply, a codicil is a short deed granted by a testator making alterations to an original will. It is particularly useful where the original will is long and complicated, and historically codicils were used to avoid the significant effort required in the drafting of an entirely new document. In these more technologically advanced times, where the electronic preparation of documents is commonplace, codicils have perhaps lost some of their attractiveness; it might well be easier to simply retrieve a document from electronic storage, make the necessary changes, and print a new copy for execution.

Nevertheless, codicils at present do still seem to play a role in contributing to testaments. One could be used, for example, to increase a general legacy to keep pace with inflation, or to add a new grandchild to a list of beneficiaries. Sometimes a will may have several codicils. The tradition, in the days of writing or typewriting, was to engross the codicil on to the main will or, alternatively, to stitch it in as an appendix. It can just as easily be an entirely separate document, which is more likely these days, but care should be taken to keep both documents together. If it is a true codicil, it will be quite clear that both the original will and the codicil(s) are to be read as one and that they are not two or more separate wills. In other words, the codicil should specifically refer to the original will and confirm the parts which are not expressly revoked.

It is worth noting that a codicil that removes or reduces a legacy under the will has the potential to cause hurt feelings on the part of the erstwhile beneficiary. Sometimes it may be obvious why someone's benefit under a will has been reduced, or why they have been deleted from its terms entirely, but this is not always so. It is also very possible that someone who has been written out of a will may never know that they were ever in the testator's contemplations at all, but again this is not necessarily the case. Although this is, of course, not a matter of any legal significance, from the point of view of professional practice it is worth making clients aware of the risk of causing distress, especially where the position of someone particularly close to the testator is being materially altered; sometimes the more sensitive approach is to draft an entirely new document. In an example known to the author, a testator instructed a codicil by which a friend's children were deleted from his will without explanation. A legacy to the friend remained, which resulted in her being shown the will including, of course, the codicil. The testator had, at times, expressed disapproval regarding certain parenting choices of his friend, leading the latter to wonder whether he was attempting to make some point from beyond the grave. As melodramatic as this sounds, the matter was upsetting for the friend and her children, and would have been better avoided altogether.

The rules regarding the preparation and execution of a codicil are exactly the same as those for a deed relating to an entire estate. So, they must be signed by the testator and, to be self-proving, must be attested by a witness.

Example of a codicil

A simple example of the wording commonly encountered in a codicil would be as follows: **7–04**

I, JENNY BROWN, designed in the foregoing will dated the Sixth day of February Nineteen Hundred and Ninety Seven (hereinafter referred to as "my Will"), being desirous of making certain alterations and additions thereto, Do Hereby (First) increase the legacy to William Smith, designed in Clause Third of my Will to Ten Thousand pounds (£10,000); (Second) direct my executor to pay, as soon as convenient after my death but without interest to the date of payment, the sum of Five Thousand pounds (£5,000) to my housekeeper and companion, Mrs Euphemia Muckle, Eight Low Street, Aberfeldy. And except in so far as amended by this Codicil, I confirm my Will in all respects (*To be attested*).

POWER TO REVOKE

If the desired changes cannot be made by codicil, it will be necessary to execute an entirely new will. This almost always necessitates revocation of all prior or existing wills, the exception being rare cases where the deceased specifically wants two (or more) documents to remain in place; this would, of course, not be advised by a legal professional. Explicit revocation is important so that there is no doubt as to what the testator's true intentions actually were. It is difficult to know which result is worse: to have someone die having mistakenly left two contradictory wills and have the "wrong" one deemed operative, or to leave a will that is deemed inoperative and have the estate (or part of it) fall into intestacy.   **7–05**

The general rule

Testamentary documents are unusual in law in that they have no effect until the death of the testator.[1] This may seem obvious, but it actually strikes at an important aspect of their legal nature. Wills are said to be "ambulatory", meaning that they are subject to change or capable of alteration. Potentially unfamiliar terminology aside, again this may seem obvious. The point, however, is that testamentary documents provide, technically, an exception to the normal rule that a properly executed deed is irrevocable once delivered by the grantor to the grantee, or someone on the grantee's behalf. With an inter vivos deed (i.e. one taking effect during the grantor's lifetime), the logic of the normal rule is that the grantor shows his intention to be bound by surrendering physical control of the deed. The same logic cannot be applied to a genuinely testamentary deed, which can only take effect upon the death of the grantor.   **7–06**

    In *Clark's Executor v Clark*,[2] a testator sent a letter to a friend in which he stated that, upon his death, the friend was to receive his (the testator's) stamp collection. Two years later the testator made a will in which he bequeathed his whole estate to the Pathologist Society of the University of Edinburgh; the will included a statement that the testator cancelled all previous wills. The court held

---

[1] Erskine, III, 9, 5.
[2] *Clark's Executor v Clark*, 1943 S.C. 216.

that delivery of the holograph document to the legatee did not deprive the testator of his right to later revoke any of its contents. (However it was also decided, although opinion was mixed, that in this particular case the testator had not in fact revoked the bequest to his friend.)

The rule allowing revocation is so firmly applied that even a statement in a will that the document is irrevocable will not, in fact, prevent its later revocation. In the very old case of *Dougall's Trustees v Dougall*,[3] a deed containing provisions for both the discharge of debts and a testamentary settlement was deemed to have been successfully revoked. The court stated that "any renunciation of a power to revoke in such a case is to no avail, because it necessarily partakes of the nature of the deed itself".[4] Having said that, there are rare circumstances in which a will, or at least specific provisions, might be deemed irrevocable.

Binding obligation

7–07   It is possible for a testator to incur a binding obligation to leave property to someone upon his death. The simplest case is where an onerous contract has been entered into. In *Paterson v Paterson*,[5] a mother and son executed a minute of agreement whereby she undertook to make an irrevocable will in his favour, in return for which he lent her money and paid her rent. Upon her death, it transpired that she had left a will revoking the previous settlement and disposing of her property in different terms. The son successfully raised a challenge that the subsequent will, and therefore the revocation of their agreement, was void.

It was relevant in the *Paterson* case that the agreement had been made in writing, and could therefore be clearly evidenced. The courts will not take the same approach where an undertaking has been made merely verbally. In *McEleveen v McQuillan's Executrix*,[6] a testator had executed a will in favour of his daughter, in particular that she was to inherit his house. This was then revoked by a later will made in different terms. The daughter alleged that the first will had been made as part of an agreement whereby she and her husband had provided funds for the purchase of the house. Whilst the court accepted that the daughter had provided the purchase funds, they held that since the agreement related to heritable property it required to be in writing, and that in any case it would be unacceptable for a verbal agreement to be employed to defeat the explicit terms of a will.

Even where there is such a binding obligation, there is nothing to prevent the testator so bound from disposing of the subject property in advance of their death. This possibility is often foreseen in the drafting of formal agreements seeking restriction, but the terms of such agreements are of utmost importance in considering the appropriate remedy should the testator breach them. In *Hutchison v Graham's Executor*,[7] the testatrix had arranged a loan for purchase of a house, which it was agreed her granddaughter would make the repayments on. In return

---

[3] *Dougall's Trustees v Dougall* (1789) Mor. 15949.
[4] *Dougall's Trustees v Dougall* (1789) Mor. 15949 at 15950 (cause reported by Lord Dreghorn).
[5] *Paterson v Paterson* (1893) 20 R. 484.
[6] *McEleveen v McQuillan's Executrix*, 1997 S.L.T. (Sh Ct) 46.
[7] *Hutchison v Graham's Executor*, 2006 S.C.L.R. 587.

the testatrix executed a will bequeathing the house to said granddaughter, and undertook not to dispose of the property either during her lifetime or by will other than as stipulated. The agreement was minuted and properly executed by both parties; it also contained provisions outlining the remedies available should the agreement be breached. When it transpired upon the death of the testatrix that she had subsequently made a will in contradiction to the terms of the agreement, the granddaughter raised an action to enforce it. The court held that the agreement did not prevent revocation of the first will, since the inclusion of remedies for breach acted as a substitute for remedies under common law. Therefore the second will stood, though the granddaughter was entitled to recover payments as per the provisions on breach.

Mutual wills

Although they are now rare in Scotland, mention can be made of mutual wills.   **7–08**
These are documents in which two testators stipulate that upon either's death, the other will inherit his or her estate. There are often further provisions favouring, perhaps, the children or further descendants of the couple. Such wills are perfectly valid, and on the face of it are subject to the normal rules regarding revocation; they can be viewed simply as two separate wills contained within the same document. It is also worth reiterating the point that property can usually be freely disposed of before death.

The question, however, is whether any stipulation in these documents can remove the power to revoke, or whether the power to revoke is impliedly surrendered. In *Hanlon's Executor v Baird*,[8] a husband and wife executed a mutual will whereby the survivor would inherit from the deceased, and upon the death of the survivor the estate would then pass to their daughter. The husband died first, after which the wife made a new will, expressly revoking her prior testamentary documents, in favour of the local church. An action taken by the daughter failed, the court holding that the mutual settlement was revocable by the surviving party.

In contemplation of such circumstances it is common for mutual wills to contain an express undertaking by each party that they will not revoke the will, either before or after death of the other. This is obviously relevant, but it not necessarily conclusive. In *Corrance's Trustees v Glen*,[9] a husband and wife executed a mutual will in the usual terms, instructing that upon the death of the survivor their combined estate should be divided equally among the respective families of each spouse. A provision limited the power of revocation so as to be effective only against the relevant spouse's family's share of the estate. The wife died first, and the husband later remarried. He revoked all previous testamentary writings and gave his second wife a liferent of his whole estate. This was successfully challenged, the court holding that he lacked the power to revoke the provisions in respect of his first wife's family's share. This can be contrasted with *Dewar's Trustees v Dewar's Trustees*,[10] where the mutual will of two spouses left the residue of the estate to the survivor in liferent, and to each spouse's nieces and

---

[8] *Hanlon's Executor v Baird*, 1945 S.L.T. 304.
[9] *Corrance's Trustees v Glen* (1903) 5 F. 777.
[10] *Dewar's Trustees v Dewar's Trustees*, 1950 S.L.T. 191.

nephews in fee. The agreement expressly reserved the power to revoke only in regards to each spouse's "respective means and estate". The wife having inherited executed a new will favouring only her own family. A challenge raised by the husband's family was unsuccessful, the court holding that despite the alleged restriction the wife was entitled to revoke the mutual will.

The law regarding mutual wills has, on occasion, been considered by the Scottish Law Commission, which remarks that it is a difficult area but have made no particular recommendations regarding its reform.[11]

METHODS OF REVOCATION

7–09   As with many legal exercises, the revocation of a will can be achieved either expressly or by implication. Again in keeping with similar areas of relevance, express revocation is the more likely to be effective. There are in addition a number of other activities that might serve to revoke a will, though perhaps not entirely reliably. It is worth reiterating that, above all, and whatever method is used, it should be as clear as possible that testator's intention was indeed to revoke a prior document or provision.

Revocation by physical destruction

7–10   The testator, if he wishes to revoke the entire will, may destroy the deed by completely tearing it up (or shredding it), either in person or by giving express authority to his law agent or some other person to do so. This revokes the will, assuming that the testator possessed the required *animus revocandi* (i.e. intention to revoke). Indeed, it may not even be necessary to completely destroy the document. In *Hare v Nasmyth*,[12] it was held that cutting off a seal attached to the end of the document constituted symbolic destruction, and therefore complete revocation.

The historical effectiveness of destruction is fairly obvious, especially when one considers how common or informal holograph wills once were. A document of which there is only one copy, which is in the testator's sole possession and has been seen by no one else, cannot of course have any effect if he destroys it. This gave rise to an important presumption applied by the courts. If it can be shown that a testator executed a will and that, thereafter, he retained that will in his own custody, but at the time of his death it cannot be found, there is the presumption that he destroyed it with the intention to revoke. Like most presumptions, it can be rebutted, but the burden of the proof is on the party who seeks to do so. In the old case of *Laing v Bruce*,[13] the deceased's will could not be found and it was presumed that it had been destroyed *animo revocandi*. Similarly in *Clyde v Clyde*,[14] a testator made a will favouring his nephew and left the document with his solicitors. Some considerable time later (and several years before his eventual

---

[11] Scottish Law Commission, *Report on Succession* (Scot. Law Com. No.215), para.6.53.
[12] *Hare v Nasmyth* (1823) 2 Addams 25.
[13] *Laing v Bruce* (1838) 1 D. 59.
[14] *Clyde v Clyde*, 1958 S.C. 343.

death) he requested that his solicitor send the will to him. At the time of his death, the will could not be found and it was held to have been intentionally destroyed by the testator.

If there *is* another copy, or if the document is held by someone other than the testator, revocation by destruction becomes a more complicated matter. Concerning the status of copies, the general rule is that changes made to a copy are not effective, and the original document will prevail where the two contradict.[15] However, it would seem that where an explanation accompanies such changes, they can be given effect on the basis that they express a new and overriding testamentary intent. In *Thomson's Trustees v Bowhill Baptist Church*,[16] a testatrix's will had been retained by her solicitor, and a typewritten copy later sent out to her. Upon her death it was discovered that the testatrix had physically cut out the residue clause, signing in the margins that remained and writing in explanation for her actions that she did not have the funds to satisfy this. It was held that this constituted a valid revocation of the residue clause, despite the fact that the testatrix had actually erred in her estimations of her own estate, with the effect that the residue fell into intestacy.

In addition to its importance for copies, the *Thomson* case also raises the matter of partial destruction. What if there is a will, but parts of the text have been scored out or obliterated? There is a very real risk that this could easily have been done fraudulently, so there would need to be some evidence that the obliteration was carried out by the testator (or with the testator's express authority) and not by some unscrupulous third party. Indeed, in keeping with the general rules of formality, the court would require some form of authentication of the deletion, such as, at least, initials or signature.[17]

If it can be shown that destruction was accidental, fraudulent or effected whilst not fully mentally capable, this might not constitute revocation. Such a situation is obviously very complicated, but it is possible for an action to be raised in court seeking to re-establish the document. This is called "proving tenor" and historically required a declarator from the Court of Session; it is now competent for such a case to be brought before the sheriff court.[18] Evidence is required as to the alleged contents of the missing will, the best examples of which would be drafts, earlier copies or instructions sent to a law agent. In the absence of writing the evidence of witnesses might be sufficient. In *Leckie v Leckie*,[19] the testator's settlement had been drafted by a law agent and thereafter given to the testator. The law agent had some time later destroyed all notes pertaining to the work, thinking them no longer of any use. Witnesses reliably reported having seen the will recently before the testator's death, but it appeared the document had been maliciously destroyed by one of the beneficiaries. A number of witnesses attested to the will's contents, and were able to give a clear and consistent, if not a verbatim account of its terms. It was held that tenor of the document had been sufficiently proven. Of course, the potential motivations of anyone giving such testimony would need to be considered.

---

[15] See, e.g. *Manson v Edinburgh Royal Institute*, 1948 S.L.T. 196.
[16] *Thomson's Trustees v Bowhill Baptist Church*, 1956 S.L.T. 302.
[17] See, e.g. *Taylor's Executrix v Thom*, 1914 S.C. 79.
[18] Courts Reform (Scotland) Act 2014 s.38(2)(h).
[19] *Leckie v Leckie* (1884) 11 R. 1088.

It is also necessary to lead evidence as to how the document was destroyed or otherwise went missing, referred to as establishing the *casus amissionis* (i.e. circumstances of the loss). The crucial point is to show that, howsoever the will was lost or destroyed, it was done so without the intention to revoke the rights expressed within it. In *Winchester v Smith*,[20] the daughter of a testator sought to prove tenor of a mutual will (executed between her parents) on which the signatures had been cancelled, therefore rendering the document invalid. The testator's widow gave evidence that she had deliberately damaged the will in a fit of anger, and that the testator had known nothing of her actions. The court held, however, that her uncorroborated testimony alone was not enough to establish the *casus amissionis*, and the will was not revived.

Revocation by later will

7–11   A common method of revocation is an express declaration in a later will that earlier wills are "hereby revoked". Generally speaking, a declaration of this kind is effective, although exceptions have been made as will be seen. If there is no express revocation, and the earlier will has not been destroyed in a regular manner, it may be that the two wills have to be read together. Of course, it is unlikely that this is what the testator would have wished, unless he perceived his second will as being in the nature of an extended codicil, in which case that fact ought to have been made clear.

In some cases, revocation (or partial revocation) may be implied in so far as the earlier will is inconsistent with the later one. A rule of thumb is that if the later will is a universal settlement, i.e. deals with the entire estate as one, without any other bequests, the earlier will is revoked by implication. In *Cadger v Ronald's Trustees*,[21] a testatrix left a number of wills, in one of which was stated "I leave all my worldly goods to my sister". This was held to be a disposal of her whole estate, and therefore the previous will was impliedly revoked. If, on the other hand, this is not the case, and especially if the two wills can broadly make sense even being read together, the general rule is that they would both be effective. In *Duthie's Executor v Taylor*,[22] a second will conveyed the testatrix's whole estate to trustees and provided for certain legacies. However, it made no direction as to the residue of the estate, something which had been done in the first will. The court held that both wills were valid, and the legacies contained in the first were effective insofar as they were not inconsistent with the second; the result was that most of the legacies in the earlier will were, in fact, effective.

If it is claimed that a later will revokes an earlier will by implication, it appears that the party alleging such revocation requires to discharge a very heavy burden of proof. In *Mitchell's Administratrix v Edinburgh Royal Infirmary*,[23] a codicil to a will was ambivalent on the matter of revocation, despite having been professionally drafted. In one provision it suggested revocation of certain legacies made in the principal will, while another provision was against it. Evidence was led that, in other documents, the testator had employed express language of

---

[20] *Winchester v Smith* (1863) 1 M. 685.
[21] *Cadger v Ronald's Trustees*, 1946 S.L.T. (Notes) 24.
[22] *Duthie's Executor v Taylor*, 1986 S.L.T. 142.
[23] *Mitchell's Administratrix v Edinburgh Royal Infirmary*, 1928 S.C. 47.

revocation. The court held that, in the circumstances, the onus of proving implied revocation had not been satisfied; accordingly, the original provisions stood.

Revocation by the conditio si testator sine liberis decesserit

There is an ancient rule of Scots common law whereby a will that makes a universal settlement of the testator's estate is presumed to be revoked by the subsequent birth of a child. This is the *conditio si testator sine liberis decesserit*.[24] The presumption raised by the *conditio* is based on the notion that the testator would not have wished such a will to stand where it made no provision for the child or children. There is, therefore, a limitation to the presumption that it will only apply where no such provision has been made.

7–12

Its basic application can be seen in *Knox's Trustees v Knox*.[25] Here, a testator had executed a will and soon after fathered another child. There was extensive evidence that he had been in the process of drafting a new will making provision for all his children, but this was not executed before he died suddenly and unexpectedly. The court held that his original will was revoked by the *conditio* and his estate fell into intestacy.

The presumption given rise to by the *conditio* can be rebutted by circumstances which show that the testator intended that his will should stand in spite of the subsequent birth of the child. It is possible that this can be established by the mere passage of time. If, after a sufficient period during which the testator instructs no changes himself, it can be argued that this rebuts the presumption. The courts seem reluctant to apply this lightly however, and the argument was rejected in *Milligan's JF v Milligan*[26] where a 10-year period was deemed insufficient. Rebuttal is far easier where evidence can be led of a conscious and positive decision by the testator. In *Stuart-Gordon v Stuart-Gordon*,[27] a testatrix died very shortly after the birth of her daughter. During her pregnancy she had expressed concerns regarding her own health and the potential difficulties she might encounter in childbirth, but did not amend her will to make provision for her unborn child. Evidence was led that this had been a conscious decision by the testatrix, who knew that her child would be well provided for by other means. Accordingly, the *conditio* was displaced and the will stood.

It is worth noting that a child invoking the *conditio* is not the same as where a child claims legal rights.[28] Successfully invoking the *conditio* results in revocation of the entire will, which as demonstrated above will likely result in intestacy. This might actually serve to disinherit the child by way of prior rights being claimed by a surviving spouse or civil partner.[29] In practice it might be safer, and ultimately more lucrative, to exercise legal rights, even acknowledging that the estate against which these can be claimed is limited.

The Scottish Law Commission have recommended that the *conditio si testator sine liberis decesserit* be abolished.[30] This was partly motivated by the fact that

---

[24] Erskine, III, 8, 46.

[25] *Knox's Trustees v Knox* (1907) 15 S.L.T. 282.

[26] *Milligan's JF v Milligan*, 1910 S.C. 58.

[27] *Stuart-Gordon v Stuart-Gordon* (1899) 1 F. 1005.

[28] See Ch.6.

[29] See Ch.4.

[30] Scottish Law Commission, *Report on Succession* (Scot. Law Com. No.215), para.6.21.

the principle had not been successfully invoked for nearly 100 years, the *Milligan* case being the most recent example at the time. However, there is now modern authority in the form of *Greenan v Courtney*.[31] Here a testator had, during a somewhat complex relationship with his first wife, executed a will in which he made provision for their children. Their relationship ended and the testator remarried, having two further children, but never amended his will. His widow sought to revoke his will based on the *conditio*, an action that was defended by the testator's first wife. She had remained in regular contact with the testator, and gave evidence that he had deliberately omitted to alter his will due to having made separate provision for the children of his second marriage. Whilst the latter of these assertions was true, the court held that this testimony alone was not enough to rebut the presumption, and the will was held to be revoked.

Regardless of the arguments to be made variously in favour of or against the *conditio*, it has not at the time of writing been abolished. The Scottish Government consulted on the issue, and the proposal to abolish was met with a generally negative response. As a result, the Government concluded that further consultation on the issue was required before a decision could be taken, and the recommendation was not implemented.[32]

Revocation by supervening agreement

7–13   It is very common upon separation for couples to enter into a formal agreement in which legal rights dependent on the relationship are either redefined in some way or expressly renounced; any rights not dealt with in the agreement are retained. This can, of course, be relevant where wills are concerned, and a well-drafted separation agreement can avoid complications later on, or at least provide a remedy as to how disputes might be resolved.[33] For certainty of effect the safest approach is for all rights in succession to be expressly renounced by both parties, provided of course this is what is intended. Problems can easily arise, however, if the language used is not clear or comprehensive.

This was recently demonstrated in the case of *Price v Baxter*.[34] Here, a husband had made a will leaving his entire estate to his wife. Subsequently the couple separated and both spouses signed a minute of agreement that, among other things, stated that its terms were made in full and final settlement of any financial entitlements due either as a result of the breakdown of the relationship or "any prior rights and rights of succession arising under the Succession (Scotland) Act 1964 or at common law". Upon the husband's death his will remained unchanged and the two remained married. An action was raised by relatives of the husband that the will had been revoked by the separation agreement, and that the wife had renounced her rights in succession not only under it, but also in respect of intestacy. It is easy to have some sympathy for this argument, since clearly the separation agreement was intended to have at least some effect regarding rights in succession. However, the court held that the action

---

[31] *Greenan v Courtney* [2007] CSOH 58.

[32] Scottish Government, *Consultation on Technical Issues Relating to Succession—Analysis of the Written Consultation Responses and Scottish Government Response* (Scottish Government, June 2015) paras 3.33–3.37.

[33] See, e.g. *Redfern's Executor v Redfern*, 1996 S.L.T. 900.

[34] *Price v Baxter*, 2009 Fam. L.R. 138.

must fail; it was not possible to construe the wording of the separation agreement as a revocation of the will, and whilst the wife had renounced her rights in succession explicitly stated, these expressions did not include renunciation of rights under a will. Accordingly, she inherited the estate.

It is worth mentioning here the related matter of revocation by subsequent marriage or divorce, or the equivalent entering into, or dissolution of, a civil partnership. This was also a matter that had been considered by the Scottish Law Commission, who recommended that divorce or dissolution should revoke an existing will insofar as it confers a benefit on the former spouse or civil partner.[35] This was implemented under the 2016 Act, but the precise mechanism by which it was done was not to revoke the will per se, but to treat the former spouse or civil partner as having predeceased the testator.[36] This actually has a broader relevance than the matter currently at hand, and as such is further considered in Ch.8.

Revival of a revoked will

There is also the question of whether a revoked will can later be revived. This issue can arise where there is some problem with the subsequent revoking will, such as lack of formality being discovered, or where it simply cannot be found. It might even itself have been revoked by yet another testamentary document! Put simply, the question is whether or not a will that has been revoked can ever again be effective.

7–14

Under common law, the (very) general rule was that if a subsequent will was itself revoked, the earlier will would revive as if the second had never existed.[37] In *Ferguson v Russell's Trustees*,[38] it was stated that:

> "In my view of the law of Scotland, if a deceased person left in his repositories a probative will, it would be irrelevant to aver that, subsequently to its execution, he had executed another will revoking it, which he had subsequently cancelled or destroyed."[39]

However, it was also acknowledged that Scottish authority on the matter was scant, and that this rule was not absolute.

Indeed, judicial opinion on the matter was mixed, resulting in inconsistent case law and consequently an unclear overall position. Often the decisions turned on what exactly had happened in respect of the earlier will. One good illustration can be found in *Bruce's JF v Lord Advocate*.[40] In this case, a testator signed a will, which remained in the possession of his law agents. Four years later, he signed a second will revoking all previous wills; but this second will he retained in his own possession. At the time of his death, the second will could not be found, and was presumed to have been destroyed *animo revocandi*. The problem, however, was that the first will still existed, and the question was raised as to whether it, having been revoked by the second will, could be revived by the

---

[35] Scottish Law Commission, *Report on Succession* (Scot. Law Com. No.215), para.6.17.
[36] Succession (Scotland) Act 2016 s.1.
[37] Erskine, III, 4, 5.
[38] *Ferguson v Russell's Trustees*,1919 S.C. 80.
[39] *Ferguson v Russell's Trustees*,1919 S.C. 80 at 84 per Lord Sands.
[40] *Bruce's JF v Lord Advocate*, 1969 S.C. 296.

second will's revocation. Not without some difficulty, the court decided that the first will was effective. It is possible that the court was influenced by the fact that if someone undertakes to make two wills over the course of his lifetime, he clearly does not intend to die intestate.

There is also the possibility that the first will has, in fact, been destroyed upon revocation. If the first will has been destroyed by the testator, or by his law agent on the instructions of the testator, it is highly likely that this, coupled with express revocation in a later will, would ensure that it could not revive. A similar result would probably arise if the solicitor had been instructed to destroy the first will but had failed to do so.[41]

7–15   The decision in *Bruce* can be contrasted with that reached in the older case of *Elder's Trustees v Elder*.[42] Here, a testator made a second will that expressly revoked his first, but was itself revoked by the subsequent birth of his son under the *conditio si testator sine liberis decesserit*. His daughters sought to claim under the terms of the first will, which favoured them. The court held that in this case the first will not revived, stating

> "wherever a last will is cut down by the operation of the rule or presumption that we are now considering, all previous testamentary settlements must fall along with it except such as are obligatory and matter of contract".[43]

Perhaps adding to the uncertainty, this principle was not followed in the later case of *Nicolson v Nicolson's Tutrix*,[44] in which the facts were similar but the circumstances were distinguished on the grounds that revocation of the first will had been implied rather than express.

In a final twist to the possible circumstances, there was also the potential for an earlier will to have been destroyed contrary to the wishes of the testator. If the subsequent revoking will is itself revoked (or flawed), what is the status of the first will? This was the question faced in *Cullen's Executor v Elphinstone*.[45] In this case, a testatrix executed a will prepared by her solicitor. Eight years later she instructed the preparation of a new will that expressly revoked the earlier one, but as she had meanwhile become blind, the second was executed notarially (i.e. on her behalf)[46] by a partner in the solicitor's firm. The first will was destroyed in accordance with normal professional practice, but this had not actually been instructed by the testatrix. Upon her death, it transpired that the second will was formally invalid, due to a case that had been decided in the intervening period[47] whereby notarial execution would be invalid if the solicitor signing stood to indirectly benefit under the will, such as in respect of fees that might be received. (There was no suggestion of any wrongdoing on the part of the solicitor, whom the court explicitly acknowledged had acted honestly and in good faith, but there was no question that the will was rendered invalid.) The court held that although

---

[41] This was a further observation made in the *Ferguson* case.
[42] *Elder's Trustees v Elder* (1895) 22 R. 505.
[43] *Elder's Trustees v Elder* (1895) 22 R. 505 at 512 per Lord McLaren.
[44] *Nicolson v Nicolson's Tutrix*, 1922 S.L.T. 473.
[45] *Cullen's Executor v Elphinstone*, 1948 S.C. 662.
[46] See Ch.5 on notarial execution.
[47] *Finlay v Finlay's Trustees*, 1948 S.C. 16.

the earlier will had certainly been destroyed, it had not been validly revoked. It was therefore revived and, since there was sufficient evidence of its provisions, declarator of tenor was granted.

In light of the complex body of case law on the matter, this is yet another area in which the Scottish Law Commission had long advised that reform was required.[48] This was achieved under the 2016 Act, which states that where a will, or part of a will, is expressly or impliedly revoked by a subsequent will which is itself revoked, this does *not* revive any part of the earlier will.[49] This effectively reverses the common law position, and undoubtedly has the advantage of certainty in its favour, but its effects in practice remain to be seen. It seems likely that there will be an increase in estates falling into intestacy, and in at least some of the cases cited above this would have led to a distribution not intended by the testator. It will be interesting to see if the new statutory rule is applied as rigidly by the courts as the legislation suggests it ought to be, or if creative judicial interpretation will require to be employed so as to resolve difficult circumstances.

---

[48] Scottish Law Commission, *Report on Succession* (Scot. Law Com. No.215), paras 6.31–6.36.
[49] Succession (Scotland) Act 2016 s.5.

CHAPTER 8

Interpretation of Wills

INTRODUCTION

It was observed in Ch.6 that most wills are generally quite easy to understand. **8–01** Despite the legal jargon that is necessarily at times employed, the basic idea of a will is straightforward, and most testamentary documents encountered in practice leave little doubt as to what the testator intended; indeed one important mark of a well-drafted will is that its terms be implemented with as little complication as possible.

Having said that, there are times when it is not altogether clear what the correct implementation of a testamentary provision would be; perhaps the terms are too vague, or perhaps circumstances have arisen that the will has failed to provide for. In other words, it is sometimes necessary to interpret the provisions of a will in order to deduce how they ought to be given effect.

Throughout this chapter reference is made regularly to different types of testamentary documents and to various types of provision that they commonly contain. As a result, technical terminology is at times employed. For sake of brevity, such terminology is not fully explained in this chapter, although its meaning can often be deduced from the context. All terms are fully explained and considered elsewhere in the text; of particular relevance are Ch.5, on the preparation of testamentary documents, and Ch.6, on common testamentary provisions. Revocation, covered in Ch.7, is also mentioned at certain points. To avoid excessive cross-referencing in the footnotes, suffice it to say that it is recommended that these chapters should be consulted wherever necessary.

RULES OF EVIDENCE

In addressing almost all questions of law, evidence must be used in order to **8–02** establish facts, support arguments, and ultimately formulate a sound legal position. The practice of interpreting testamentary documents is no different. The most important source of evidence in this matter is the will itself, and the most fundamental principle of interpretation is to give effect to the intention of the testator as expressed in the will. The testator's meaning must be deduced from the words he used. This is called using "intrinsic evidence", i.e. considering the provisions contained within the boundaries of the will. It is possible, though only in limited circumstances, to consider evidence from sources other than the will itself; this is called using "extrinsic evidence".

Intrinsic evidence

8–03 Put simply, then, the most basic question to ask in any matter of interpretation is "what does the will actually say?". This seems obvious in the extreme, but it is far from unknown for disappointed beneficiaries to attempt to challenge a will's terms simply because they cannot believe that the testator would have actually done what it appears is instructed by the will. A will that contains provisions that are perfectly clear, regardless of how unexpected or upsetting those are, cannot be challenged through the mechanism of interpretation; though of course it might well be subject to challenge on other grounds.

The court's general approach to interpretation was neatly summarised in *Blair v Blair*[1]:

> "We must find the intention of the testatrix within the four corners of the deed which she has legally executed ... it is only if the terms of the deed appear to be in themselves doubtful in their import or legal construction that it is either necessary or legitimate to affect or explain them by extraneous circumstances."[2]

If possible, the will shall be read in such a way that intestacy is avoided. This is based chiefly on the idea that, as the testator has taken the positive step of making a will, it can legitimately be inferred that he wanted to avoid intestacy. There is also the generally accepted principle that it is better to give effect to the deceased's wishes if at all possible rather than surrender the estate, or any part of it, to the strictly applied rules of intestacy.

In considering the contents of the will, the court must read the document as a whole. Attempts must be made, if necessary, to deduce the testator's overall intention rather than simply implementing each provision in isolation. The court must also include in this whole any additional or ancillary testamentary writing such as codicils and even, if appropriate, any informal writings such as letters. Where provisions conflict with each other, the court will try to reconcile them; if this is not possible, effect will be given to the most recently executed.

8–04 Words are presumed to have their ordinary, primary meaning unless the context clearly indicates otherwise.[3] Having said that, where words have a technical legal meaning they will be given this effect; there are very real dangers with "homemade" wills in which a testator might use a technical term such as his "issue" when he actually just means his "children". Indeed, usage of the terms "child" and "children" is particularly troublesome, and gives rise to the possibility of confusion regarding which particular generation of descendants is being indicated by a will's provisions. In the case of *Yule's Trustees*,[4] it was held that in order for the will to make any sense, the term "child" had to be interpreted as meaning "grandchild".

Where the provisions of the will are clear and unambiguous, they cannot normally be contradicted by claims that the testator meant something else, even if such claims can be supported by evidence. Verbal statements made by the testator

---

[1] *Blair v Blair* (1849) 12 D. 97.
[2] *Blair v Blair* (1849) 12 D. 97 at 107 per Lord Moncreiff.
[3] See, e.g. *Hay v Duthie's Trustees*, 1956 S.C. 511.
[4] *Yule's Trustees*, 1981 S.L.T. 250.

beyond his testamentary writings are not relevant,[5] since of course people might be motivated to say what they believe the listener wants to hear, if for no other reason than to "keep the peace". Spiritual and theological arguments aside, the emergence of a contradictory document upon the testator's death will not be a matter of his own concern! Similarly, an alteration in circumstances of which it can be shown the testator was aware is not relevant either; a well-drafted will attempts to accommodate potential future circumstances, so it is not competent to argue that changing circumstances in themselves justify artificially altering the terms of the will.

It is possible that revoked clauses, where they have not been removed entirely and their contents are still evident, might be considered in order to aid interpretation of the provisions still in effect. In *McLachlan v Seton's Trustees*,[6] it was necessary to interpret the terms of a will that had been amended at least six times between its initial drafting and the death of the testatrix; consideration of the amended versions was appropriate in the circumstances, particularly as duress was alleged. It is probably fair to say that this was an unusual case, and that the courts are generally reluctant to allow this form of evidence.[7]

Extrinsic evidence

Having said all the above, there are times when the court will allow extrinsic evidence. As can be inferred from the observations of the *Blair* case, its use is permitted if the will is unclear, and the ordinary rules of interpretation provide no solution. In considering extrinsic evidence, the court's general approach of attempting to deduce the intention of the testator remains. To this end, the court attempts to place itself in the position of the testator at the time the will was made; the aim is always to explain the will, not contradict it.[8]

8–05

Extrinsic evidence is admitted for a number of overlapping purposes. First, and for practical purposes above all else, extrinsic evidence can be used where it is necessary in order that a will can actually be read. Although admittedly rare, it is possible for a will to be written in a foreign language, in which case reference to that language is obviously required so that it may be translated. In *Re Cliffs Trusts*,[9] an Englishman made a will in French whilst living abroad. Both the original and an English translation were certified by a notary public in the relevant country. The court decided that it was entitled to look at both the original and the translation, and that assistance from French lawyers would be required in order to properly construe the will's contents.

Secondly, where the primary or ordinary meaning of a word fails to give logical effect to a provision, it might be permissible to consider evidence suggesting that words should be given an unusual or secondary meaning personal to the testator. In *Borthwick's Trustees v Borthwick*,[10] a testator directed that the fee of his estate was to be divided among his "next of kin". He was survived by

---

[5] *McEleveen v McQuillan's Executrix*, 1997 S.L.T. (Sh Ct) 46.
[6] *McLachlan v Seton's Trustees*, 1937 S.C. 206.
[7] See, e.g. *Devlin's Trustees v Breen*, 1945 S.C. (HL) 27 and *Currie's Trustees v Collier*, 1939 S.C. 247.
[8] *Hill v Crook* (1873) L.R. 6 HL 265.
[9] *Re Cliffs Trusts* [1892] 2 Ch. 229.
[10] *Borthwick's Trustees v Borthwick*, 1955 S.C. 227.

cousins on both his father's and his mother's side; under the law at the time, only his paternal relatives would be included in the category of "next of kin". However, provisions elsewhere in the will made reference specifically to a maternal cousin; the court held that in the circumstances it was likely the testator had intended to include relatives of both sides. As Lord Justice-Clerk Thomson remarked,

> "a testator may give his own meaning to the words which he uses. His will becomes the dictionary from which the meaning of the terms used in it is to be ascertained".[11]

It may also be relevant to prove that the testator was aware of circumstances material to the construction of his will. This is not the same as attempting to infer alterations as mentioned earlier in this chapter. The principle is rather more narrow, and is designed to cover situations where facts cogent to the estate were clearly known by the testator, in which case the terms can be construed as incorporating those facts. The case of *Dunsmure v Dunsmure*,[12] considered in Ch.6, is relevant again here, where a legacy was left of any money the testator was entitled to under his late father's estate. Extrinsic evidence was admitted in that case to prove that the testator knew he was also entitled to money from his parent's marriage contract; these funds were held to be included in the legacy. It is worth noting that the circumstances of this case were relevant to the decision. The testator had left a brief holograph will naming only his wife as a beneficiary. In addition to the legacy in question, two other legacies, broad in scope, also favoured her. Had the money under the marriage contract not been included, it would have fallen into intestacy and been claimed by the testator's mother and siblings. His intention had been clear, even if his exact wording was not, that his wife ought to inherit his entire estate.

CASES OF UNCERTAINTY

8–06   As perhaps already illustrated, matters of interpretation very often concern ambiguity over the intent of the testator. As might also be apparent, the most common questions that arise concern the subjects and objects of legacies; the former relates to what property the legacy actually comprises, and the latter relates to who is entitled to receive it. It is, again, that classic question central to succession of "who gets what?".

It is perhaps obvious to say that, in order to be given effect, a legacy must have both a subject and an object that are identifiable. If there is uncertainty as to either element of this, there is a chance that a legacy will fail. In such cases of ambiguity, intrinsic evidence is, as in all cases, of primary importance. However, extrinsic evidence can be admitted within the parameters outlined above, if necessary.

---

[11] *Borthwick's Trustees v Borthwick*, 1955 S.C. 227 at 230 per Lord Justice-Clerk Thomson.
[12] *Dunsmure v Dunsmure* (1879) 7 R. 261.

Identifying the subject

On balance, fewer problems are encountered in identifying the subject of a legacy   **8–07**
than the object; the latter is more prone to bedevilment by technical terminology.
That said, issues of uncertainty do of course arise, as in the *Dunsmure* case.

The same basic rule is applied that if there is no ambiguity in the wording of a
legacy, and it makes sense without going outwith the document, it will stand or
fall on its own; extrinsic evidence cannot be led to alter it. In *Fortunato's JF v
Fortunato*,[13] the testator made a bequest of two public houses to a mother and
daughter, the mother having worked for him as a manager. Above each public
house was a connected dwelling, which the manager claimed should be included
in the legacy. In support, she sought to have evidence admitted that before his
death the testator's relationship with his wife had deteriorated, to the point that he
wished her (i.e. the claimant) to be his main beneficiary; averments were also
made of a relationship between the two. She also sought to admit evidence of the
haste in which the will was made, arguing that exclusion of the dwellings had
been an oversight. The court held that, whilst some latitude in interpretation
might be justified, there was no requirement in this case to look beyond the limits
of the will; the meaning of the legacy was clear by itself and thus it required to be
so implemented.

Even where the subject of a legacy lacks detail, it may not be so uncertain as
to fail. Where the intention of the testator can be deduced from the will's general
instructions, the court can stipulate an appropriate sum to give effect to a legacy.
In *Magistrates of Dundee v Morris*,[14] testamentary trustees were directed to set
up a school (which eventually became the well-known Morgan Academy) but no
actual cash sum was stated. However, as the will did specify the size of the
proposed school, the amount of the legacy required could be ascertained and the
provision did not fail from uncertainty.

A question can arise when the same legatee receives a number of benefits
under a will. A second or subsequent legacy given to the same person can be
either cumulative or substitutional; if it is cumulative then it is payable in
addition to the first legacy, if it is substitutional then it is payable instead of the
first legacy. The general rule to be applied was stated in *Arres' Trustees v
Mather*[15]:

> "When a testator by one or several instruments gives two or more legacies to the
> same person, he presumably intends that all shall have effect. The presumption may,
> however, be overcome, not only by distinct expression that the later bequest was
> intended to be substitutional, but by anything which satisfies the Court that it was so
> intended."[16]

It is actually not unusual for the same legatee to receive more than one legacy,
particularly where a testator has been very exacting in their instructions.
However, there is a particular problem if a benefit has been duplicated, or a

---

[13] *Fortunato's JF v Fortunato*, 1981 S.L.T. 277.
[14] *Magistrates of Dundee v Morris* (1858) 20 D. (HL) 9.
[15] *Arres' Trustees v Mather* (1881) 9 R. 107.
[16] *Arres' Trustees v Mather* (1881) 9 R. 107 at 109 per Lord Young.

second legacy given in very similar terms to the first. The correct approach in such a situation was stated with authority in *Edinburgh Royal Infirmary v Muir's Trustees*[17]:

> "When exactly the same amount is given twice in the same paper, the presumption is that it is a mere repetition arising from some mistake or forgetfulness; but where the same amount is bequeathed in two distinct testamentary papers, both equally formal, then both legacies are payable, unless it can be shown from the settlement of the deceased, or by other competent evidence, that his intention was to give one legacy only."[18]

The rule above has been variably applied according to the circumstances of each case, leading to some notable exceptions being made. In *Gillies v Glasgow Royal Infirmary*,[19] a testator directed that the residue of his estate be divided into four equal parts, and named Glasgow Royal Hospital twice in the list of legatees; there were only two others. The court held that the hospital was entitled to receive two quarters of the residue. In *Livingstone v Livingstone*,[20] a father left £500 to his son, with the instruction that it be invested in property, in which the son would have a liferent and his own children the fee. Before his death the testator had instructed the building of a property, worth around £500, in which he gave the same son a liferent and the same son's children the fee. He had written a letter in which he stated that the house was in satisfaction of his son's inheritance; but this letter had never been delivered. The court held that the son was not entitled to the double benefit.

Identifying the object

8–08   The beneficiary, or "object", of a legacy is in most cases identifiable without difficulty, although as already mentioned problems can, and do, arise. If a matter of uncertainty cannot be remedied, the legacy will fail. As stated in *Salveson's Trustees v Wye*[21]: "if there can be reasonable doubt as to who [the testator] comprehended ... the courts will treat the bequest as void".[22] In that case, the testator's legacy to "any poor relations, friends or acquaintances of mine" was void for uncertainty.

Errors

8–09   Minor errors made in respect of names or designations are not normally fatal, although the courts will not lightly depart from applying a legacy literally if its terms are clear. This is the case even where it is strongly suggested that an error has occurred. In *Naysmith's Trustees v NSPCC*,[23] a Scottish testator left a number of legacies to charities, all of which were Scottish except the National Society for

---

[17] *Edinburgh Royal Infirmary v Muir's Trustees* (1881) 9 R. 352.
[18] *Edinburgh Royal Infirmary v Muir's Trustees* (1881) 9 R. 352 at 355 per Lord President Inglis.
[19] *Gillies v Glasgow Royal Infirmary*, 1960 S.C. 438.
[20] *Livingstone v Livingstone* (1864) 3 M. 20.
[21] *Salveson's Trustees v Wye*, 1954 S.C. 440.
[22] *Salveson's Trustees v Wye*, 1954 S.C. 440 at 444 per Lord Carmont.
[23] *Naysmith's Trustees v NSPCC*, 1914 S.C. (HL) 76.

the Prevention of Cruelty to Children, which operated in England. A claim was raised by the *Scottish* National Society for the Prevention of Cruelty to Children (NSPCC), a separate organisation not identified in the will, on the basis that it was surely this charity that was intended by the testator. The court held that where the description of a legatee applies exactly to one party, this does not preclude inquiry as to whether a different party was in fact intended; however, there is a strong presumption in favour of the correctly-described party, which cannot be overcome except by cogent positive evidence. In this case, there was not sufficient evidence, and the legacy fell to be paid to the (English) NSPCC.

The court is perhaps more inclined towards generous interpretation where there is not an outright correctly-described party. Where there are various parties who *might* fall within the description, extrinsic evidence can be admitted to facilitate clarification. A classic example is found in *Cathcart's Trustees v Bruce*,[24] where a legacy was left to "General Alexander Fairlie Bruce". There were two possible beneficiaries; General Alexander J. Bruce and Mr Alexander F. Bruce. Extrinsic evidence allowed the legacy to be paid to the General.

Two related cases demonstrate the lengths the courts have been willing to go to in order to identify a legacy's object. In the first, *Wedderspoon v Thomson's Trustees*,[25] the testator had left £500 to "Janet Keiller or Williamson, confectioner in Dundee". There was, in fact, no such person, which could easily have resulted in failure of the legacy. The testator did have a cousin named Janet Keiller, but she was not a confectioner, and in fact did not lodge any claim. However, her sister Agnes Keiller, also, of course, a cousin of the testator, had previously been married to a confectioner, in Dundee, by the name of Wedderspoon. In considering her claim to the legacy, the court allowed extrinsic evidence in the form of letters demonstrating her correspondence with the testator, and also old testamentary documents in which he referred variously to a "Janet Keiller", "Keiller, spouse to Wedderspoon" and "Mrs Wedderspoon". The court was satisfied that only a minor error was involved, and that no other person could logically be meant; accordingly the claim succeeded. In the related case of *Keiller v Thomson's Trustees*,[26] the same testator had left a legacy to "William Keiller, confectioner in Dundee". Again, there was no such person. This time, there were actually two claimants in the action; James Keiller, a well-established confectioner in Dundee, and William Keiller, who had previously worked for James in Dundee but had established himself in Montrose some time before the testator's death. Extrinsic evidence was admitted to demonstrate that the testator had had a close relationship with James, and that he was apt to commit errors in respect of peoples' names; which the previous case supported. On consideration of the evidence, the court decided that the testator had intended the legacy to go to James Keiller of Dundee.

Classes of relation

The potential problems that can arise with legacies left to classes of relation were alluded to earlier in this chapter; they warrant further consideration here.

8–10

---

[24] *Cathcart's Trustees v Bruce*, 1923 S.L.T. 722.
[25] *Wedderspoon v Thomson's Trustees* (1824) 3 S. 396.
[26] *Keiller v Thomson's Trustees* (1826) 4 S. 724.

Terminology is key, and as already stated will be given its primary, ordinary meaning unless it can be proved that this was not the testator's intent. Some terms are simply too vague to be given effect at all. In *Robertson's JF v Robertson*,[27] a testatrix made a holograph will leaving the residue of her estate to her niece and nephew "and their dependents". The court observed that the latter term could encompass a very wide range of persons, including both relatives and associates beyond those tied by family, and held that the entire legacy was void. The portion of the estate it related to therefore fell into intestacy. This case is interesting because the term "dependent" does have a legal definition for various other purposes, for example when conducting the national census.[28] It is perhaps understandable, therefore, that the lay person would assume it also has a legal definition for succession purposes; but again, this highlights the potential dangers of informal testamentary documents.

Even where a term has a precise legal meaning, there might be a problem regarding the point at which the appropriate qualifying person is to be identified and their status ascertained; this might have a bearing on who actually inherits. Use of the term "heir" has on occasion given rise to this technical question, particularly where the term is used to identify the secondary legatee in a destination-over. In *Baillie's Trustees v Whiting*,[29] a testator directed that his heritable property be held for his widow in liferent and upon her death be conveyed to his nephew in fee, whom failing the testator's "heir" would inherit. The nephew died before the testator's wife, and the question arose as to the relevant point at which the testator's "heir" should be ascertained. It was held that the testator's heir should be ascertained as at the death of his widow.[30]

At common law, a "child" meant only legitimate, genetic offspring unless the context clearly indicated otherwise. This was a presumption not easily rebutted. In *Scott's Trustees v Smart*,[31] a testator left part of his estate to his two daughters in liferent and to their respective "children" in fee. One of his daughters had a legitimate child, the other a child who was illegitimate. Evidence showed that the testator was aware of all the relevant circumstances in respect of these children. The court observed that the term "child" could potentially refer to an illegitimate child if this was necessary to make sense of the legacy; for example where a bachelor died leaving *only* illegitimate children. However, in this case as there was a legitimate beneficiary, the presumption applied and the illegitimate child was not entitled to any share in the estate.

8–11   Adopted children were also excluded at common law unless otherwise stated.[32] As discussed at length in Ch.4, the position of illegitimate children was altered considerably under statute, with their rights gradually increased until the status of illegitimacy itself was finally abolished in 2006. The entitlements of adopted children were similarly established over time, again as discussed in Ch.4. Wills executed before the various statutory amendments are still interpreted according to the legal position as at the time of their execution.

---

[27] *Robertson's JF v Robertson*, 1968 S.L.T. 32.
[28] Scotland's Census, *Dependent Children in Family*, available at *http://www.scotlandscensus.gov.uk/variables-classification/dependent-children-family* [Accessed 11 May 2017].
[29] *Baillie's Trustees v Whiting*, 1910 S.C. 891.
[30] The same principle was later followed in *Macdonald's Trustees v Macdonald*, 1974 S.L.T. 87.
[31] *Scott's Trustees v Smart*, 1954 S.C. 12.
[32] *Hay v Duthie's Trustees*, 1956 S.C. 511.

Having established the relevant qualifying criteria, it is also sometimes necessary to determine whether the testator intended the class to treated as closed as of the point of execution of the will, or open to being expanded before his death. In *Millar's Trustees v Rattray*,[33] a testatrix directed that the residue of her estate be divided equally among a number of legatees including "the children of my brother, of whom there are 10". The testatrix's brother did indeed have 10 children as of the date of the will, but he fathered three more before her death; it was held that these additional children were entitled to share in the residue.

It is also common for children (in the literal sense of underage persons) who are the objects of legacies to be given some form of postponed right until they reach adulthood. A term often used historically was the reaching of "full age", which itself has been the subject of interpretation. Under common law it meant the traditional 21 years old, but this was reduced to 18 by the Age of Majority (Scotland) Act 1969.[34] Under this statute a number of additional terms are also given the same meaning, including "perfect age", "complete age" and "lawful age".[35] Although a raft of statutory substitutions were implemented under the 1969 Act, wills executed before its commencement are unaffected, even where amendments have been made subsequent to its coming into force.[36] The related matter of the age at which a person has capacity to make a will himself is considered in Ch.5.

Spouses and the effects of divorce

A legacy to one's "wife" or "husband" could also give rise to problems.[37] The position until recently was to apply the general presumption that, no matter how old a will is, it indicates the wishes of the deceased at the time of death; the justification being that any change in the testator's intentions would have been executed by an updated testamentary document. This presumption is not always helpful or even strictly accurate, and particular problems could arise in relation to spouses who had separated or even divorced. Under common law, a legacy that does not name the recipient and identifies him or her purely by familial designation will be given its literal meaning, allowing inheritance by whomever occupies the stated position at the time of death. This applies regardless of relevant changes in circumstance. In *Burns' Trustees*,[38] a testator made extensive provisions in favour of "my nephew and his wife and children". After the testator's death his nephew divorced and then, years later, remarried. It was held that the second wife was entitled to benefit under the will.

Where a legacy identifies a legatee and also designates the family relationship, under common law a change in the status of that relationship would not necessarily defeat the provision; though it must be said that the relevant case law

8–12

---

[33] *Millar's Trustees v Rattray* (1891) 18 R. 989.
[34] Age of Majority (Scotland) Act 1969 s.1(1).
[35] Age of Majority (Scotland) Act 1969 s.1(2).
[36] Age of Majority (Scotland) Act 1969 s.1(6).
[37] It is acknowledged that the same point could be made in relation to civil partners; however the age of the case law and the relatively less frequent use of "civil partner" as a designation means that practical examples are rare.
[38] *Burns' Trustees*, 1961 S.C. 17.

is somewhat inconsistent. In *Towse's Trustees v Towse*,[39] the court held that a wife who divorced the testator before his death had forfeited her right to the provisions made for her under his will. By contrast, in *Couper's JF v Valentine*,[40] the testator left his estate to "my wife, Mrs Dorothy Couper" but divorced her for desertion eight months before his death; despite this, the court held that she was entitled to inherit under the will. A similar decision was reached in *Ormiston's Executor v Laws*[41] regarding use of the term "fiancée", where the person identified was allowed to claim under the will despite having married someone else before the testator's death. It *was* possible to avoid such problems by the addition of a suspensive condition to the effect that the legatee would only inherit provided the relationship endured until the testator's death, but there would be no general presumption to this effect.[42]

There had long been calls for statutory reform of this somewhat complicated area,[43] and indeed this was recently achieved by the 2016 Act. This Act clarifies the position so that provisions made in favour of a spouse or civil partner by way of a testamentary document will effectively be revoked by termination of the relationship. The specific mechanism by which the 2016 Act achieves this is that the beneficiary shall be treated as having predeceased the testator for all purposes under the will, subject to an exception in respect of any provision relating to appointment of a legal guardian.[44] So, any benefit conferred upon the former spouse or civil partner is lost, as is any right under the will to be appointed as a trustee or executor,[45] but the right to be appointed legal guardian of children is preserved. The necessity for this exception is clear when one considers that the usual method of appointing legal guardians is to name a substitute if the individual identified dies before the testator; it would be illogical for a former spouse or civil partner's right in this regard to be lost artificially.

There is an important qualification in that the provisions of the 2016 Act will not apply where the will expressly provides that the benefit or appointment should continue to be effective even if the relationship comes to an end.[46] It is possible, therefore, for a testator to "opt out" of the statutory revocation, should he wish to do so.

The same provisions apply where a named legatee later becomes the spouse or civil partner of the testator, but the relationship is terminated before the testator's death.[47] "Termination" is defined as a decree of divorce, dissolution or annulment,[48] which has been granted in the UK or the validity of which is otherwise recognised in Scotland.[49]

On this final point, the 2016 Act does not make any addition to the rules regarding breakdown of a relationship falling short of the formal methods

---

[39] *Towse's Trustees v Towse*, 1924 S.L.T. 465.
[40] *Couper's JF v Valentine*, 1976 S.L.T. 83.
[41] *Ormiston's Executor v Laws*, 1966 S.L.T. 110.
[42] See, e.g. *Henderson's JF v Henderson*, 1930 S.L.T. 743.
[43] Scottish Law Commission, *Report on Succession* (Scot. Law Com. No.215) paras 6.12–6.17.
[44] Succession (Scotland) Act 2016 s.1(2).
[45] Succession (Scotland) Act 2016 s.1(1).
[46] Succession (Scotland) Act 2016 s.1(3).
[47] Succession (Scotland) Act 2016 s.1(1)(b).
[48] Succession (Scotland) Act 2016 s.1(4).
[49] Succession (Scotland) Act 2016 s.1(5).

outlined. Such situations continue to be regulated by separation agreements, in so far as they are regulated at all, and continue to require careful treatment in practice.

DISPOSITIVE DISCRETION

It is not unusual for a testator to give his executors or testamentary trustees some degree of latitude in deciding who exactly will benefit under a legacy. This is called "dispositive discretion" and is perfectly acceptable provided the parameters set by the will are sufficiently well defined. Where the dispositive discretion given to executors or trustees is too wide, or otherwise uncertain, there is a chance the legacy will be deemed void, with the result that the affected portion of the estate falls into intestacy. In common with other issues already discussed in this chapter, the courts will try to interpret such conditions so as to avoid intestacy if possible.

8–13

The general rule

A testator cannot delegate his power to test entirely. The whole purpose of a will is that it allows the testator's wishes to be known and this purpose is undermined if the testator transfers his powers in their entirety; there is an argument that such a delegation is no more practically useful than surrendering the estate to intestacy. A classic case is *Anderson v Smoke*,[50] where there was a direction to trustees to dispose of the residue of the estate in any way they should think fit; this provision was void from uncertainty. Nearly 100 years later a similar decision was reached in *Wood v Wood's Executrix*.[51] Here, a testator left a holograph will appointing his sister as executrix and providing only one testamentary instruction; "I give everything I have to her to share out as she knows I would wish it". The deceased's brother argued that the will was void from uncertainty. The court held that, as the deed was silent as to potential beneficiaries, and there being no suggestion by the executrix that she was aware of the wishes of the deceased, the instruction was indeed void; however the appointment of the sister as executrix stood.

8–14

That is not to say that dispositive discretion is particularly restricted; only that *some* scope must be outlined by the testator. Two common ways of setting such parameters are to direct distribution among a certain class of person, or direct distribution for a certain purpose. In the latter case, this is almost always a purpose charitable in nature.

Distribution among a class of persons

A testator can instruct that his estate, or part of it, be distributed among a class of persons as the executor or trustee sees fit. As stated in *Crichton v Grierson*,[52]

8–15

---

[50] *Anderson v Smoke* (1898) 25 R. 493.
[51] *Wood v Wood's Executrix*, 1995 S.L.T. 563.
[52] *Crichton v Grierson* (1828) 4 E.R. 1390.

"a party may, in the disposition of his property, select particular classes of individuals and objects, and then give to some particular individual a power, after his death, of ... applying any part of his property to any particular individuals among that class".[53]

The class identified must itself be sufficiently certain. This particular matter had already been addressed by the court in respect of the will again at issue above in *Crichton v Crichton's Trustees*.[54] The testator had instructed that his remaining estate was to be applied "in bequests to such of my friends and relations as may be pointed out by my said dearly beloved wife". The class "friends and relations" was deemed to be sufficiently certain, in spite of its potential wide scope, and the provision was held to be valid. Where the class of persons intended to benefit is not sufficiently certain, the clause will be void. In *Sutherland's Trustees v Sutherland's Trustees*,[55] a somewhat complex collection of testamentary writings gave discretionary powers to trustees regarding the residue of the estate. Although indications had been variously made as to whom the testator might wish to benefit, the provision was void for uncertainty.

It is possible for a legacy to be given effect where an instruction as to distribution can be viewed as a mere suggestion rather than a positive direction. This was the issue in *McGinn's Executrix v McGinn*,[56] where a testatrix in her holograph will bequeathed her house to her children, with the following instruction:

"Regarding the division of the house if they wish to sell it, then I think the fairest way would be each one of the four members at home [receiving] a share in proportion to their contribution to the upkeep of it."

Among the questions to be addressed by the court was that of whether this statement created sufficient ambiguity to render the legacy void for uncertainty. The court decided that it did not; in the judge's words, the statement was

"not integral with the bequest itself ... it is simply an expression of wish, a suggestion, a piece of advice offered to the beneficiaries as to a matter that she was inviting them to take into account if they ever came to sell the house".[57]

Distribution for charitable purposes

8–16   It is very common indeed for testators to make bequests to charity. Sometimes a specific charity is identified, in which case there is no problem implementing the provision; unless of course there is some other matter of uncertainty as discussed earlier in this chapter. A situation that can be problematic is where a testator directs that part of his estate be applied to charitable purposes, but does not sufficiently specify which charitable purposes are intended.

The term "charitable purposes" itself has, in England, been stated with authority to have a distinct definition encompassing

---

[53] *Crichton v Grierson* (1828) 4 E.R. 1390 at 1393 per Lord Lyndhurst LC.
[54] *Crichton v Crichton's Trustees* (1826) 4 S. 553.
[55] *Sutherland's Trustees v Sutherland's Trustees* (1893) 20 R. 925.
[56] *McGinn's Executrix v McGinn*, 1994 S.L.T. 2.
[57] *McGinn's Executrix v McGinn*, 1994 S.L.T. 2 at 5 per Lord McCluskey.

"trusts for the relief of poverty; trusts for the advancement of education; trusts for the advancement of religion; and trusts for other purposes beneficial to the community".[58]

In Scotland the definition is much looser, although the above is used for tax purposes,[59] and it is probably fair to say that the concept is applied more generously than it is south of the border. A particular problem is encountered when additional terms are combined with the word "charity", since this immediately widens the scope and increases the possibility of failure for uncertainty. The decision in any case is dependent on the circumstances; so in *McPhee's Trustees v McPhee*[60] the term "religious and charitable" was held to be valid, whilst in *Rintoul's Trustees v Rintoul*[61] the term "charitable or social institutions" was not. It is necessary, therefore, to again look to cases for guidance in order to determine the precision with which a testator must outline his wishes. It should be noted that the body of case law in this matter is vast, and as a result only a selection is presented here.

It is worth reiterating the basic principle that where the boundaries of dispositive discretion are too wide, the provision will fail for uncertainty. In *Blair v Duncan*,[62] the testatrix made a bequest for the residue of her estate to be applied for "such charitable or public purposes as my trustee thinks proper". This was held to be void, due at least partly to the inclusion of the term "public purposes". The distinction between "charitable" and "public" purposes was discussed at length, and it was observed that whilst the scope of the former was potentially very wide, it was still far more narrow than the latter. As observed in the judgment it

"leaves the trustee at large with the whole world to choose from. There is nothing affecting any community on the globe which is outside the ambit of his choice".[63]

From this, it can be inferred that an acceptable parameter might be set in terms of a geographical boundary. In *Hill v Burns*,[64] a testatrix directed that the residue of her estate be applied for "charitable and benevolent purposes in the city of Glasgow or neighbourhood thereof". Whilst the court was divided on the matter, and unfavourable views were expressed regarding such instructions, it was held that the instructions were sufficiently specific in their purpose.

In the absence of a geographical boundary, it is possible for a particular cause to be identified. It is certainly not required that the testator nominate a single charity, though of course the better defined the purpose, the more chance there is that the provision will be given effect. In *Whicker v Hume*[65] it was held that an instruction to distribute an estate for the aid of "advancement and propagation of education and learning all over the world" was a valid charitable bequest.

---

[58] *Commissioners of Income Tax v Pemsel* [1891] A.C. 531 at 583 per Lord MacNaghten.
[59] See, e.g. *Inland Revenue v Glasgow Police Athletic Association*, 1953 S.C. (HL) 13.
[60] *McPhee's Trustees v McPhee*, 1912 S.C. 75.
[61] *Rintoul's Trustees v Rintoul*, 1949 S.C. 297.
[62] *Blair v Duncan* [1902] A.C. 37.
[63] *Blair v Duncan* [1902] A.C. 37 at 47 per Lord Robertson.
[64] *Hill v Burns* (1824) 3 S. 389.
[65] *Whicker v Hume* (1858) 11 E.R. 50.

Similarly, in *Bannerman's Trustees v Bannerman*,[66] a legacy was held to be sufficiently certain by instructing that the estate be disposed of in favour of "religious or charitable Institutions ... conducted according to Protestant principles".

It is worth noting that the court does not appear particularly interested in considering the merits of the cause identified; provided of course that it is lawful. *McLean v Henderson's Trustees*[67] offers an interesting example. Here, a testator directed that his entire estate be distributed "for the advancement and diffusion of the science of phrenology". This particular branch of science had enjoyed a period of popularity in the early 19th century, but by the date of the case in question its veracity had long been under question, with some arguing even that it had been entirely discredited decades previously. The court limited its considerations to that of whether the cause was sufficiently certain rather than the utility of applying funds to it,

> "in considering this objection it must be borne in mind that the expression phrenology denotes a known, although not a flourishing, branch of science. However much people may differ as to the utility or tendencies of phrenology in some aspects ... the advancement and diffusion of it is [not] unlawful".[68]

Accordingly, the bequest stood.

Delegating discretion

8–17   It would seem that dispositive discretion can only be exercised by someone specifically identified by the will. As will be seen in Ch.11, there are different mechanisms by which someone becomes executor of an estate, or otherwise becomes responsible for the administration of someone else's property. In *Angus' Executrix v Batchan's Trustees*,[69] a testatrix left a holograph will which provided for the residue of the estate to be given to "charities". The will failed to appoint an executor, so one was appointed as an "executor-dative"; it was held that an executor so appointed does not have dispositive discretion and the bequest to charities failed from uncertainty; had the will appointed an executor, the direction would almost certainly have been valid. Similar rules would apply where the court has appointed a "judicial factor", essentially a legal agent responsible for another's property. In *Robbie's JF v Macrae*,[70] the deceased had directed her executors to pay the residue of her estate to such charities as they thought proper within a stated class. On the face of it, this direction was specific and therefore valid. Unfortunately, all of her executors died before exercising their discretion and a judicial factor was appointed by the court. It was held that the discretion could not be exercised by a judicial factor.

---

[66] *Bannerman's Trustees v Bannerman*, 1915 S.C. 398.
[67] *McLean v Henderson's Trustees* (1880) 7 R. 601.
[68] *McLean v Henderson's Trustees* (1880) 7 R. 601 at 608 per Lord Ormidale.
[69] *Angus' Executrix v Batchan's Trustees*, 1949 S.C. 335.
[70] *Robbie's JF v Macrae* (1893) 20 R. 358.

CHAPTER 9

Will Substitutes

INTRODUCTION

Reference has been made in previous chapters to various mechanisms that **9–01** operate either to tackle certain complexities that arise during the process of succession, or to provide an alternative to succession having to operate at all. In terms of the latter, Scots law recognises a number of methods whereby one can make provisions for succession on death, but without actually leaving a will. Various types of lifetime deed operate to have a testamentary effect, without themselves being testamentary documents. These are worthy of discussion beyond a passing mention since some, in particular the "special destination", have become an everyday part of legal practice. Others are outlined for sake of completeness and historical interest.

SPECIAL DESTINATIONS

In the context of ownership of property, the purpose of a "destination" clause is to **9–02** regulate the order in which people will have rights over part of an estate. In Ch.6, consideration was given to a common testamentary device called a "destination-over", whereby an alternative beneficiary is named to provide for the possibility of the person named first dying before the deceased. The special destination is rather different, in that it regulates ownership of property during an individual's lifetime and also directs the inheritance of it upon death. Therefore, it is not a testamentary writing but it has an equivalent testimentary effect. A special destination can apply in respect of heritable or moveable property,[1] but it is far more commonly encountered in respect of heritage.

Nature and context

At its simplest, a special destination is where property is held in common by two **9–03** living parties, with the stipulation that upon the death of one, ownership will pass in full to the other. This is expressed in the title deeds, or other document outlining ownership, as the property being held "in joint names and the survivor", or words having similar effect. It is possible for more than two parties to hold

---

[1] See, e.g. *Connell's Trustees v Connel's Trustees* (1886) 13 R. 1175.

property in common under the same arrangement, which is more complex but only slightly so; the agreement is that ownership will ultimately pass to the last surviving party.

The essence of a special destination is that it defeats many of the normal rules of succession, in particular those applying on intestacy, since property passes under its terms rather than passing to the respective heirs of the parties. It is termed "special" because it deals with ownership rights in respect of a particular item of property (as opposed to an entire estate) and in respect of a particular person or persons (as opposed to classes of person). Judicial definitions are rare, and not unanimously accepted, but one offered in *Cormack v McIldowie's Executor*[2] was

> "a special destination [is] one in which the particular property in the deed is disponed to the particular person (or persons) specifically nominated by the granter, without regard to the normal law of succession on intestacy".[3]

For sake of accuracy, it is important to point out that the arrangement outlined above is actually a specific *type* of special destination called a "survivorship destination". Whilst this is undoubtedly a valid and interesting distinction, it is probably fair to say that the terms are used interchangeably in practice, and that the subtle difference between the two rarely causes a problem in execution. Under scrutiny, it can be seen that the majority of special destinations encountered are, in fact, survivorship destinations. For sake of brevity and simplicity, the former term is used throughout this chapter, unless the context insists on use of the latter.

Regardless of the precise term used, to fully understand this somewhat curious device, a little bit of history is required. Under common law, it was not possible to dispose of heritable property in Scotland by testamentary provision, unless certain rather technical steps were taken.[4] The heritable property had to follow the feudal succession, which favoured the first-born and male.[5] A will, accordingly, normally only dealt with moveable property and, even until the passing of the 1964 Act, an executor could only act in respect of moveable estate.

Whatever criticisms people might wish to make of the legal profession, it could never be seriously suggested that lawyers lack inventiveness or initiative. As an owner of heritable property could not easily dispose of it by will, the question arose as to whether there might be some way around this restriction. Necessity being the mother of invention, the legal profession came up with a solution, namely building a survivorship clause into the actual title to the property. So, if the property was held, for example, by "A and B and the survivor" or "A whom failing B", the general effect was testamentary. This was highly ingenious and, more importantly, it worked.

---

[2] *Cormack v McIldowie's Executor*, 1975 S.C. 161.
[3] *Cormack v McIldowie's Executor*, 1975 S.C. 161 at 177 per Lord Justice-Clerk Wheatley.
[4] Erskine, III, 8, 20.
[5] As discussed in Ch.4.

Use in modern practice

The need to employ special destinations effectively disappeared under the Titles to Land (Consolidation) Act 1868, which abolished restrictions on making testamentary provisions over heritable property.[6] One would have thought that in light of this, the special destination would only have a limited remaining useful life. This did not prove to be the case, and the device in fact grew in popularity, among legal practitioners at least, over the course of the 20th century. Their increased prevalence was not, however, universally welcomed by the academic community, nor indeed by the judiciary. Although special destinations could prove useful beyond merely circumventing an inconvenient restriction, for example in simplifying certain aspects of executry practice,[7] they were also liable to give rise to unforeseen complications, or arguably undesirable results. For example, in *Barclays Bank Ltd v McGreish*,[8] a couple held the title to their heritable property in joint names and survivor. The wife had provided all of the original funds for the purchase. The bank obtained a decree against the husband's half-share in respect of certain debts he owed but, before they could enforce it, he died. It was held that the special destination not only transferred his half-share of the house to his wife but also did so free of debt. The reasoning behind this "have your cake and eat it" result was that as the property did not pass through the hands of the executor, it could not be subjected to debts constituted against the estate. The soundness of this reasoning has, however, been doubted, and the judgment was not followed in later cases.

9–04

The unpredictability of their effects led to special destinations being famously criticised in *Hay's Trustees v Hay's Trustees*,[9] where it was observed that it seemed

> "unfortunate that the device of a special destination ... should still be utilised in circumstances which, as our reports show, are more likely to be productive of litigation than of any compensating advantage to the parties concerned".[10]

This was echoed almost half a century later in *Fleming's Trustees v Fleming*,[11] a further case that considered the position of creditors where a deceased's insolvent heritable estate had passed to his widow under a special destination. It was commented that "the present case is yet another example of the inconvenience of this unnecessary quirk of feudal conveyancing".[12] In this case, the *McGreish* decision was not followed and the creditors were granted a remedy.

In some ways, its use has become a habit and there is clearly divided opinion as to whether that habit is good or bad.[13] Some solicitors recommend putting a special destination into the title of heritable property to be owned in common almost as a matter of course; it is probably a point of good practice to suggest that

---

[6] Titles to Land (Consolidation) Act 1868 s.20.
[7] See Ch.11.
[8] *Barclays Bank Ltd v McGreish*, 1983 S.L.T. 344.
[9] *Hay's Trustees v Hay's Trustees*, 1951 S.C. 329.
[10] *Hay's Trustees v Hay's Trustees*, 1951 S.C. 329 at 334 per Lord President Cooper.
[11] *Fleming's Trustees v Fleming*, 2000 S.C. 206.
[12] *Fleming's Trustees v Fleming*, 2000 S.C. 206 at 213 per Lord Sutherland.
[13] See, e.g. Brand, D., *Time for Special Destinations to Die?*, 2000 S.L.T. 203 and Kerrigan, J., *Special Destinations—the Debate Continues*, 2014 S.L.T. 175.

a special destination should only be included when there are clear and specific instructions from the clients to do so, or at the very least that there should be an explanation of the relevant options.

A special destination was, and still is, particularly useful where the co-owners of heritable property are not spouses or civil partners, but rather are cohabitees, friends or siblings; this is even the case taking into account recent legislation increasing the rights afforded to cohabitants.[14] Where there is a special destination, the succession to the property is clear. One could just as easily add that if people made proper wills, this would be an equally satisfactory solution and there would be no need to use a special destination.

It is important, finally, here, to make one distinction very clear. If a property is taken in the name of "A and B", this is not, nor does it imply, a special destination. If A dies, his half-share of the property would form part of his estate in the usual way, and be distributed according to either testate or intestate succession as appropriate. Of course, depending on the identity and relationship of the parties, B might not be A's heir. This is particularly worthy of mention since the opposite presumption is made under English law, and this divergence can lead to problems where the estate of a deceased domiciled in Scotland contains property located in England. This was one of several matters that required to be addressed in *Cunningham's Trustees v Cunningham*,[15] in which a Scottish deceased held War Stock and National War Bonds, administered in England, that were the subject of a special destination. In the question of which territory's rules should prevail in respect of the destination, it was held that as they were essentially British (or "Imperial") investments, rather than being genuinely foreign, they fell to be ascertained according to Scots law.

Effects of a special destination

9–05 Given the "dual nature" of special destinations in that they at once regulate ownership of property during life and upon death, it is appropriate to consider their effects during both states of affairs. While both parties are still alive, the effect of the special destination depends upon the "true" status of ownership as regards the subject property. This, in turn, is likely to be influenced by whether the property is heritable or moveable.[16]

It can credibly be argued that moveable property presents the more complicated situation, since explicit statements of ownership are far less common, and the near endlessly variable nature of moveables means that presumptions relevant to the particular property must often be applied. For example, in *Dinwoodie's Executrix v Carruthers' Executrix*,[17] it was held that bank deposits made by two siblings repayable "to them or to the survivor of them" were not owned equally; rather they were owned in proportion to the amount each sibling had originally contributed. The same principle can be applied to joint bank accounts,[18] which are often mistakenly believed to become

---

[14] See Ch.4.
[15] *Cunningham's Trustees v Cunningham*, 1924 S.C. 581.
[16] On this distinction see Ch.3.
[17] *Dinwoodie's Executrix v Carruthers' Executrix* (1895) 23 R. 234.
[18] *Forrest-Hamilton's Trustee v Forrest-Hamilton*, 1970 S.L.T. 338.

the outright property of the survivor when one party dies.[19] This can be particularly troublesome when the parties to the account are not married or in a civil partnership, and their rights in succession therefore limited.[20]

Ownership of heritable property, on the other hand, is a matter in which very little is left to doubt. Title to heritable property requires to be registered,[21] with the result that the respective rights of the parties are clearly expressed. The most common arrangement is for property to be held equally, though other proportions can be stipulated. Taking the norm as an example, the two named parties are common owners during their lifetime, with each having a pro indiviso share (i.e. an undivided right) to half the property. This ownership is unrestricted, neither having rights over the other's share. This was confirmed to bleak effect in *Steele v Caldwell*,[22] where a husband sold his half-share of a house to strangers who took up residence; his wife, who owned the other half, failed in an action seeking to void the disposition. That said, depending on the exact terms of the agreement, it is possible that ownership can be literally "joint" over the whole property rather than "in common", in which case it does seem possible for a restriction on either party selling their share to be incorporated into the conditions.[23] The very fine distinctions between property held jointly and property held in common were considered at length and with authority in *Magistrates of Banff v Ruthin Castle*,[24] but are beyond the scope of this book. Suffice it to say that, as in many things, the exact rights of the parties depend on the circumstances and the terms of the agreement. It fair to say that the rules of common ownership are more often applied, even though it is normal professional practice to use the phrase "in joint names and the survivor".

Upon death, as mentioned above, the essence of a special destination is that most normal rules of succession are subverted. The practical effect of this is that property that passes under a *survivorship* destination does not form part of the deceased's estate for most purposes,[25] although account is taken of it for the calculation of inheritance tax.[26] With heritable property, the special destination actually moves the ownership of the property to whoever is "called", i.e. the survivor, and no conveyance is required unless the destination is unusually complicated. It is well established that, in the case of a straightforward survivorship destination, the share belonging to the deceased passes automatically at the time of his death.[27] In the case of an existing sasine title, no further formality is required and, perhaps surprisingly, the public record will continue to show all original proprietors as owners unless and until such time as the survivor disposes of his share. In the case of a registered title, it is possible

9–06

---

[19] See, e.g. Kerrigan, J., *Special Destinations—Survivorship and Bank Accounts Revisited*, 2011 S.L.T. 5.

[20] *McCarthy's Executors v McCafferty*, 2000 G.W.D. 14-549.

[21] This was previously effected by an entry in the Register of Sasines, but all registrations are now made in the Land Register; entries still contained in the former will gradually migrate to the latter. See, e.g. the Land Registration etc. (Scotland) Act 2012 and associated legislation.

[22] *Steele v Caldwell*, 1979 S.L.T. 228.

[23] See, e.g. *Munro v Munro*, 1972 S.L.T. (Sh Ct) 6.

[24] *Magistrates of Banff v Ruthin Castle*, 1944 S.C. 36.

[25] Succession (Scotland) Act 1964 s.36(2)(a).

[26] Inheritance Tax Act 1984 ss.2–4.

[27] See, e.g. *Bisset v Walker*, 26 November 1799 (M Deathbed, App No.2).

(and highly desirable) to request the Keeper of the Registers to rectify the Land Register to show the effect of the operation of the destination.

With other types of special destination, it is very occasionally required for an executor to seek confirmation (i.e. authority to deal with the estate) in respect of the subject property for the limited purpose of conveying it to the beneficiary. In such a case, the value of the property is counted as nil and it is made clear that the executor is only confirming to it for this limited purpose.[28] Otherwise, to confirm to heritable property passing under a special destination amounts to professional negligence.[29]

There can be pitfalls in using the special destination, and the judicial disapproval mentioned earlier in this chapter is not without merit. A further potential complication can be illustrated by the case of *Christie's Executrix v Armstrong*.[30] Here, a couple were cohabiting partners in a property which they had bought "in joint names and the survivor". The male partner was actually married to another woman, and there were children of the marriage. The couple had borrowed the purchase funds from a building society, and according to standard practice had granted a security over the property. They had also assigned to the building society a life insurance policy taken out over the life of the male partner. Unfortunately he died suddenly, and the proceeds of the insurance policy almost exactly paid the outstanding loan amount due over the house, the title to which duly passed to the female partner under the special destination. A dispute arose, however, when the deceased's daughter argued that her late father had, in effect, paid off the whole loan, and that therefore his estate was entitled to recover half that sum from his cohabitee. The effect, of course, would be that the amount of estate claimable by his relatives might potentially increase. This was a valid argument, though perhaps a slightly underhanded tactic, which might have succeeded had it not been for the court taking the view that since the policy was not part of the deceased's estate at the time of his death (because it had been validly assigned to the lender), he could not be considered as having paid the debt. If the policy had not been assigned in security, the result would have been very different, since the deceased's estate would only have been liable for one half of the outstanding debt over the house.

Revocation

9–07   The question is bound to arise as to whether or not a special destination can be superseded by a later will. Suppose that title to property was taken between two people "in joint name and the survivor", but upon one party's death it emerges that he has left his half-share to someone else in his will. This is a complex area but (at the risk of being over-simplistic) the general rule under common law is that a later will does not evacuate an existing special destination. It certainly does not do so where the destination is contractual, i.e. where two co-owners have contributed to the cost, as is the case with many destinations between spouses and civil partners.[31] If only one party has contributed to the purchase, that party does

---

[28] Succession (Scotland) Act 1964 s.18(2).
[29] See Ch.11.
[30] *Christie's Executrix v Armstrong*, 1996 S.L.T. 948.
[31] See, e.g. *Perrett's Trustees v Perrett*, 1909 S.C. 522.

have power to evacuate the destination but the non-contributing party does not.[32] If the funds were provided by a third party, neither of the named parties has the power to evacuate.[33]

In any event, the matter was subject to statutory development under the 1964 Act. Since the commencement of this Act, a will cannot evacuate a special destination unless it contains a specific reference to the destination *and* a declared intention to evacuate.[34] This is strictly construed by the courts,[35] and is still the subject of litigation more than 50 years after the provision came into force. In the recent case of *Hill v Hill*,[36] a husband and wife had owned heritable property, taking title in joint name and the survivor. The relationship ultimately broke down, leading the wife to execute a codicil purporting to revoke the special destination in favour of her son. The court held that she did not have the power to do this, and the destination stood. In *Hamilton v Campbell Smith*,[37] a disappointed beneficiary raised an action alleging professional negligence against a firm of solicitors for failure to advise that a will might not revoke an existing special destination.

Also of relevance is the effect of married couples divorcing, or in the case of civil partnerships formal dissolution of the relationship. At common law, a divorce did not automatically evacuate a special destination any more than it revoked a will. In *Gardner's Executor v Raeburn*,[38] a couple divorced; the title to their house was in joint names and survivor. As part of the divorce settlement, the wife conveyed her half-share to the husband; in fact, he paid her for it. Unfortunately, the half-share belonging to the husband remained subject to the special destination, with the result that, when he died, this half-share passed to his former wife. This result almost certainly did not reflect the true wishes of the husband. To prevent such a situation arising, it became good practice to ensure that *both* parties conveyed the entire property to the party who was taking the title. This ensured that the destination was properly "washed out" of the title.

This rule has also been the subject of statutory reform. First, the Family Law (Scotland) Act 2006 significantly changed the common law position. It provides that where heritable property is held by spouses in joint name and to the survivor, or where there is otherwise a special destination in either spouse's favour, then divorce or annulment will render the arrangement ineffective. The mechanism by which this is achieved is to treat a former spouse who would stand to benefit from the destination on succession as having failed to survive the deceased, for the purposes of the destination only.[39] This is exactly the same as the method by which legacies in favour of a former spouse or civil partner are effectively revoked, as seen in Ch.8. More recently, the 2016 Act extended the same rule to

9–08

---

[32] *Henderson's Trustees*, 1911 S.C. 525.
[33] *Renouf's Trustees v Haining*, 1919 S.L.T. 15.
[34] Succession (Scotland) Act 1964 s.30.
[35] See, e.g. *Stirling's Trustees v Stirling*, 1977 S.C. 139 and *Marshall v Marshall's Executor*, 1987 S.L.T. 49.
[36] *Hill v Hill* [2016] CSOH 10.
[37] *Hamilton v Campbell Smith*, 2015 G.W.D. 10-174.
[38] *Gardner's Executor v Raeburn*, 1996 S.L.T. 745.
[39] Family Law (Scotland) Act 2006 s.19 (as enacted). Equivalent provisions for civil partners were at the same time inserted into the Civil Partnership Act 2004 s.124A (as enacted).

moveable property and replaces both previous sets of provisions.[40] In keeping with the provisions regarding legacies, the Act does permit parties to opt out of the statutory provisions by express provision in the destination that it will not be evacuated by subsequent divorce or annulment.[41] A purchaser in good faith and for value is protected in the event that he buys the property from a party who has no title due to divorce or dissolution.[42]

It was observed in Ch.8 that under the provisions of the 2016 Act only divorce, dissolution or annulment have any effect on legacies; the same applies to special destinations. For neither purpose is mere separation of the parties sufficient to effect revocation, however if this is expressly stated in a formally minuted agreement then it will be enforced. In *Redfern's Executor v Redfern*,[43] the spouses signed a separation agreement renouncing any rights of succession in the estate of the other and agreeing to sell their house and share the proceeds. Before the house could be sold, the husband died. The property was subject to a survivorship destination. The question at issue was obvious: did the entire heritable property now belong to the wife, or had the destination been evacuated by the separation agreement? It was held that rights of succession (at least in this context) included those normally passing under a special destination. The separation agreement had therefore effectively evacuated the destination.

Finally, it is important to note that a special destination only operates where one party actually survives the other. Thus, if husband and wife hold property in joint names and survivor and both are killed in a common calamity, neither is presumed to survive the other, unless evidence shows otherwise. Thus, the special destination could not operate and their executors would require to confirm to the respective half-shares.

ALTERNATIVE SUBSTITUTIONARY DEVICES

9–09   As outlined in the introduction to this chapter, there can be no doubt that the special destination is the most relevant will substitute. However, there are a number of others that warrant brief discussion, some of which will actually be encountered very commonly in practice. Others are included for historical interest, or because they have been the subject of recent reform. It should also be pointed out that many of the devices considered here have broader legal relevance beyond merely the law of succession; this further justifies their inclusion, but this general application outside the present purpose will not be considered in any detail.

---

[40] Succession (Scotland) Act 2016 s.2; repeal of the previous provisions is effected by Sch.1 paras 3 and 4.
[41] Succession (Scotland) Act 2016 s.2(3).
[42] Succession (Scotland) Act 2016 s.2(4).
[43] *Redfern's Executor v Redfern*, 1996 S.L.T. 900.

Nominations

The deceased may have nominated another party to receive certain funds, such as   **9–10**
a bank account or benefits under a pension scheme, on the event of his death.
Such a nomination, like a special destination, has a general testamentary effect
but it is not necessary for the executor to confirm to such funds. A true
nomination will be based on a statutory provision, which will require to be
checked out in each particular case; the most common examples relate to mutual
societies, which are regulated by the Financial Services Act 2012 and associated
legislation. In some cases (not many) the funds may still require to be first
delivered to the executor.

In fact, payments of relatively modest sums to a deceased's next-of-kin are
frequently allowed by financial institutions as a matter of privilege, rather than
right. If a holder of funds belonging to a deceased person chooses to pay them to
anyone other than an executor with confirmation, he generally does so at his own
risk and a confirmed executor would have the right to demand payment again.
Usually the maximum value to be paid out under a nomination will be £5,000.[44]
The payer will require evidence of death and entitlement. The beneficiary may be
required to sign an indemnity, in case an executor with confirmation appears at a
later date.

Generally speaking, a nomination is not evacuated by a subsequent will,
although the nomination itself may be revoked by the appropriate statutory
documentation. In most cases, the nomination is invalidated if the nominator
subsequently marries or enters into a civil partnership.[45] Similarly to a
testamentary provision, if the beneficiary (nominee) dies before the nominator,
the nomination simply falls.

Policies of insurance

It has been alluded to elsewhere that if someone takes out a life assurance policy   **9–11**
on his own life, the status of the proceeds upon his death depend upon the person
to whom they are payable. If they are payable to the deceased, they form part of
his estate and are subject to the normal rules of succession. However, if they are
payable to another person, then the proceeds are paid directly to the beneficiary
and are excluded from the deceased's estate; thus they will escape inheritance tax
and will also not be subject to claims such as prior and legal rights.[46] Thus, this is
another useful mechanism whereby a testamentary result can be achieved without
a testamentary document; in fact it could be observed that the effect of this is
preferable to a testamentary document because it is far more difficult to challenge
a life assurance policy than a will.

There is a specific exception to the general rule outlined above in the form of
the Married Women's Policies of Assurance (Scotland) Act 1880 (as amended).
If, and only if, a policy of life insurance is written under this Act, it counts as a

---

[44] Administration of Estates (Small Payments) Act 1965 s.2; current limit set by the Administration of
Estates (Small Payments) (Increase of Limit) Order 1984.
[45] For relevant cases see, e.g. *Ford's Trustees v Ford*, 1940 S.C. 426 and *Clarke's Executor v
Macaulay*, 1961 S.L.T. 109.
[46] This was seen in *Christie's Executrix v Armstrong*, 1996 S.L.T. 948, discussed earlier in this
chapter.

separate estate and is not confirmed to nor does account need be taken of it for calculation of inheritance tax. Despite the title, the Act applies to both husbands and wives as a result of subsequent amendments.[47] The spouse who takes out such a policy is counted as a trustee and the beneficiaries have vested rights from the time the policy is taken out. The policy proceeds are payable to the surviving spouse and/or children on production of the death certificate. It is not necessary for the policy to make specific mention of the Married Women's Policies of Assurance (Scotland) Act 1880, provided the creation of the trust is clear.

It should be noted that the law of insurance is a highly specialist area, and the above is a gross oversimplification only intended to draw attention to the broad concepts. Further reading and/or the seeking of professional advice is highly recommended.

Marriage contracts

9–12   These somewhat cumbersome arrangements were popular with our Victorian forefathers, particularly among the more prosperous classes. They could (and still can) be entered into by a couple upon marriage (or civil partnership), but more commonly this would occur before the marriage and be termed an "anti-nuptial marriage contract" or "pre-nuptial agreement".[48] It has to be remembered that, in former times, married women were often treated as little better than wayward children when it came to the administration of their own property. A lady of means might have had much to lose if her fortune was entirely at the mercy of her husband. This is no longer a concern in light of subsequent legislative reform.[49]

Shortly before the marriage, the woman transferred her property to trustees but, normally, retained an alimentary liferent in her own favour. Since the consideration of the contract was the marriage taking place, that contract could not come into operation until such time as the marriage was actually solemnised. However, once the contract came into force, it was irrevocable, on the grounds that it gave rights to children *nascituri* (i.e. yet to be born), unless the contract itself gave express powers of revocation. The law in regards to this was significantly amended by the Law Reform (Husband and Wife) (Scotland) Act 1984, which abolished many of the rules that positioned a wife's rights as inferior to those of her husband.

Some marriage contracts contain provisions that are clearly intended to be testamentary. It appears to be the case that such provisions are always revocable, even if the contract declares them to be irrevocable.[50] On the other hand, in keeping with the approach taken in similar areas, if a provision is deemed contractual it cannot be revoked, and may give an indefeasible right.[51] The potential effects of a marriage contract on intestacy are discussed in Ch.4.

---

[47] The Civil Partnership Act 2004 makes certain separate provision for civil partners in respect of life assurance.
[48] See also Ch.4.
[49] See, e.g. the Married Women's Property Act 1920 and the Family Law (Scotland) Act 1985 ss.24–25.
[50] *Barclay's Trustees v Watson* (1903) 5 F. 926.
[51] See, e.g. *Mackie v Gloag's Trustees* (1884) 11 R. (HL).

Donations mortis causa

Generally speaking, donations (gifts) given mortis causa (in contemplation of death) are, in and of themselves, not uncommon, especially when small items of sentimental value are involved. An elderly person may wish to pass such items to members of family or to close friends and this is scarcely controversial. However, where these gifts increase in value, so too does their potential to be of legal relevance, not least of which is the question of whether they ought to be liable to inheritance tax. The broader legal question that may arise is whether the donation counts as an out-and-out gift or a donation mortis causa. It is certainly distinct from a legacy, as established in the classic case is *Morris v Riddick*.[52] Here, a terminally ill man endorsed a bank deposit receipt in his friend's favour, payable on the condition that he did not recover from his illness. The court held that this was not a legacy, but a donation mortis causa; as a result, the sum went directly to the friend and did not form part of the deceased's estate. **9–13**

Thus, a donation mortis causa is somewhere between a straightforward gift and a legacy. The law always presumes against donation and there may be difficulties of proof.[53] Although the law requires writing to convey particular property (such as an interest in land), writing is not required as a matter of proof of donation.[54] Most donations are not, in practice, fortified by written documentation. The normal rule in donation mortis causa is that there has to be delivery (or equivalent) to the recipient, although the rule has not always been strictly applied.[55]

If a donation made as an out-and-out gift, it is generally irrevocable. If it is a donation mortis causa, the donor can revoke the donation during his own lifetime. If the recipient predeceases, the donation reverts to the donor. In the case of an insolvent estate, the value of the donation could be reclaimed by the executor or trustee. In terms of division of assets, a donation mortis causa ranks after legal rights, but before legacies.

In modern times the popularity of donations mortis causa diminished significantly. Indeed, the Scottish Law Commission observed that the rules relating to them are archaic and obsolete, and thus a recommendation was made that they ought to be abolished.[56] This was for all intents and purposes achieved by the 2016 Act, which removes the status of donation mortis causa from all gifts other than those that are expressly made on conditional terms.[57] So, in effect it is still possible for a gift to be made mortis causa, although it must be made explicitly so, and it seems highly unlikely that anyone would actually do this in practice.

---

[52] *Morris v Riddick* (1867) 5 M. 1036.
[53] See, e.g. *Brownlee's Executor v Brownlee*, 1908 S.C. 232.
[54] *Aiken's Executor v Aiken*, 1937 S.C. 678.
[55] See, e.g. *Macpherson's Executrix v Mackay*, 1932 S.C. 505 and *Gray's Trustees v Murray*, 1970 S.L.T. 105.
[56] Scottish Law Commission, *Report on Succession* (Scot. Law Com. No.215), paras 7.38–7.41.
[57] Succession (Scotland) Act 2016 s.25.

REARRANGEMENTS AFTER DEATH

9–14 It is possible for the beneficiaries under a will to enter into a formal agreement whereby the division of the estate is varied in whatever form they wish. Whilst this is a distinct matter from those previously discussed in this chapter, since it involves deviation from a will after death rather than the utilisation of a substitutionary device beforehand, it warrants discussion here because, in essence, the formal agreement reached will itself become a substitute for the terms of the will.

Freedom to rearrange

9–15 It is possible to observe from commentary in previous chapters that rights falling under succession are, at times, not as well-protected as certain other rights relevant to property. By the same token, there is no guarantee that the wishes of a deceased will be followed after his death, even if a perfectly valid testamentary document has been left expressing them. Although it is in some ways a contentious issue, it is perfectly acceptable (at least in a legal sense) for rearrangements to be made after death regarding who will get what from a deceased's estate. As stated in *Gray v Gray's Trustees*,[58]

> "when ... every possible beneficiary desires and consents to a particular course being adopted ... then no-one has any right or interest to object".[59]

In this case, the reasons for rearrangement were purely practical. The testator had directed that his estate be put in the hands of trustees, who were to pay an annuity to his widow and distribute the estate to his daughters in half-yearly payments, but only so far as would be consistent with ensuring his widow's annuity. The practical effect of this was that the moveable estate was exhausted after only four years, and that no further distribution could be made to the daughters without borrowing against the heritable property. While the value of the heritage was considerable, and in excess of that required to secure the widow's annuity, it was felt that borrowing against it would be contrary to everyone's interests. In short, the trust had become unworkable, and so a rearrangement of the trust provisions was proposed. Whilst the court did not allow for the full range of proposals to be implemented, the essence of the rearrangements were upheld.

Motivations and effects

9–16 It is important to note that, other than where a special legacy is concerned, beneficiaries have a right only to cash, not specific assets. In practice, an executor will frequently come to a private arrangement with beneficiaries as to which specific assets they might wish, such as company shares or even items of valuable corporeal moveable property. This is motivated purely by convenience, and offers no problems except where beneficiaries themselves cannot agree as to the items

---

[58] *Gray v Gray's Trustees* (1877) 4 R. 378.
[59] *Gray v Gray's Trustees* (1877) 4 R. 378 at 383 per Lord Gifford.

each will receive. It should also be remembered that, by the same token, no one is obligated to accept any legacy if he does not wish to. He may disclaim a legacy or any right of succession entirely, or he may only take a proportion of his entitlement. This in itself can be motivated by several factors, including the desire to pursue an alternative claim as seen in Ch.6.

A more "wholesale" rearrangement of the estate's distribution can be rather more controversial. A written election to vary is required, called a "deed of post-death variation" or in older terminology a "deed of family arrangement". This must be made within two years of the deceased's date of death.[60] Sometimes there may be tax advantages to such a rearrangement, in which case the only legal implication is to ensure that the meticulous rules of taxation are adhered to. What might be problematic is where the rearrangement is motivated by feelings of injustice among the beneficiaries. Provided all are genuinely of the same mind then there is no problem and the proposals will be upheld. There is a risk, however, of influence being exerted by more assertive beneficiaries against those less inclined to argue, even if their interests are compromised as a result. Statutory protections are limited; previously it was necessary to give a written election of the variation to the Capital Taxes Office within six months,[61] but this requirement was removed in 2002.[62] It can be noted, however, that while a young person has capacity to sign a deed of post-death variation from the age of 16 years,[63] he might raise a subsequent challenge, up to the age of 21, that doing so had caused him substantial prejudice.[64] There is also a process whereby an executor may seek judicial ratification of the discharge or variation,[65] which would certainly be prudent in practice.

---

[60] Inheritance Tax Act 1984 s.142.
[61] Inheritance Tax Act 1984 s.142 (as enacted).
[62] Inheritance Tax Act 1984 s.142 (as amended by the Finance Act 2002 s.120).
[63] Age of Legal Capacity (Scotland) Act s.1.
[64] Age of Legal Capacity (Scotland) Act s.3.
[65] Age of Legal Capacity (Scotland) Act s.4.

CHAPTER 10

Vesting

INTRODUCTION

It was mentioned in Ch.1 that property law is of great significance to the law of **10–01** succession. The importance of property classifications, and how this might affect a person's inheritance, was discussed in Ch.3. Also of relevance are a number of fundamental principles regarding rights in property, for example the clear distinction that exists between ownership and possession. "Vesting" is another concept that relates to rights in property, and is crucial to the operation of succession. There are a number of issues related to vesting that can lead to problems for the legal practitioner.

RIGHTS IN PROPERTY

To understand vesting, it is first necessary to appreciate the differences between **10–02** certain rights in property. This is another area of the law that is specialist in its own right, so the commentary here should not be taken as a comprehensive guide. As when dealing with other fields of legal study, the purpose is to draw attention to the broad concepts and explain how they impact on succession.

Ownership and possession

In everyday language, there are certain terms which are commonly used **10–03** interchangeably; people refer to the items belonging to them as their "property", their "possessions" or perhaps simply as the things they "own". Outside of legal study and practice, there is no problem with such loose application of terminology, but when considering matters of law, it is vitally important to understand that these terms are very different in their meanings.

"Property" is commonly understood to mean any item, howsoever it may be classified, which can be owned, i.e. "an item of property". The term is often used in a more narrow sense, intended to imply only that which is heritable, e.g. "property situated in Scotland". With regard to *rights*, however, the term property is used to describe a right of ownership *over* something, e.g. "having property" in a house. This can, admittedly, be confusing. It is important therefore when considering such matters to pay attention to the context in which the term is used; the intended meaning will usually be quite clear.

The current context is to consider the concept of ownership itself. Erskine defined ownership as

> "the right of using and disposing of a subject as our own, except in so far as we are restrained by law or paction".[1]

In other words, the owner of an item of property can do with it whatever he wishes, provided he is not restricted in doing so by the law, or by an agreement he has voluntarily entered into. Taking a simple example, the owner of a car can use that car, but he must comply with relevant laws whilst so doing, e.g. by having valid insurance in place and by adhering to the speed limit while driving. He can also dispose of that car if he wishes, by selling it, giving it away, or destroying it, but again these actions must be done according to relevant laws. Ownership, then, is the most extensive right in property that someone can have.

"Possession" is quite different, although on the face of it the distinction may be difficult to perceive without knowing something of the circumstances that lie behind what can immediately be observed. Having possession of an item of property simply means having it in one's custody, or otherwise under one's immediate control.[2] Of course, the person who owns property very often also has possession of it, but this is not necessarily the case; there are many reasons why the owner of property might surrender possession of it to another. Assuming that possession has been obtained legally, the rights the possessor has over the subject are only those as stipulated by the owner. In other words, a right of possession allows use (and perhaps even disposal) of property except in so far as restricted by the owner. Staying with the example of a car, the owner of that car can also make it available for hire, again providing he complies with all relevant laws in so doing. If the owner surrenders possession of the car to someone who has agreed to hire it, the hirer has a lawful right of possession, but can only use the car as agreed, e.g. there might be a restriction placed on using it for a commercial purpose. The most important restriction is that the hirer cannot purport to sell the car or give it away; if he does, there could be consequences under both the civil and criminal law.

One important implication of the above distinction is determining whether or not items that were in the possession of a deceased before his death are also items he owned and, consequently, whether or not they form part of his estate.[3]

Real and personal rights

10–04 This distinction is also relevant to both property law and succession. A "real" right is one that can be defended against anyone in the world.[4] Ownership is the most common example of a real right, since an owner can defend his rights against anyone; if an owner is forced or duped into surrendering possession of his property, he can enforce his right of ownership to recover possession later.[5] Real rights are also encountered in leases and securities taken over heritable property.

---

[1] Erskine, II, 1, 1; "paction" means an agreement or contract.
[2] Erskine, II, 1, 20.
[3] Some of the potential difficulties that can be encountered are discussed in Ch.4.
[4] Stair, I, 1, 22.
[5] See, e.g. *Morrisson v Robertson*, 1908 S.C. 332.

Personal rights, on the other hand, are enforceable only against a particular person (or persons).[6] For example, almost invariably the right to receive something under a contract is personal against the other contracting party, who owes the corresponding obligation. A personal right is much weaker than a real right; an owner who is duped into surrendering both possession *and* ownership of his property will only be able to seek a personal remedy against the other contracting party, and will not be able to recover the property itself.[7]

The concept of vesting

Property is said to "vest" in someone when he acquires an indefeasible right to it. **10–05** This is not the same as a right of ownership, nor does it imply a right to immediate possession. Rather, a vested right in property is a personal right to receive that property *in due course*, usually at a specified point in the future, or on the occurrence of a specified event. For example, a person who is in employment has a vested right to be paid his agreed wages for each day that he works. However, he does not actually receive payment until the appropriate specified point in the future, i.e. on pay day.

It should be clear from this that acquisition of a vested right can happen at an entirely separate time from acquisition of ownership or possession. However, in many circumstances a vested right will be as important as a right of ownership already acquired; for example, if someone dies. It is this that makes vesting such a relevant concept for the law of succession. To continue the example given above, say an employee dies during the stipulated payment period, e.g. in the middle of the month. In calculating the value of his estate, account must be taken not only of the property he already owned, but also of the portion of accrued wages he had not yet actually received. In other words, due to the deceased's vested right, this unpaid portion would be payable to his estate.

It is difficult to precisely define the rights which vesting gives to a beneficiary in succession. In *Haldane's Trustees v Murphy*[8] it was stated that

"to predicate vesting is to predicate a right of property in the thing vested … in right of the person in whom it is vested".[9]

It is clear that this right falls far short of those enjoyed by an owner, since, for example, someone who has a vested right might not be able to recover the subject property from someone who has acquired it in good faith and for value.[10] Nor is he necessarily entitled to receive possession, since, for example, payment or transfer might be postponed under the terms of the will.[11] That said, he is entitled to exercise certain rights, such as assignation of the vested right,[12] and he also has liabilities in regard to it, for example since the value of the right may be taken

---

[6] Stair, I, 1, 22.
[7] Contrast *Morrisson* with the later case of *MacLeod v Kerr*, 1965 S.C. 253.
[8] *Haldane's Trustees v Murphy* (1881) 9 R. 269.
[9] *Haldane's Trustees v Murphy* (1881) 9 R. 269 at 295 per Lord Young.
[10] Succession (Scotland) Act 2016 s.24.
[11] This issue is considered later in the current chapter.
[12] *Trappes v Meredith* (1871) 10 M. 38.

into account for taxation purposes.[13] A right of ownership in the subject property
will not be acquired until it is transferred by delivery, in the case of moveables, or
registration of title in the case of heritage.

VESTING OF LEGACIES

10–06   It is quite possible, then, to have a vested right in something but not to have
possession or full enjoyment of it for a variety of different reasons. It is possible,
in fact, for someone to have a vested right in something but not to have full
possession and enjoyment for many years to come. Indeed, it is even possible for
someone to die with a vested right, never having enjoyed possession at all.
Nevertheless, the question as to whether a right has vested is not merely
academic; it is crucial in determining the correct application of succession. One
example is in cases of common calamity[14]; it could be of the utmost importance
to determine the actual order of death, even if that is perceived by members of the
family as macabre and insensitive.

General rules

10–07   It is necessary to start with the basics. Until a testator dies, there can be no vested
right for a beneficiary. The most the beneficiary can enjoy during the testator's
lifetime is a *spes successionis* (i.e. a chance to inherit) or, put more colloquially,
he may only entertain expectations. The problem with expectations, of course, is
that they can be dashed. Thus, if a testator names a sole beneficiary under a will,
and even if he delivers that will into the hands of the beneficiary, the beneficiary
does not acquire a vested right. This is because any number of changing
circumstances might occur before the testator's death. He might execute another
will, revoking the one in the possession of the erstwhile beneficiary.[15] Indeed, the
beneficiary himself might die before the deceased, rendering the will useless
unless an alternative legatee has been named. The point is that any perceived
rights under a will are largely meaningless before the point of vesting.

It is only on the death of the testator that rights in succession can actually vest.
Indeed, to put this another way, it can be stated quite categorically that the earliest
date on which a legacy can vest in a beneficiary is the date of the testator's death.
Thus, if there is a clear unconditional bequest, whether special, general or
residuary,[16] and the legatee is alive at the time of the testator's death, the legacy
vests *a morte testatoris* (from the testator's death). If that legatee subsequently
dies before taking possession of the legacy, it will, in turn, pass under his will or
his intestacy, as the case may be. It is important to again stress the general rule
that rights in succession will only vest in someone who survived the deceased.

---

[13] See, e.g. *Inland Revenue v Wemyss*, 1924 S.C. 284.
[14] See Ch.2 on survivorship.
[15] See Ch.7 on revocation.
[16] See Ch.6 on types of legacy.

Conditional vesting

It may be that vesting is postponed for one reason or another, if a legacy is conditional on the passage of time or the occurrence of a specified event. The will should make the position clear, but if there is any doubt, the normal rules of interpretation apply.[17] To briefly summarise the approach taken, the courts will attempt to determine the testator's intentions

10–08

> "in so far as they can be discovered or reasonably inferred from the deed ... and from the circumstances, legitimately collected, under which the deed was made".[18]

The general presumption is in favour of early vesting, i.e. on the death of the testator, but if that is not possible then it seems the courts will look to the other extreme, which is that vesting occurs only on distribution of the estate.[19] In absence of express provisions to the contrary, there is no "middle ground" recognised between these two points.

So, the question arises as to why vesting should ever be postponed. To find an answer it is necessary to examine two different types of condition that can be applied to a legacy. Some events are, by their nature, inevitable; death being the classic example in the realm of succession. Other events, no matter how likely they may seem, are not certain to occur; marriage being one such condition that was often traditionally attached to a legacy. The former type is known as a *dies certus* (loosely, "certain day") and the latter as a *dies incertus* ("uncertain day"). A condition that is *dies certus* will not suspend vesting, while one that is *dies incertus* might. In *Mackintosh v Wood*,[20] a testatrix left her son one legacy that was due on her daughter's marriage, and another that was due on the same daughter's death. When the son died, the daughter was alive and unmarried. It was held that the first legacy, being conditional on an uncertain event, lapsed by the second, being conditional on a certain event, did not, because it had already vested.

It might be observed that the rules relating to the above principles can seem counter-intuitive when practically applied. It is useful, therefore, to consider some examples.

Example 1. " ... to my nephew John, provided he survives me by 30 clear days
    ... "
Example 2. " ... to my wife Josephine in liferent and to my son Marmaduke in
    fee ... "
Example 3. " ... to my wife Delilah in liferent and to our children, whom failing
    their issue, in fee ... "

Looking at the first example, it is a clear condition of the will that John will not acquire any vested right unless and until he survives the testator by 30 clear days. This kind of provision is increasingly common to prevent a double passing of property in quick succession, as was demonstrated in Ch.2. In this example,

---

[17] See Ch.8 on interpretation.
[18] *Carleton v Thompson* (1867) 5 M. (HL) 151 at 153 per Lord Colonsay.
[19] *Marshall v King* (1888) 16 R. 40.
[20] *Mackintosh v Wood* (1872) 10 M. 933.

the date of vesting is tied to an *uncertain* day. That may sound illogical since such a date can clearly be traced on any calendar by taking the deceased's date of death and adding on 30 days. But, although that date is easily identified, the fact that John will survive for those 30 days is not certain. The chances are that he will, but until the uncertainty disappears, there can be no vested right. If he does survive for the 30 days, the uncertainty is removed and on that 30th day he acquires a vested right. This concept is sometimes expressed in the rather grand Latin maxim *dies incertus pro conditione habetur* (an uncertain day is treated as a condition). Even if he was unfortunate enough to die on that day, the legacy would have vested and his heirs would be able to claim it. This tying to an uncertain day is also sometimes known as a suspensive condition, simply because vesting is suspended until the uncertainty is removed.

10–09   The second example perhaps brings a more surprising result, if we look at it from the point of view of Marmaduke. His right is tied to a *certain day*, namely a day that sooner or later *must* arrive. It is not possible to plot it on the calendar, but nevertheless it is certain. This is because it is a fact that, sooner or later, the liferent must come to an end. It will end when (not if) one of the following events take place: the liferenter dies; the liferenter renounces the liferent; or, if the will expressly provides for this, the liferenter remarries.

Marmaduke's right of fee, accordingly, is tied to a certain day, i.e. the end of the liferent. This means that the fee vests in him on the death of his father. Obviously, he does not have possession, but the fee belongs to him, subject to the burden of the liferent. Thus, he can dispose of his right of fee as he wishes, subject always to the rights of the liferenter, and if he predeceases his mother, his right of fee will vest in his heirs. When, eventually, the liferent ends, Marmaduke will enjoy what is called the fee absolute or fee simple, i.e. the fee without any encumbrance of liferent. However, although he will then have full possession, his ownership does not begin at that point, it merely continues.

The third example gives yet another outcome, and has the greatest potential for complications. Here, the fee cannot vest on the death of the testator, despite the fact that, as above, the liferent must come to an end at some point. The reason it cannot vest is because the ultimate beneficiary is, as yet, uncertain; it could be the testator's children, his further descendants, or a combination of various classes. In short, the identity of the fiar is dependent upon who is alive at the point the liferenter dies; therefore, the fee cannot vest until the death of the liferenter.[21] This in itself is unproblematic, but historically a difficult situation could emerge if the liferenter renounced the liferent; if the fee could not vest, a question arose over what should be done with the income from the property accrued during the life of the liferenter after renunciation. Under common law, this depended very much on the wording of the will; it might fall to the residue, or it might fall into intestacy.[22] However, matters have been simplified somewhat by the 2016 Act, which states that, unless the will expressly provides for the contrary, then in the event of a liferent terminating other than by death of the liferenter, the fee will vest on the date of termination.[23] In effect, this means that

---

[21] *Muirhead v Muirhead* (1890) 17 R. (HL) 45.
[22] See, e.g. *Buyer's Trustees v Nunan*, 1981 S.C. 313.
[23] Succession (Scotland) Act 2016 s.7.

renunciation of a liferent is seen as the equivalent of death for the purposes of vesting, and so in the example above the fiars would be ascertained at that point.

Among the more problematic legacies in respect of vesting are those where there is some tie to a beneficiary reaching a particular age. As explained above, this is normally counted as a suspensive condition, thus there can be no vesting until the beneficiary attains the stipulated age. However, it is necessary to read the will very carefully as the above rules are actually no more than presumptions where a will is silent on the matter. There is a crucial difference between a legacy vesting *now* in a young person, but being held on his behalf by trustees until he attains, say, the age of 21, and a legacy that gives a particular benefit *provided* the beneficiary survives to age 21, which suspends vesting until that age is attained.[24]

Defeasance

The whole purpose of vesting is that it gives an element of security to a   **10–10** beneficiary. All the parties (in theory) are aware of their position. It may come as a surprise to learn that there are, however, cases when even a vested right may be defeated or, in legal jargon, may be subject to defeasance. This is also known as a resolutive condition in a legacy. Unlike a suspensive condition, a resolutive condition *allows* a legacy to vest, subject to the possibility of this being defeated later by occurrence of the stipulated event. If the event is required to occur before a certain point and it does not, once that point has been reached vesting is absolute and can no longer be defeated.

The classic case of defeasible vesting requires the birth of a child, either to the legatee or to someone else, before the legacy becomes payable at the end of a liferent. In such a situation property vests in the legatee and he is permitted to benefit from it. The rationale behind this was explained in *Johnston's Trustees v Dewar*[25]:

> "When a gift is made in such terms that it would take effect absolutely ... but for the single contingency of the possible birth of issue to a particular person, that is a possibility which interferes so little ... with the primary legatee treating the legacy as his own ... it must be presumed that the testator intended that he should so treat it. [H]e should be able to deal with his expectant interests as if they were vested in him ... rather than that he should be prevented from dealing with them at all on the ground that they are kept in suspense."[26]

The same logic can be used to apply the principle to other situations, and although this is rare it has been done where a legacy was conditional on a named person remaining unmarried,[27] and where a legacy was conditional on someone not having a sufficient mental capacity.[28] It should be noted, however, that this form of the concept is relatively new, and that it was subsequently doubted in *Moss's Trustees v Moss's Trustees*.[29]

---

[24] See, e.g. *Murray's JF v Murray* (1899) 6 S.L.T. 276.

[25] *Johnston's Trustees v Dewar*, 1911 S.C. 722.

[26] *Johnston's Trustees v Dewar*, 1911 S.C. 722 at 729 per Lord Kinnear.

[27] *Smith's Trustees v Smith* (1883) 10 R. 1144.

[28] *Yule's Trustees v Deans*, 1919 S.C. 570.

[29] *Moss's Trustees v Moss's Trustees*, 1958 S.C. 501.

Sometimes there may not be complete defeasance, in which case it is said to be partial. Again, some examples might help to illustrate. Suppose John leaves property to his wife Jean in liferent and to "our children" in fee. If there are two children at the time of John's death, they take an immediate vested right in the fee, i.e. half each. Suppose Jean was pregnant with their third child at the time of her husband's death. When that third child is born, he will acquire an immediate vested right to a share in the fee. This means that the right of the other two children is partly defeated. All three children now have a vested right in one third of the fee. Whilst this is straightforward, disputes are very possible when the arrangements are more complex.[30]

An example of full defeasance would be where Peter leaves his estate in liferent to his widow Sharon and to their as yet unborn child, whom failing his sister Gertrude. On Peter's death, Gertrude takes an immediate vested right in the fee. If Sharon was pregnant at the time of her husband's death and their child is subsequently born, Gertrude's right of fee is fully defeated. However, if the pregnancy is lost and Sharon cannot bear Peter's child, Gertrude's right to the fee becomes indefeasible.[31]

Vesting and destinations

10–11   Vesting is a complex subject in its own right. It can often arise in the context of a destination-over. If the testator directs his trustees to pay a legacy on the occurrence of an event (frequently the testator's death) whom failing to another, obviously the original beneficiary does not take any immediate vested right. So, if the original beneficiary dies before the testator, he cannot acquire any vested right (hopefully, this is by now self-evident) and the destination-over takes effect on the death of the testator.

There are cases where the legacy does not vest until a later (uncertain) date; but the same rules will apply, in that survivorship is essential to the acquiring of a vested right. Thus, even if the institute does survive the testator but dies before the time of vesting, the destination-over will operate on the death of the institute and any right will pass to the conditional institute or substitute (and, at this point, the distinction between the two does not matter).[32]

The conditio si institutus sine liberis decesserit

10–12   Having been at great pains to stress the importance of vesting, it is right to point out an exception to the general rule about survivorship being of the essence. Normally, if a legatee dies without acquiring a vested right, the legacy simply lapses. Unless the provision constitutes a destination-over, or is of a nature allowing accretion (considered later in this chapter), the subject of the bequest falls into residue or intestacy. The *conditio si institutus sine liberis decesserit* (better known as the *conditio si institutus*) is an exception to this rule. It is vitally important not to confuse this doctrine with the *conditio si testator sine liberis*

---

[30] See, e.g. *Nicol's Trustees v Farquhar*, 1918 S.C. 358.
[31] See, e.g. *Taylor v Gilbert's Trustees* (1878) 5 R. (HL) 217.
[32] For a case in which these concepts were extensively and authoritatively considered see *Thompson's Trustees v Jamieson* (1900) 2 F. 470.

decesserit discussed in Ch.7; despite the two sounding very similar, and arguably being based very broadly on related presumptions, they are very different and in application have no practical connection to one another. It was long a favourite question of examiners to ask what the difference is between the two; that is an artificial question since they are entirely different apart from the fact that they look alike.

The *conditio si institutus* is an equitable doctrine that implies into the will a conditional institution of the legatee's children to inherit in his place if he fails to survive; translated the phrase itself means "the condition that the institute shall have died without children". The doctrine is derived from Roman law,[33] and its effect is significant; the legatee's children will inherit in preference to a substitute named in the will, a residuary legatee, an heir on intestacy and anyone to whom the legacy would otherwise accresce, such as the surviving members of an identified class.

The *conditio si institutus* can only apply where the predeceasing institute is closely related to the testator. The theoretical rationale behind it is based on the presumption that, if the testator had foreseen that the institute might die before him, he would have wished the institute's children to take the place of their parent.[34] In practice this will only happen when the predeceasing institute is a direct descendant of the testator; in keeping with the law's common approach to stepchildren, it would not include someone related to the deceased in this way. In theory, it can apply if the institute is a nephew or niece but only if the testator has placed himself in loco parentis to them, i.e. treated them in the will as a parent would normally do.[35] In practice, the relevance of the *conditio si institutus* to nephews or nieces is slight.

In effect the *conditio si institutus* is presumed automatically from the relationship, but it can be rebutted; the onus of proof is on those seeking to displace it rather than those seeking to assert it. The *conditio* will not apply if the will indicates expressly or by clear implication that the testator did not intend it to. So, if it is clear that a testator made a bequest to a nephew out of personal favour to that individual, rather than mere relationship, the *conditio* would not apply.[36] Also, it would not apply where the testator makes express provision elsewhere in the will for the institute's descendants.[37] This kind of situation could not normally arise unless in the context of litigation or by agreement among the family. It would be a rash executor who would take the law into his own hands and apparently bypass another claimant without the authority of the court or a formal writing from the beneficiaries who would lose by the invocation of the *conditio*.

Although the *conditio si institutus* has its basis firmly in common law, the rule has now been made statutory under the 2016 Act. The position has been clarified so that only direct descendants of the testator can claim a deceased legatee's

---

[33] Erskine, III, 8, 46.
[34] See, e.g. *Devlin's Trustees v Breen*, 1945 S.C. (HL) 27.
[35] *Hall v Hall* (1891) 18 R. 690.
[36] *Knox's Executor v Knox*, 1941 S.C. 532.
[37] *McNab v Brown's Trustees*, 1926 S.C. 389.

legacy, and that any claim will be defeated where the testator has made provision for the contingency of the legatee's death; for example by way of a survivorship clause or a destination-over.[38]

Practical example of vesting

10–13 The following is a copy of an actual will, drawn from the family archives of Alasdair Gordon, former lecturer at Aberdeen College (now North East Scotland College) and original author of the *LawBasics* title on succession.

I, MRS ISABELLA MORTIMER or GORDON residing in South Street, Elgin, widow of the late John Gordon, plumber in Elgin, in order to settle my affairs in the event of my death, Do hereby Give, Grant, Assign and Dispone to and in favour of my son George Gordon, my daughter Elsie Gordon and my brother-in-law, Thomas Forsyth, Flesher in Elgin and the acceptors and acceptor, survivors and survivor of them as Trustees and Trustee for the ends, uses and purposes aftermentioned, my whole means and estate, heritable and moveable, real and personal, wheresoever situated, presently belonging or which shall pertain and belong to me at the time of my death with the writs, vouchers and instructions thereof, and I nominate my said trustees to be my executors, declaring that these presents are granted in trust: (First) For payment of all my just and lawful debts, deathbed and funeral expenses and the expenses of this trust; (Second) That my trustees shall give the use of the dwelling-house now occupied by me or in lieu thereof another dwelling-house, being part of my heritable property, together with the household furniture belonging to me, to my unmarried daughters so long as any of them remain unmarried; and after payment of the rates, taxes, burdens, necessary repairs and interest of borrowed money on the heritable property shall divide the annual proceeds thereof among my daughters Elsie, Isabella, Christina Jane and Williamina Mortimer and the survivors of them, share and share alike, and on the death of all my said daughters to realise the property and divide the proceeds equally share and share alike among my sons John, George and James, the lawful issue of any of my said sons predeceasing the term of division taking their parent's share, the furniture to be divided among my daughters equally on the whole being married or on the death of the last surviving unmarried one; (Third) Any other property which I may be possessed of at the time of my death I direct my trustees after fulfilment of the first head of this trust to divide among my daughters share and share alike and I hereby authorise my trustees if they in their discretion consider it necessary or advisable for carrying out the purposes of this trust, to sell the whole or any part of the heritable or moveable property or to borrow money on the security thereof and in the event of a sale I direct the trustees to invest the trust funds and pay the interest thereof to my daughters in the manner provided by the second purpose of this trust; and I authorise my trustees to appoint one or more of their own number or others to be factors or agents in the trust and to pay them suitable remuneration to invest the trust funds on such securities heritable or moveable as to them may seem fit; And I reserve my own liferent and I consent to registration for preservation: IN WITNESS WHEREOF these presents written on this and the preceding page by James Cameron, Clerk to Forsyth & Stewart, Solicitors, Elgin, are subscribed by me at Elgin upon the Fifteenth day of February, Eighteen hundred and eighty nine, before these witnesses, Hugh Stewart, Solicitor in Elgin and Archibald Taylor, Clerk to the said Forsyth & Stewart.

This will caused considerable controversy among the heirs, particularly in respect of the second purpose and is an excellent illustration of a vesting problem.

---

[38] Succession (Scotland) Act 2016 s.6.

The will is archetypically Victorian in that it provides for the protection of the unmarried daughters. The testatrix died in the 1890s but her last surviving unmarried daughter, Isabella, survived until 1947. The second purpose provides for the heritable property to be sold and divided among the sons, John, George and James. If these sons were to predecease the "date of division" (the date of death of the last unmarried daughter in 1947) their lawful issue could take their share. All three sons predeceased the date. John and James both left lawful issue. The problem lay with George who, as a young man, had gone abroad to seek his fortune. While living abroad, he married a German woman but died quite soon after the marriage. There were no children and it was believed that his widow had returned to Germany. The question was whether George's widow had any claim against the estate. Counsel's opinion was sought from Professor R. Candlish Henderson, QC, the leading expert on vesting and author of a much respected book on the subject.[39]

His opinion was quite clear: the date of division was a certain day because, although the estate could not be divided until there ceased to an unmarried daughter, that day was bound to come eventually. All the unmarried daughters would eventually either marry or die unmarried. Because the bequest to the three sons was tied to a certain day, the legacy vested *a morte testatoris* but subject to defeasance in the case of any son who should: (a) die before the date of division; and (b) also leave issue. George did die before the date of division but he did not leave issue. Accordingly, his vested right was not subject to defeasance. The heirs of George's widow, who were unknown to the family and not a blood relative of the testator, could claim his one third share.

ACCRETION

A concept related to vesting is that of accretion, which in essence means "increasing by addition". It was mentioned earlier in this chapter in the context of failure of a legacy, and indeed is one method whereby a legacy shall not necessarily fail on the death of a beneficiary. It is relevant in legacies made to more than one beneficiary, particularly where the object is a class of beneficiary such as "children" or "issue". Essentially, accretion occurs where one or more of several beneficiaries dies before the testator and his share is added on to the share of the others, i.e. it "accresces". **10–14**

Vesting and accretion

It is not the case that accretion will necessarily apply in cases of bequests to multiple legatees. Perhaps the simplest rule to consider is whether or not a vested right has been acquired when the legatee dies. If all the legatees survive long enough to acquire a vested right, each takes a proportionate share of the legacy; if one of them later dies before actually receiving payment, then his share forms part of his estate and therefore passes to his heirs. In this case there is no accretion. If, on the other hand, a legatee dies *before* acquiring a vested right, the **10–15**

---

[39] Candlish Henderson, R., *The Principles of Vesting in the Law of Succession*, 2nd edn (Edinburgh: W. Green, 1938).

situation becomes more complicated, and the question of what happens to his share is more difficult to answer. There is a chance it will fall into intestacy, or a destination-over might provide an alternative legatee. There is also the possibility that, contingent on a number of factors, it will indeed accresce to the surviving legatees.

The correct solution depends upon whether the legacy is treated as "several" or "joint". If deemed to be several, each share passes separately and there is no accretion. If joint, the legacy remains undivided and the share accresces to the survivors. The underlying issue is, as in many such questions, the intention of the testator; was the legacy intended to be an aggregate shared among the beneficiaries, or were there actually to be a number of separate legacies merely payable out of a common fund?

Rules of accretion

10–16 In determining an answer to the question posed above, the first place to look for guidance on the matter is the will itself and hopefully it will make the position clear. If it does not, a number of fairly simple presumptions will apply, derived from the leading case of *Paxton's Trustees v Cowie*.[40] It does not matter whether the property is heritable or moveable, nor is the nature of the bequest important, e.g. whether it is special, general or residuary, in liferent or in fee.

In the simplest case of a clearly joint legacy, e.g. "to A and B", there is accretion to the survivor should either die without acquiring a vested right. If, however, "words of severance" are used, this implies that the testator intended separate legacies and accretion is excluded; the deceased's share of the legacy would therefore fall into intestacy. The matter for interpretation by the courts is very often what constitutes sufficient "words of severance" so as to render the legacy several rather than joint. Two factors relevant to this are the identification of individual beneficiaries as opposed to a class of legatees, and the specifying of a set portion or share of the fund. As stated in the *Paxton* case,

> "when a legacy is given to a plurality of persons named or sufficiently described for identification 'equally among them'', or 'in equal shares', or 'share and share alike', or in any other language of the same import, each is entitled to his own share and no more, and there is no room for accretion in the event of the predecease of one or more of the legatees".[41]

The adding of individual beneficiaries' names, therefore, tends to indicate that a legacy is several; it does not necessarily matter if the legatees also happen to form a class. In the case of *White's Trustees*,[42] a residuary legacy was left by a testatrix to be divided amongst her two nieces and two nephews, all of whom were named. There was a proviso that should any predecease, their share should pass to their issue. One niece died but left no issue, and the question arose as to what ought to happen to her share. The court held that sufficient words of severance had been used in the provision, and the predeceasing niece's share fell into intestacy. On the other hand, if names are included merely as subsidiary

---

[40] *Paxton's Trustees v Cowie* (1886) 13 R. 1191.

[41] *Paxton's Trustees v Cowie* (1886) 13 R. 1191 at 1197 per Lord President Inglis.

[42] *White's Trustees*, 1957 S.C. 322.

identification, this will not necessarily bar accretion; in *Menzies' Factor v Menzies*,[43] the words "to the grandchildren of my brother William Menzies, who are … " were held to constitute a joint legacy, and accretion was allowed.

As regards the specifying of a portion, it is also the case that the presumption can be rebutted and accretion held to apply. The term "equally among the children" did not bar accretion in *Muir's Trustees v Muir*.[44] A particularly good example is found in *Roberts' Trustees v Roberts*.[45] Here, a one-third share was left to each of three children; dividing anything into three parts is a very clear example of severance. However, in the overall context of the will, it was clear that the legatee was intended to inherit as one of three sons, and so the legacy was deemed to be a joint legacy to a class; accordingly, accretion applied in respect of a predeceasing son's share.

10–17

The importance of careful wording can be demonstrated by *Mitchell's Trustees v Aspin*,[46] in which a residuary legacy was directed to go in equal shares to children in liferent and to their issue in fee. Provision was made for "failure" of issue by stipulating that any such share should be divided *per stirpes* among the survivors. This could easily be taken to imply an intention in favour of accretion. However, the will did not contain provision for the event of issue never having existed at all; when two daughters died without issue, it was held that their shares fell into intestacy.

Finally, accretion can take place as a result of events other than the death of a potential beneficiary, although the same rules as outlined above will apply. Revocation provides a good example, as in *Fraser's Trustees v Fraser*.[47] In this case, a testator had provided a liferent of the residue of his estate for his wife, the fee to pass to his two named brothers in equal share or their heirs. By a later codicil the testator provided for the removal of one's brother's name, and also that of his children. Upon the death of the testator's widow, a dispute arose among the surviving heirs of the testator's brothers (who themselves were by this time deceased). The heirs of the brother whose legacy had *not* been revoked claimed the full residue by accretion, whilst those of the brother whose legacy had been revoked claimed an interest in a half share of the residue under intestacy. It was held that the codicil did not provide for accretion to the other claimants, and therefore one half of the residue did indeed fall into intestacy.

---

[43] *Menzies' Factor v Menzies* (1898) 1 F. 128; see also *Young's Trustees v Young*, 1927 S.C. (HL) 6.
[44] *Muir's Trustees v Muir* (1889) 16 R. 954.
[45] *Roberts' Trustees v Roberts* (1903) 5 F. 541.
[46] *Mitchell's Trustees v Aspin*, 1971 S.L.T. 166.
[47] *Fraser's Trustees v Fraser*, 1980 S.L.T. 211.

CHAPTER 11

Executry Practice

INTRODUCTION

Succession is an area that involves a great deal of legal theory, and also a great   **11–01**
many potential complications putting that theory into practice. When a person
dies, his estate must be "ingathered" and distributed to his beneficiaries; it should
be clear by now that this is the whole purpose of succession! The task of ensuring
that a deceased's estate is correctly administered, i.e. distributed and wound up,
falls to the executor. This in itself is a role of no small responsibility, but when
one also considers the possibility of an executor being held personally liable for
any mistakes he makes, it becomes clear that it is also a role of great legal
significance. Therefore, the office of executor, and executry practice, merit
separate consideration even if exhaustive coverage of the area is not possible in a
book of this size.

THE OFFICE OF EXECUTOR

The office of executor is one that is steeped in history. By common law tradition,   **11–02**
only the moveable property of a deceased's estate passed via the executor;
heritables passed directly to the heirs of the deceased by "service".[1] The rules
regulating the role of executor and his interactions with a deceased's moveables
evolved over centuries, from the church officials who dealt with succession under
canon law prior to the Reformation in 1560, to their replacement by commissary
courts under royal control which lasted into the early 19th century, until
ultimately jurisdiction was transferred to the sheriff court in modern times.[2]
Throughout this long period of changing times the fundamental essence of the
office has remained unaltered.

Appointment of the executor

Executors come in two main categories, the main distinction being whether or not   **11–03**
they have been appointed to the position of executor by the deceased. If the
deceased died testate (i.e. having left a will) he should also have made
arrangements in that will for the appointment of an executor; certainly a
professionally drafted testamentary document will contain such a provision. An

---

[1] Erskine, II, 3, 18.
[2] Under the Sheriff Courts (Scotland) Act 1876.

executor appointed under a will is given the title of "executor-nominate". Provided the individual is willing and legally competent to act, he assumes office with no immediate formalities required. On the other hand, if the estate is intestate (i.e. the deceased left no will), then the court will have to appoint an executor, whom in this case is given the title of "executor-dative".

There is also the possibility that the deceased dies testate, having left a will, but that the will does not contain relevant provisions appointing an executor; this might well be the case with informal or "homemade" wills. In another potential twist, a nominated executor might decline to act; nobody can be compelled to assume the office simply by nomination in a will. An alternative problem might be that the person nominated becomes incapax (incapable of carrying out the duties) before taking up office; there is even the possibility that he might die. Here the situation is somewhat more complicated than if there is no will at all. In any of these eventualities, the rules of appointment are set out in statute, under the Executors (Scotland) Act 1900. Under its terms, if there are testamentary trustees named in the trust disposition and settlement (as it would accurately be called in this case, rather than a simple will), then these trustees will be deemed the executors-nominate.[3] However, frequently there are no such trustees, or if there are, they are the same persons as the executors; so any of the problems listed would still apply. In such a case the office of executor, under the same statutory provision, falls on any general legatee, universal legatee or residuary legatee.[4] If there are several legatees, they are all required to accept or decline the office expressly.

Many testators express the desire for a family member or close friend to act as executor. This is traditional and entirely understandable, since the testator obviously wants to entrust his affairs to someone he feels will carry out his wishes and not act in their own interests. It is good professional practice, however, for a solicitor or firm of law agents to be appointed as co-executors alongside any individual specifically selected by the testator. At the very least, a provision should be inserted appointing a solicitor or law firm as legal representatives of the executor-nominate. This strikes a useful balance of maintaining the desired close connection whilst also ensuring that there is a legal professional on hand to give advice and deal directly with the more technical aspects of the process.

Appointment of an executor-dative

11–04 So, where the deceased died intestate, it will be necessary to petition the sheriff to appoint an executor-dative. In order for an executor-dative to be appointed, an application has to be lodged in the form of a petition to the sheriff court of the sheriffdom in which the deceased was domiciled. Generally speaking, parties are not in competition with one another to be appointed to this office, although occasionally sibling rivalry will rear its head. In *Russo v Russo*,[5] a widow died

---

[3] Executors (Scotland) Act 1900 s.3.
[4] In context, a general legatee is found where the estate is a mixture of heritage and moveables. A universal legatee is found where the estate is entirely moveable. A residuary legatee is anyone entitled to the "residue" (remainder) of the estate after prior ranking legacies.
[5] *Russo v Russo*, 1998 S.L.T. (Sh Ct) 32.

leaving three sons, one of whom had been "decerned" (appointed) as executor-dative, but had not been confirmed to the estate. One of the other sons also wished to be appointed joint executor. The sheriff principal agreed that the appointment of an executor-dative was an administrative and not a judicial function. The court had no discretion to choose between two brothers of the same blood.[6]

The parties entitled to appointment are, in order of priority:

(1) the surviving spouse, if that spouse has prior rights which exhaust the estate;
(2) the deceased's "next-of-kin" (now relations entitled to succeed under intestate succession);
(3) other persons in the order in which they are entitled to succeed according to the rules of intestate succession;
(4) creditors of the deceased;
(5) legatees; and
(6) the procurator fiscal or a judicial factor.

At common law, "next-of-kin" referred to the class nearest in degree to the deceased in which there was at least one surviving member. It would be perfectly in order for a surviving spouse, particularly if elderly, to decline the office and for, say, the eldest son to petition for appointment. In cases where there are two or more applicants within the same category, they are all entitled to be appointed jointly.

The lay person often fails to appreciate that the appointment of an executor does not permit that person to intromit with the estate (i.e. uplift, dispose of or distribute it). Whether executor-nominate or executor-dative, he must apply to the sheriff for "confirmation". Put simply, this is an inventory of the items in the deceased's estate and gives the executor legal title to intromit with the estate as listed. Anyone taking the law into his own hands without being appointed as executor and being confirmed will be classed as a "vitious intromitter" and may be held liable for all the debts of the deceased. This could be the case even when there was no actual fraudulent intention.

The bond of caution

Historically, it was considered necessary that an executor-dative should give a guarantee to the sheriff under which he agrees to perform his duties properly; essentially that he will distribute the estate as required rather than embezzling it (or any part of it) himself. This involves the executor-dative lodging what is called a "bond of caution"[7] with the sheriff that he will make the estate "furthcoming", i.e. that he will hand it over to those entitled to it. In practice the bond is actually provided by a third party, usually an insurance company, in return for a single premium payment. Its practical effect goes beyond merely that of a promise by the executor; it indemnifies creditors or beneficiaries of the estate

11–05

---

[6] In light of recent statutory amendments this might not remain the position; these amendments are discussed later in this chapter.

[7] Pronounced "kay-shun".

against losses caused by fraud, negligence, or maladministration of the estate on the part of the executor. A bond of caution has never, as a rule, been required to be lodged by an executor-nominate, except in very rare circumstances,[8] and in more recent times "finding caution" was deemed unnecessary where a surviving spouse (or now civil partner) inherits the entire estate through prior rights.[9]

This is an area that has seen some development of late. The Scottish Law Commission had long considered the question of whether or not the requirement for an executor-dative to find caution was still a practical necessity. It was observed that whilst the requirement certainly affords a degree of protection to beneficiaries, especially children,[10] the time and cost involved is arguably disproportionate to the value of that protection given the rarity of claims in practice.[11] In light of support from industry and other respondents to the relevant discussion papers, the Commission therefore recommended that the requirement to find caution ought to be abolished.[12]

The response from the Scottish Government was not to abolish the requirement entirely but, in recognition of the cost and the broader context of the insurance industry, to amend the position so as to make the requirement less onerous. The relevant provisions are contained within the 2016 Act. The most significant amendment is removal of the requirement to find caution in relation to small intestate estates[13]; what constitutes a "small estate" is considered later in this chapter. Provision was also made paving the way for further amendment, either by adding to the cases where caution is not required to be found[14] or by, if necessary, abolishing the requirement altogether.[15] At the time of writing these provisions have only recently been brought into force, so it is not possible to say what further development there might be, or when such development will occur. What *can* be said is that the court has already given a strict interpretation to these provisions; in the very recent case of *Garnett's Executor*,[16] a request was made by the son of an intestate deceased for the sheriff to exercise discretion and confirm him as executor-dative without requiring a bond of caution. The estate was relatively small (although not such so as to constitute a "small estate") and there were only two beneficiaries so maladministration was unlikely. The court held that the 2016 Act had *not* altered the previous position in terms of the exercise of discretion by a sheriff; whilst the sum required to be guaranteed can be reduced, it cannot be reduced to nil, and the requirement for caution certainly cannot be waived entirely.

It is finally worth noting here that also included in the 2016 Act are provisions allowing further amendment to be made whereby the court can require conditions to be met before appointing any person as an executor-dative.[17] The thrust of the

---

[8] For discussion on this point, and indeed on various matters raised in this chapter, see Currie, J.G. and Scobbie, E.M., *The Confirmation of Executors in Scotland*, 9th edn (Edinburgh: W. Green, 2011).
[9] Confirmation of Executors (Scotland) Act 1823, as amended.
[10] Though there are separate protections under the Children (Scotland) Act 1995.
[11] Scottish Law Commission, *Report on Succession* (Scot. Law Com. No.215), paras 7.6–7.8.
[12] Scottish Law Commission, *Report on Succession* (Scot. Law Com. No.215), para.7.11.
[13] Succession (Scotland) Act 2016 s.18, amending the Intestates Widows and Children (Scotland) Act 1875 s.3.
[14] Succession (Scotland) Act 2016 s.19.
[15] Succession (Scotland) Act 2016 s.20.
[16] *Garnett's Executor*, 2017 S.L.T. (Sh Ct) 50.
[17] Succession (Scotland) Act 2016 s.21.

relevant section is that the office should only be taken by "persons suitable for appointment"; this is to accommodate the possibility that insurers will cease agreeing to provide bonds of caution, and so would act as an alternative form of protection, at least in the sense that those appointed will have been subject to judicial scrutiny.

Registration of documents

It goes without saying that a will is an important document, even if it is open to challenge or even having its terms rearranged by the beneficiaries. It makes sense, therefore, to register it for preservation, either in the Books of Council and Session (sometimes referred to as the Register of Deeds) in Edinburgh or in the books of the local sheriff court.[18] The latter is slightly cheaper but the outcome is exactly the same in both cases. The original will is retained in perpetuity and becomes part of the public records of Scotland. A certified photocopied extract is issued which has the same legal status as the original, no more and no less. Thus, if the will is open to challenge, it remains so. Registration does not make it any more "legal". **11–06**

There has, for a long time now, been statutory provisions in place to allow registration of a will by a living person.[19] These have never been brought into force, although the possibility of them being so remains. At the present time, however, only the will of a deceased person can be registered. When seeking confirmation, the inventory and associated documents are recorded in the books of the sheriff court.

Duties of the executor

Regardless of whether an executor assumes office as an executor-nominate or is appointed to it as executor-dative, the main function is identical, and should by now be becoming obvious; to ensure that the deceased's estate is correctly distributed to those entitled to receive it. Within this broad function are a range of specific duties, which are outlined in brief below. Many of the relevant issues that can arise are within these tasks are discussed later in this chapter, and terminology that is unfamiliar will be explained in due course; one or two others have already been considered. For the purposes of convenience and overview at this point, however, the duties of the executor can be summarised as follows: **11–07**

(1)   The executor arranges for the valuation and safekeeping of the estate until such time as he can obtain confirmation, i.e. the authority to intromit. This is not the same as actually intromitting with the estate, although may of course involve him taking possession of it; anything that might be considered vitious during this period is "purged" by the executor obtaining confirmation within a year and a day. He may consider advertising the death in the papers, although death is legally a public or "notorious" fact, of which notice need not be given to third parties.

---

[18] Confirmation of Executors (Scotland) Act 1858 s.8.
[19] Administration of Justice Act 1982 s.23.

(2)   An executor represents the deceased, i.e. he is debtor to the deceased's creditors and creditor to the deceased's debtors. An executor must take particular care to attempt to pursue debts that were due to the deceased; he has title to for a debt owed, although he will need to obtain confirmation before seeking an extract decree or enforcing the debt through diligence (meaning, very loosely, debt recovery procedures).

(3)   The executor must frame an "inventory" of the estate, i.e. provide a comprehensive account of its contents. This can be a major exercise, but it is important to ensure that it is done correctly as it is the basis for confirmation and, if necessary, inheritance tax.

(4)   When the inventory is framed and signed (and any inheritance tax paid), it is lodged with the commissary office of the area in which the deceased was ordinarily resident. In the case of an executor-nominate the will, usually in extract form, is also lodged at this point. Where there is an executor-dative, the inventory is accompanied by a bond of caution (if required).

(5)   The sheriff clerk issues the confirmation, which is the executor's title to intromit with the estate. If an executor (or anyone) intromits without confirmation, his intromissions may count as vitious, and he may become personally liable for any errors made.

(6)   If an item has been missed out of the original inventory or requires correction, a corrective inventory can be lodged and the executor will be given an "eik"[20] (supplementary document) to his original confirmation.

(7)   Liability of the executor for the debts of the deceased is limited to the amount of the deceased's estate, unless he vitiously intromits.

(8)   He will proceed to ingather the estate. Some items, such as bank accounts, are personal to the deceased and must be liquidated. The vast majority of property comprising most estates, such as heritable property, stocks and shares and so on, need not be liquidated at once and will be retained intact; though of course this may change before actual transfer to beneficiaries.

(9)   He will pay preferential debts (such as deathbed and funeral expenses) as soon as possible. Ordinary debts intimated within six months of death rank pari passu.

(10)   Eventually, he will pay the beneficiaries: special legacies first, general legacies next and residue last. Interest is payable on legacies from date to death to date of payment. Very frequently, the will provides for legacies to be paid without interest. Where interest is due, the rate is what the property or funds earned, or should have earned, if properly administered.

DRAFTING THE INVENTORY

11–08   Drafting the inventory is a practical skill that cannot be obtained merely by reading books. Nevertheless, it is useful to make a few comments about this crucial part of the executry process. It stands to reason that every estate is different. The following are only very general rules which, according to best legal practice, should only be applied after due care and enquiry.[21] Items in the

---

[20] Pronounced "eek".

[21] For the statutory basis see the Administration of Estates Act 1971 and associated legislation.

inventory are recorded, along with other details of both the deceased and the executor, in a document called a "confirmation form C1" and, if necessary, on a "confirmation continuation form C2". Both can be obtained online from Her Majesty's Revenue and Customs.[22]

An executor does not want to overvalue the estate; the greater the value, the higher the confirmation dues. Even more important is the need to mitigate the possible demands of inheritance tax. It is, however, equally important to ensure that the valuations on the inventory are realistic and honest. It is not only a waste of time, but it is also professional malpractice for a solicitor to knowingly enter an item at less than its true value. Having said that, valuation is not always an exact science. The general rule is that all assets are worth their open market value as at the date of death.

When listing the estate on the inventory form, the order to be followed is:

(a)   Estate in Scotland (heritable first).
(b)   Estate in England and Wales.
(c)   Estate in Northern Ireland.
(d)   Summary for confirmation.
(e)   Estate elsewhere.

Each item should be consecutively numbered. At the end of the list of property in the UK, the summary referred to above appears. An example might be:

Summary for confirmation

Heritable Estate in Scotland	£96,000.00
Moveable Estate in Scotland	£21,798.68
Personal Estate in England and Wales	£23,291.02
	£141,089.70

Heritable property

How heritable property is described for confirmation is partly a matter of taste when it comes to an existing sasine title. The description must be sufficient to identify the subjects, so that: "Flat One, No.10 Glebe Street, Anyburgh" would be adequate. However, it is not altogether satisfactory if, say, it is a flat in a tenement house where several properties might share the same street number. It would normally be better to use at least a general conveyancing description, e.g.:   **11–09**

> "ALL and WHOLE the westmost first floor flat forming part of the tenement dwelling-house entering by the common passage and stair at 10 Glebe Street, Anyburgh in the County of Naeplace together with all rights and privileges effeiring thereto."

The above assumes a sasine title. If the title has previously been registered, a general description is not needed but it is essential that the registered title number

---

[22] Available at *https://www.gov.uk/government/publications/inheritance-tax-confirmation-c1* [Accessed 12 May 2017].

is quoted, e.g. "Flat One, No.10 Glebe Street, Anyburgh registered as title number NAE998765". In the case of an existing sasine title, conveying the property to a beneficiary does not induce a first registration and any disposition in his favour will continue to be recorded in the appropriate Division of the General Register of Sasines. If the property is to be sold by the executors, the disposition to the buyer will induce a first registration.

It has become almost invariable practice for married couples, cohabitees or others who share the use of heritable property to take title in joint names. The difference between holding in joint names and holding in joint names and survivor has already been covered in Ch.9. At the risk of repetition, in the former case a one half *pro indiviso* share ought to be confirmed to when the first of the parties dies. In the latter case, the half-share passes automatically under the special destination and is not confirmed to. The value of the property has to be accounted for elsewhere in the inventory form, but only for the purposes of calculating any inheritance tax that may be due.

Because a mortgage is a heritable debt, it is deducted from the heritable estate at this stage. Thus, if a property was valued at £96,000 but there was an outstanding secured loan of £50,000, this would be shown in the inventory and the net value would be the figure for confirmation purposes, along the following lines:

ALL and WHOLE the dwelling-house, etc.	£96,000
less outstanding secured loan due to, etc.	£50,000
	£46,000

Occasionally, a deceased may have been a creditor in a standard security, although most heritable creditors are financial institutions. As mentioned in Ch.3, the value of the standard security counts as a moveable asset for the purposes of confirmation but it counts as a heritable asset in respect of legal rights or taxation. The obvious effect is that legal rights cannot be claimed out of the value of the security, as they can only be claimed out of the net moveable assets.

Cash in house

11–10   Any balance of cash in the deceased's possession, no matter how small, should be handed over to the executor and accounted for in the inventory. Any legal currency in pounds sterling will, of course, be given its face value. The value of any legal foreign currency will likely need to be converted. Also, there is obviously a distinction to be made between mere currency and collectible coins or notes; items of numismatic interest are more in the manner of personal effects, and would therefore require to be valued by an expert in such things.

Household furniture and personal effects

In theory, all household furniture and personal effects of the deceased require to   **11–11**
be accounted for. In practice, however, families very often engage in "tidying up"
of a deceased's home and often items are discarded. Provided this is being done
in good faith it is a matter of no controversy, at least in a legal sense; bitter family
disputes can, of course, arise over such decisions if they are perceived to have
been taken arbitrarily. In many cases it is a matter of judgement whether it is
necessary to go to the expense of a professional valuation. If inheritance tax is
likely to be payable, a valuation on a professional basis may be required, and
indeed is sensible, otherwise a reasonable approximation will probably be
adequate. It is not usually necessary to list all the separate items of furnishing
within the deceased's house; one global sum is sufficient. If the furnishings have
been professionally valued, the valuer will normally produce a detailed inventory
of items. Reference may be made to this report on the Form C1, something along
the following lines:

Furnishings in house,
as valued by Messrs Black & Whyte   £2,310.00

The valuation is what the effects are worth as at the date of death, not what it
might cost to replace them with new (as in many insurance policies). In the case
of one of a married couple or civil partnership dying, the furniture and effects in
the house would be confirmed to in respect of a half-share, unless the true facts
were different. Items such as jewellery, antiques or specialist hobby equipment,
again, may require professional valuation.

Assets of a business

If the deceased had business interests which involved rights over property, these   **11–12**
will also need to be accounted for in the inventory. In theory these are treated
exactly like personal effects, but there are complications. It can first be observed
that assets held by a registered company remain the property of that company; the
deceased had no ownership interest over them in life, so nor will he in death.[23] In
the case of a single-member company, death of the sole member can give rise to
great complications that are more a matter of company law and therefore beyond
the scope of this book. What is more relevant for succession is where the
deceased had an interest in a business organisation not subject to such separation
as that which divides a company from its members. Partnerships are a good
example, since whilst these organisations are afforded a degree of separate
identify, ownership of assets is certainly not detached from the partners entirely.
If the deceased had interests in a partnership, it is likely that the partnership
agreement will provide for the occasion of a partner's death; if not, statutory
provisions apply.[24] The norm would be for the deceased's aggregate share of any
partnership assets to be entered on the inventory as one item.

---

[23] See, e.g. *Macaura v Northern Assurance Co Ltd* [1925] A.C. 619.
[24] Partnership Act 1890.

The assets of a sole trader enterprise are indistinguishable from the assets of the deceased. The same disputes as might arise with personal effects are, therefore, once again relevant, only it is now probably fair to say that the potential for problems is intensified due to the importance that might be placed by some relatives on the continuation of a family business, and also from a very practical point of view because the monetary values involved might be considerably higher. It is therefore much more likely that disputes will actually reach the court.[25]

Motor car

11–13　As mentioned in Ch.4, in professional practice a motor car is not normally counted as part of the household effects. It is still, of course, a potentially valuable asset and so account must be made of it. A car may be valued by using one of the trade guides or obtaining a professional valuation. The car should be identified by its make, model and registration number. There are no presumptions about half-shares in cars.

Bank and building society accounts

11–14　These figures can be obtained from the institution itself with interest accrued to date of death. Having been informed of the death of its customer, the institution should freeze the account, unless it is a joint account. Irrespective of the location of the head office, if the deceased used a local branch, the monies are counted as property in Scotland. If an account is held in joint names, as is common with spouses, and one of the holders dies, the inventory should state the proportion contributed by the deceased. There is no presumption about half-shares, though it is possible to demonstrate that the deceased has gifted his share to the co-holder; this requires very clear proof.[26]

National Savings

11–15　These are entered as property in Scotland, irrespective of their centre of administration. National Savings Certificates are valued free of charge by the appropriate National Savings Centre and this applies to other National Savings products. Premium Savings Bonds are valued at par, although they remain eligible for a prize draw for a period of 12 months after date of death and should not be liquidated before that date.

Company shares

11–16　All companies in the UK count as British but the location of a company's registered office determines whether shares are counted as property in Scotland or England and Wales. Valuation of shares in a publicly quoted public limited company is straightforward and, in practice, is usually carried out by a

---

[25] See, e.g. *Lamont v Mooney* [2012] CSIH 43.
[26] See, e.g. *Forrest-Hamilton's Trustees v Forrest-Hamilton*, 1970 S.L.T. 338; see also the commentary on bank accounts in Ch.9.

stockbroker. The stockbroker should be informed that the valuation is for the purpose of confirmation. The shares are valued as at the date of death. The lower of the two valuation figures quoted in the *Financial Times* is taken and that figure is "quartered up". An example would be if shares were quoted at 380p/384p. The basis of the valuation would be 380p plus one quarter of the difference between the higher and lower figures, in this case 1p. Thus, the shares are valued at 381p each. If the deceased died on a Saturday or Sunday, or on a bank holiday, the figure chosen may be based on the nearest business day before or after. Surprisingly, the executor may select the date giving the most favourable valuation. Even more surprisingly, he need not, assuming there is more than one shareholding, confine all the valuations to the same day, but the inventory must make it clear in every case which date is being used.

Shares in a private company or in a public limited company whose shares are not quoted on the stock market will require professional valuation. The basis of valuation is the price the shares would (in theory) fetch on the open market on the assumption that the prospective purchasers had available to them all the information that a prudent buyer might reasonably require if negotiating a sale by private bargain from a willing seller at arm's length. In practice, the articles of association of many private companies place restriction on the transferability of their shares, but this restriction is not taken into account in the valuation.

Government securities

Like National Savings, these are British, so they count as estate in Scotland. **11–17** Government securities will normally be valued by a stockbroker on the same basis as shares in a public limited company, but accrued interest will either be added to or subtracted from the valuation figure. If the stock is quoted during the period between the announcement of a dividend and it actually being paid, the normal dividend will be due for payment shortly after the date of death. The apportionment of interest from date of death to date of payment is deducted from the valuation. Thus if the date of death were 1 May and payment was due on 1 June, the proportion of the interest due for the month of May would be deducted. If the stock is quoted with the dividend included, the interest from the last payment date to date of death is added to the valuation figure.[27]

Unit trusts, ISAs and PEPs

These are treated in a similar way to company shares. They can be valued by a **11–18** stockbroker but the fund manager will normally do it free of charge. Approved unit trusts are not subject to the quarter-up rule. The valuation is the manager's buying back or bid price, i.e. the lower of the two figures quoted.

Income tax

Quite frequently, a repayment of tax may be due to the deceased but the exact **11–19** amount is not known. It is common professional practice to insert a notional sum, say £50.

---

[27] Apportionment Act 1870.

Uncashed dividend warrants

11–20   If a dividend from shares is payable after the death of the deceased but prior to confirmation being obtained, there is a potential problem. Obviously, the payment can no longer be passed through the deceased's bank account, as it will have been frozen. The actual warrant should be returned to the company registrar with a request for the funds to be retained by the company, pending confirmation. The amount of the dividend should be shown on the inventory as an addition to the value of the shares in that particular company.

Moveable debts

11–21   Unlike the heritable debts, moveable debts are not directly deducted from the listed assets but are accounted for separately in another part of the inventory form. Thus, the global values of deceased estates, sometimes published in local newspapers, do not always reveal an entirely accurate picture. The published figure will not include heritable property passing under a special destination. Whilst the heritable property is net of debt in the inventory, the figure for moveables is gross. Thus, an estate might appear to be substantial but the moveable debts might, in fact, considerably reduce the real value.

CONFIRMATION AND INTROMISSION

11–22   It has been observed several times that an executor cannot proceed to intromit with the estate until he has obtained confirmation from the sheriff. This is a requirement often misunderstood by the lay person; indeed many people are entirely ignorant as to its existence. The keenness of family members for a speedy resolution of the deceased's affairs, and the frustrations that can be caused by delay, are entirely understandable. However, regardless of how pressurised the executor may feel to start distribution immediately after the funeral is over (if not sooner), he must firmly decline to do so. A solicitor who has been appointed executor should have no problem fending off such insistence; a family member might be less inclined to such obstinance. Anyone who gives in, or takes it upon himself to act without confirmation, does so at his own risk.

The significance of confirmation

11–23   The confirmation is, in fact, the executor's legal title to intromit. As already mentioned, if an executor (or anyone else) intromits with the property of the deceased without having confirmation, this intromission is counted as being vitious, which means that the vitious intromitter has to take personal liability for the debts of the deceased.[28] The legal basis for this is the venerable Vitious Intromitters Act 1696 which, despite its age and status as an "historic" Act, is still cited in modern cases.[29] It is important to note that liability of the executor (or anyone else) as regards vitious intromission is only to creditors of the deceased,

---

[28] *Fraser v Gibb* (1784) Mor. 3921.
[29] See, e.g. *Dobbie v Patton*, 2015 G.W.D. 32-530.

not beneficiaries,[30] although the latter might have grounds for action based on professional negligence where the executor is a practicing solicitor[31]; there is of course no guarantee that actions taken on such grounds will succeed.

Obtaining confirmation

The process starts with the executor completing the detailed inventory of the estate belonging to the deceased as outlined above. This inventory has a two-fold purpose of calculating whether any inheritance tax will be payable and of obtaining actual confirmation. **11–24**

Once the drafting of the inventory is complete, the executors are required to swear that, to the best of their knowledge and belief, the inventory contains a full and accurate account of the deceased's estate. If there is a will and any relevant codicils, the executors also have to swear that these are the only operative ones known to them. One executor may take the oath on behalf of all of the executors. It may be sworn before a justice of the peace, certain officials at the sheriff court or a notary public. Most solicitors are also notaries public. For those who do not wish to swear an oath, it is possible as an alternative to "solemnly affirm".

With the inventory prepared (and any inheritance tax paid), and having sworn or affirmed, the executor can proceed to apply for confirmation. This is achieved by lodging the signed inventory with the sheriff clerk of the commissariot in which the deceased was domiciled, accompanied by the will appointing the executor-nominate or, in the case of an executor-dative and if required, a bond of caution. It is not necessary to lodge an extract of the decree appointing the executor-dative, and in practice, such decrees are rarely extracted. The sheriff clerk will, in due course, issue the confirmation. When issued, this is, to all intents and purposes, a copy of the inventory previously lodged by the executor but with an official warrant to the executor to intromit with the estate.

It is not uncommon for an executor to find that he has omitted or even just undervalued or misdescribed part of the estate under his charge, e.g. a bank passbook may be found which the deceased had hidden away and of which the executor had no knowledge. In such a case, if confirmation has already been granted, the executor will prepare a corrective inventory incorporating the additional item for submission to the Capital Taxes office and then the sheriff clerk. The executor will be granted an eik to his confirmation. An eik is simply an additional confirmation that supplements or corrects the original document. If the original executor has died and additional property is discovered, it is not competent for his successor to apply for an eik. Instead, the new executor would be able to apply for confirmation *ad omissa* (in respect of things omitted).

If the deceased owned estate outwith Scotland, confirmation may not be acceptable in that country. Thus it may be necessary for the confirmation to be re-sealed in the probate register of that country. A Scottish confirmation is recognised throughout the UK by virtue of reciprocal arrangements and may include property in England, Wales or Northern Ireland, if the deceased had his domicile in Scotland.[32]

---

[30] Erskine, III, 9, 54; reaffirmed in the *Dobbie* case.
[31] See, e.g. *Steven v Hewats* [2013] CSOH 61.
[32] Administration of Estates Act 1971.

The executor's dealings

11–25 Armed with this document, the executor now has title to collect and ingather all the listed property, both heritable and moveable, which belonged to the deceased (apart from heritable property passing under a survivorship destination). The confirmation (or separate certificate of confirmation for any individual item on the inventory) can now be exhibited to whoever is in possession or custody, or whoever registers the item, such as a bank. The item will be encashed, sold, endorsed into the executor's name or transferred to a beneficiary. As money comes into the hands of the executor, he may proceed to pay off debts due by the deceased.

In carrying out his duties, an executor acts as the representative of the deceased. He is debtor to the deceased's creditors, and as a consequence he may have to perform or conclude contracts undertaken by the deceased, although not if they involve an element of *delectus personae* (choice of person), i.e. where the personal skill or qualities of the deceased were relied on. An obvious example is the deceased's contract of employment, which dies with him. The executor is also creditor to the deceased's debtors, and is entitled to sue for the recovery of debts due to the deceased. It would seem that this role as representative does not necessarily extend to *all* legal actions relevant to the deceased's estate; the courts have been reluctant, for example, to allow claims taken by an executor against solicitors for reductions in value of the estate occurring after death.[33]

There is then the no small matter of distributing the estate to beneficiaries. This will be done either according to the rules of testacy or intestacy as appropriate, and an executor must, of course, ensure that distribution is effected correctly. Potential claimants of legal rights should be notified and asked to elect whether or not to claim. Reasonable time must be given to ensure that all who might wish to claim have had the chance to do so. The executor is not required to wait indefinitely, however, and normal practice is that if the estate is solvent, funds will begin being paid out after around 12 months; this is, of course, often subject to delays, so again the need for patience on the part of expectant beneficiaries should be emphasised.

In respect of distribution, the role of the executor is equivalent to that of a trustee; this is considered in greater detail in Ch.12. It is sufficient at this point to say that the executor owes "fiduciary duties" to the beneficiaries, and thus must act in their best interests as opposed to his own,[34] and that conflicts of interest ought to be avoided.[35] An executor is potentially liable for mistakes in distribution,[36] although he is afforded certain statutory protections.[37]

---

[33] See, e.g. *Matthews v Hunter & Robertson* [2008] CSOH 88 and *Milligan's Executor v Hewats* [2013] CSOH 60.

[34] *Inglis v Inglis*, 1983 S.C. 8.

[35] *Johnston v Macfarlane*, 1987 S.L.T. 593.

[36] See, e.g. *Armour v Glasgow Royal Infirmary*, 1909 S.C. 916.

[37] Most recently by way of the Succession (Scotland) Act 2016 s.23.

Small estates

At the time of writing, a "small" estate is one whose gross value, i.e. before deduction of debts, is not more than £36,000.[38] This figure can be raised by statutory instrument, the most recent increase occurring in February 2012[39]; the previous figure was £30,000. The small estates procedure provides a simpler option for winding up a relatively modest estate. The sheriff clerk will give assistance in completing the inventory Form C1 and there is no requirement for a separate petition for the appointment of an executor-dative, should such appointment be required. No one is obliged to use this system, if they do not wish to. The sheriff clerk must be satisfied that there is no competition for appointment of the executor, that the executor is the person entitled to be appointed and that the value of the gross estate does not exceed £36,000. Once the inventory is completed, the sheriff clerk is unable to provide further advice on the winding up of the estate or other legal matters.

11–26

Cessation of office

There are a number of situations in which an executor might have to vacate office. An executor-nominate may resign, although if acting alone he should first appoint a new executor; an executor-dative can neither resign nor assume new executors.[40] There are also a number of situations that would justify removal of an executor, such as loss of capacity to act or if he is absent from the UK for an extended period.[41] There is also, of course, the possibility as mentioned earlier that an executor might die; if one of several executors die, the others may continue in office,[42] but if a sole executor dies then the office lapses.

11–27

If all the executors in whose favour the confirmation was granted die or become incapacitated, this is obviously a very difficult situation. In brief, it can be remedied by the executor of the deceased executor taking on the function in respect of *both* estates,[43] or a procedure whereby creditors or other interested parties can apply for confirmation *ad non executa* (in respect of property not administered), and this authorises them to complete the administration of the estate.[44]

Of course, the vast majority of executries end with the successful winding up of the estate, i.e. with all assets having been properly distributed. In their own interests, executors should normally seek formal discharge at the close of their administration. As with other related matters of administration, discharge is considered further in in the context of trusts in Ch.12.

---

[38] Intestates Widows and Children (Scotland) Act 1875 s.3, as amended.
[39] Under the Confirmation to Small Estates (Scotland) Order 2011.
[40] Succession (Scotland) Act 1964 s.20.
[41] Trusts (Scotland) Act 1921 s.23.
[42] Executors (Scotland) Act 1900 s.4.
[43] Executors (Scotland) Act 1900 s.6.
[44] Executors (Scotland) Act 1900 s.7.

CHAPTER 12

Trusts

INTRODUCTION

Trusts, in one form or another, have been recognised by the law of Scotland for **12–01** centuries, and remain an important part of private law. Trusts were particularly popular with the Victorians, but have been adapted to a wide variety of modern uses. Trusts can arise either inter vivos (taking effect during the creator's lifetime) or mortis causa (taking effect upon death) and it should be fairly obvious that the latter is the situation that is relevant to succession. Indeed, it was outlined in Ch.5 that many documents that would commonly be called "wills" should in fact more accurately be termed "trust dispositions and settlements" where the estate is retained in the hands of testamentary trustees. There is further connection between succession and trusts in the functions of the executor, who is in essence occupying a role equivalent to that of a trustee. In this final chapter, it is only morta causa trusts that will be considered in detail, although many of the principles discussed are applicable to both types.

NATURE AND LEGAL BASIS

As the name suggests, "trusts" occupy an area that is based first and foremost on **12–02** trust rather than law. As will be seen, the essence of a trust is that one person is exercising control over property that has been transferred to him by its original owner, but only on the proviso that it is administered for the benefit of another person or persons. It is unsurprising that historically such responsibilities would only be "entrusted" to those whom the original owner of the property felt could be relied upon to occupy the office with the utmost of honesty and good faith; and whilst the majority of trustees rose to the task, inevitably legal disputes arose and had be adjudicated upon by the courts. Of course, the motivations and expectations of the "truster" have remained the same, although in modern times as one might expect, there has been a requirement for significant statutory regulation to ensure that matters run as smoothly as possible.

Legal development

Formerly, trusts were largely governed by common law, with the result that the **12–03** rules regulating their administration developed in a piecemeal fashion over time; this is, of course, the nature of the common law. Particularly during the 19th century, a great many cases were heard involving trusts that had been established for various business purposes, and constituted new and innovative ways of taking advantage of this novel legal mechanism.

To this latter end, there were considerable legislative inroads made into the administration of trusts during the 19th century, but the main governing statutes are now the Trusts (Scotland) Act 1921 (the TSA 1921) and the Trusts (Scotland) Act 1961 (the TSA 1961). The common law, as with many areas, has continued to play an important role.

It is also worth noting that, at the time of writing, the Scottish Law Commission has recently concluded a thorough review of trusts law, and has made deep and wide-ranging recommendations for its reform.[1] These proposals are currently being reviewed by the Scottish Government.[2]

The concept of a trust

12–04 At its simplest, a trust is a legal arrangement, which bears similarity to other arrangements that impose legally enforceable rights and obligations. What sets it apart immediately from other, simpler situations however is that it is a relationship involving three parties; it is sometimes said therefore that a trust involves a "tripartite" relationship. It can be defined as

> "an interest created by the transfer of property to a trustee, in order that he may carry out the truster's directions, respecting its management and disposal. This definition includes the two essentials of a trust, viz, the conveyance or transfer of the legal estate to a trustee, and the constitution of a trust purpose".[3]

In essence, then, a trust is created when one person transfers property to a second person, who is then under a legal obligation to administer that property for the benefit of a third person. To consider the roles involved in more detail, the three parties are:

(1) The "truster", who is the person having instructed the creation of the trust and the owner of the trust property. In the context of succession, this is the testator, and the trust becomes effective only upon his death.

(2) The "trustee", who is the person appointed to administer the trust property once the trust becomes effective. In succession, since executors are trustees by statutory definition, there is considerable overlap between the two roles. Nevertheless, there are distinctions. The executor obtains confirmation, ingathers the estate, pays the debts and then distributes the estate to entitled beneficiaries. At that point, the executor's duties are at an end. If there are continuing trust purposes, such as a liferent or an ongoing charitable benefit, the administration of these begins when property or funds are transferred to the trustees. In practice the executor will also take the role of trustee, but this is not necessarily the case, and in any event the two roles are separate.

---

[1] Scottish Law Commission, *Report on Trust Law* (Scot. Law Com. No.239, 2014).

[2] Updates available at *http://www.gov.scot/Topics/Justice/law/damages/Trusts* [Accessed 15 May 2017].

[3] *Allan's Trustees v IRC*, 1971 S.L.T. 62 at 63 per Lord Reid, quoting McLaren, 1510.

(3)   The "beneficiary", who is the person for whose benefit the trust is designed to operate. In the context of succession, the beneficiary will often be family members of the deceased, but this is not always the case; it has already been mentioned that mortis causa trusts are also commonly established for charitable purposes.

As a general rule of trusts, it is perfectly possible for there to be more than one person simultaneously occupying any of the above roles, and it is also possible (in theory at least) for the same person to occupy more than one role, although in mortis causa trusts the potential for the latter is obviously limited by practicality. There is also the exception, which applies to both inter vivos and mortis causa trusts, that a sole trustee cannot also be a sole beneficiary; this is legally impossible since the rights and obligations of both roles become conjoined in one person, and so the legal concept of *confusione* ("confusion") would serve to extinguish the trust relationship.

Whilst the law of trusts certainly falls within the broad scope of the law of obligations, it can be said that a trust is not by nature a contract, and that the obligations it gives rise to are more delictual than contractual.[4] The trust is a peculiar legal institution, an entity that exists separately and independently of others; whilst it is not in itself a legal person, the trustees do acquire a new legal personality which is separate from their own status as natural persons.[5]

Public and private trusts

Every trust will be either private or public. In practice, the majority of trusts are private. In a private trust, the beneficiaries will always be private individuals, either expressly named or easily identified as a private class, e.g. "my children". Only beneficiaries or others with a direct interest have any title to sue. If a private mortis causa trust fails before it even comes into effect, the property will revert to the deceased's estate.

12–05

There are provisions for variation of the purposes of a private trust once it has come into operation. The common law possibilities for variation were limited and, in any event, required the consent of all beneficiaries. The TSA 1961 brought in reasonably wide powers to allow either the beneficiaries or the trustees to petition for variation of its terms or purposes.[6] The common law position whereby all beneficiaries (including potential beneficiaries) must consent is retained; however, provided the court is satisfied that relevant interests are not being prejudiced, it may consent on behalf of one or more of them. This provision includes a beneficiary of non-age or other incapacity, a potential future beneficiary and any person unborn. The court must be satisfied that such implied consent is not prejudicial to the beneficiaries, or potential beneficiaries, concerned. The Court of Session has considerable powers to approve an arrangement varying or revoking any of the trust purposes or to enlarge the given powers of trustees, as will be seen below.

---

[4] *Croskery v Gilmour's Trustees* (1890) 17 R. 697.
[5] See, e.g. *Heritable Reversionary Co Ltd v Millar* (1891) 18 R. 1166.
[6] Trusts (Scotland) Act 1961 s.1.

One fairly obvious reason for varying the provisions of a private trust is the mitigation of tax liability, and in *Colville, Petitioner*,[7] it was held that this was a proper use of the TSA 1961 provisions. The court may also revoke an alimentary liferent as long as it is satisfied that the arrangement is reasonable, taking account of the beneficiary's other income and all the circumstances of the case. As indicated in Ch.6, at common law an alimentary liferent could not be revoked once it was operational, although it could be revoked before it actually commenced.

A public trust, as the name would suggest, is for the benefit of the public, or a proportion or class of the public. Normally, such a trust will be of an educational, religious or charitable nature, or a mixture. The fact that such trusts are public has nothing to do with their size. Some public trusts are small, although the Law Reform (Miscellaneous Provisions) (Scotland) Act 1990 (the 1990 Act) first opened the way to amalgamation or disbursement of certain small and outdated public trusts. Many, but not all, public trusts are also charitable. The Charities and Trustee Investment (Scotland) Act 2005 (the 2005 Act) introduced major changes to the law affecting charities in Scotland, setting up, for the first time, the Office of the Scottish Charity Regulator (the OSCR). There is now a public register of charities and the OSCR has wide powers to monitor, investigate and take action to ensure good practice and protect assets where appropriate.[8] The 2005 Act also provides statutory definitions of what are recognised as charitable purposes.[9]

12–06   In the case of a public trust, any member of the public having an interest to do so has a title to sue. Occasionally, there has been doubt as to whether a particular trust is public or private. In *Salvesen's Trustees v Wye*,[10] there was a legacy to "poor relatives, friends or acquaintances". The court held that the beneficiaries' connection with the testator was the dominant factor rather than their poverty and, accordingly, it was a private trust. On the other hand, in the older case of *Andrews v Ewart's Trustees*,[11] a trust set up for the establishment of a school was held to be a public trust and title to sue rested with members of the public who might wish to avail themselves of this educational provision.

The major difference from a private trust was traditionally found in the mechanism for changing the purposes of an existing trust. If public trust purposes fail, the trustees may petition the Court of Session to ask it, under its *nobile officium,* to approve a cy-près (pronounced "see pray") scheme, i.e. to rearrange or reorganise the trust as closely as possible to the original directions.[12] If, however, the truster had expressed a clear intention only to benefit one restricted purpose or a particular institution (i.e. no general public purpose can be implied) a cy-près scheme is not appropriate and the trust purposes would fail from the beginning. In *Burgess' Trustees v Crawford*,[13] a bequest provided for the establishment of an industrial school for females. Due to a change in the law, it

---

[7] *Colville, Petitioner*, 1962 S.C. 185.
[8] The OSCR website is available at *http://www.oscr.org.uk/* [Accessed 15 May 2017].
[9] Charities and Trustee Investment (Scotland) Act 2005 ss.7–9; see also the Charities Act 2011 in so far as its provisions extend to Scotland.
[10] *Salvesen's Trustees v Wye*, 1954 S.C. 440.
[11] *Andrews v Ewart's Trustees* (1886) 13 R. (HL) 69.
[12] The basis for this is common law, but the procedure to be followed is stipulated by the Act of Sederunt (Rules of the Court of Session 1994) 1994 para.14.
[13] *Burgess' Trustees v Crawford*, 1912 S.C. 387.

was impossible to carry out these directions. The bequest lapsed entirely as no other public or charitable purpose was stated or implied, so cy-près was inappropriate. In strict theory, a cy-près scheme will not be approved unless the original purposes are impossible (not merely difficult) or are ludicrous,[14] although this principle has not always been slavishly followed.[15]

The 1990 Act broadened the law by providing that where it is no longer possible for trustees to carry out the trust purposes in the manner prescribed, the court may approve a statutory reorganisation.[16] This may take place where, having regard to social or economic changes, the trust purposes are obsolete or lacking in usefulness. The 1990 Act also contains provisions for dealing with other problems in the administration of smaller public trusts, allowing very small trusts (i.e. having an annual income of not more than £5,000) to amalgamate or wind up their affairs and transfer funds to another charity, under the supervision of the court.[17] The 2005 Act did not repeal the provisions of the 1990 Act in its entirety, but many provisions of the latter relating to charities (other than those mentioned here) have been replaced. In terms of those remaining in force, the 2005 Act introduced a regime under which the OSCR will be able to oversee amalgamations and reorganisations of charitable trusts.[18]

CONSTITUTION AND ADMINISTRATION

There is no general restriction imposed by the law as to whom may create a trust. **12–07**
The normal rules of capacity apply, briefly that a truster must have reached at least the age of 16 and must have the required mental capacity.[19] Similarly, there is no general restriction on the type of property that can be subject to a trust. In short, anyone who holds property on the basis that he is permitted to dispose of it, and has capacity to do so, can transfer that property to a second person on the basis that it administered for the benefit of a third.

The same laissez-faire approach cannot be taken, however, to the administration of the trust itself. This has already been alluded to earlier in this chapter. In particular, the position of the trustee is, unsurprisingly, subject to significant legal regulation.

Constitution

A trust may be set up either voluntarily or by legal implication. Ideally, a trust **12–08**
should be constituted expressly, although no technical wording is required.[20] As a general rule creation can be expressed verbally, but if the trust is testamentary, writing is an absolute requirement, as in the case of any bequest.[21] It is necessary for there to be a clear intention to set up a trust, and if express words are not

---

[14] A leading case on the relevant principles is *Davidson's Trustees v Arnott*, 1951 S.C. 42.
[15] For an example of a recent application see *Macdonald Trustees, Petitioner*, 2009 S.C. 6.
[16] Law Reform (Miscellaneous Provisions) (Scotland) Act 1990 s.9.
[17] Law Reform (Miscellaneous Provisions) (Scotland) Act 1990 s.10.
[18] Charities and Trustee Investment (Scotland) Act 2005 Chs 5 and 7.
[19] Age of Legal Capacity (Scotland) Act 1991 ss.1 and 2; see Ch.5 on mental capacity.
[20] *Macpherson v Macpherson's CB* (1894) 21 R. 386.
[21] Requirements of Writing (Scotland) Act 1995 s.2.

employed then it will depend on what meaning can be implied from the words that were used. In many cases, some of which have been outlined earlier in this book, the question has arisen as to whether a testator intended to create a trust or not; if there is any doubt, the courts will approach the issue in a manner similar to all questions of interpretation.[22]

There are two other requirements for a valid trust, both of which are fairly obvious. There must be actual property, heritable or moveable, and there must be some purpose for this property being held by trustees. The purpose may, in practice, be very simple, such as holding property until a beneficiary attains a particular age. Charitable purposes have been given some consideration earlier in this chapter. There are certain restrictions on the purposes for which a trust may be constituted both under common law and under statute. These are, to all intents and purposes, identical to those applying to testamentary provisions.[23]

A mortis causa trust can only be created by a testamentary writing, normally a trust disposition and settlement. Such a trust does not come into effect until the death of the truster. As long as the truster is living and competent, he can revoke the testamentary writing.[24] If the purposes of a mortis causa trust fail or do not exhaust the estate, the surplus property can be claimed by those entitled by succession, e.g. a residuary legatee or heirs in intestacy.

Trustees

12–09   At the heart of the common law of trusts is the concept of property vesting in trustees. A trustee has legal title to the property and effectively owns it,[25] but his title is not beneficial to himself, and nor does it form a part of his own estate that would be available to creditors on his insolvency.[26] Persons who receive the benefit, i.e. the beneficiaries, whether of property, capital or income have the beneficial interest or *jus crediti* (right to the benefit). Therefore, whilst a trustee is the legal owner of the property, he owns it only in order to administer it on behalf of the beneficiaries.

Trustees under the 1921 Act include not only trustees appointed by a deed of trust, but also trustees ex officio, executors and judicial factors[27]; on the latter see later in this chapter. However, the common law also applies to any person in a position of trust, such as a company director, a partner on behalf of his firm or an agent on behalf of his principal. The late Professor Andrew Dewar Gibb, somewhat whimsically, defined a trustee as

"a person who is animated either by extreme good will towards the person who made him a trustee or by a light hearted ignorance of what he is undertaking".[28]

---

[22] See Ch.8.
[23] See Ch.6.
[24] See Ch.7.
[25] See *Sharp v Thomson*, 1995 S.C. 455.
[26] *Heritable Reversionary Co Ltd v Millar* (1891) 18 R. 1166.
[27] Trusts (Scotland) Act 1921 s.2.
[28] Gibb, A., *A Preface to Scots Law*, 4th edn (Edinburgh: W. Green, 1964), p.28.

It is common for a person to be specifically named as trustee in the deed creating the trust, but a description sufficient to allow identification of the individual would also be acceptable.[29]

Although normally a trustee carries out his duties gratuitously, the responsibilities are onerous and the courts tend to be fairly strict in the area of enforcement. No one can be compelled to accept the office of a trustee.[30] No specific form of consent to acting as a trustee is insisted upon by law, but writing is clearly desirable, especially in the case of someone being appointed to an existing trust or, in the appropriate terminology, "assumed" to the existing trust.[31]

The 2005 Act introduces a new form of trustee, the charity trustee, who now has clear statutory duties and for whom mismanagement can also be interpreted as misconduct.[32]

Duties of trustees

The actual duties of trustees are largely governed by common law although certain trustees, such as charity trustees mentioned above, are governed by statutory provisions. It is obvious that a trustee must administer the trust estate in line with the directions of the truster. In many ways, the common law duties of a trustee are similar to that of an executor, though they are not quite identical. The main duties of a trustee can be summarised as follows:

12–10

(1) A trustee must ingather, administer and distribute the estate. Frequently, in a mortis causa trust, the trustees and executors are the same individuals. If a testator appoints trustees but fails to provide for executors, the trustees are entitled to be appointed as executors.[33] This is more likely to arise in a "homemade" trust disposition and settlement.

(2) Trustees are under a general duty to complete title to property which forms part of the trust estate. This is imposed strictly, as seen in *Forman v Burns*.[34] Here, an executor failed to recover monies due under a promissory note; he had gone to not inconsiderable lengths in respect of the debt, including making requests for payment from the debtor and obtaining a collateral security, but his efforts proved fruitless. It was held that he was personally liable to account for the loss, though opinion was divided and the difficulty of the circumstances was acknowledged.

(3) A trustee is expected to exercise due care. The standard of care is that of a reasonably prudent person in the management of his own affairs.[35] What a trustee's own personal standards are in the care of his own property is of no consequence. Under common law, if a trustee fails to meet a reasonable standard, he may lay himself open personally to an action for damages, though normal relevant defences to these apply.[36] Under statute there are a

---

[29] *Martin v Ferguson's Trustees* (1892) 19 R. 474.
[30] *St Silas Church Vestry v St Silas Church Trustees*, 1945 S.C. 110.
[31] *City of Glasgow Bank, Re* (1879) 6 R. (HL) 52.
[32] Charities and Trustee Investment (Scotland) Act 2005 Ch.9.
[33] Executors (Scotland) Act 1900 s.3.
[34] *Forman v Burns* (1853) 15 D. 362.
[35] *Raes v Meek* (1889) 16 R. (HL) 31.
[36] See, e.g. *Millar's Trustees v Polson* (1897) 24 R. 1038.

number of protections, such as possible relief at the court's discretion if he has acted "honestly and reasonably",[37] and for certain errors in distribution; on which see later in this chapter.

(4) The office of trustee is essentially one of *delectus personae* (choice of person) and demands his personal attention. He cannot delegate his ultimate responsibility to another party, no matter how skilled that party might be.[38] This does not mean that a trustee cannot take professional advice,[39] and indeed there are times where this is clearly wise and prudent.[40] Advice should be written and come from a person who is reasonably believed by the trustees to be qualified to give it. However, ultimately, trustees must take the responsibility of decision. It is wise, in practice, to keep records not only of what the decisions of the trustees were but also why they were made. The 2005 Act imposes a duty to take advice on matters of investment of trust funds,[41] and allows trustees to select nominees and delegate the investment and management of funds where the trust deed is silent.[42]

(5) One particularly important duty of a trustee is, in fact, a negative one, not to be *auctor in rem suam* (one who acts in his own interest). This means that a trustee's interests as an individual must not, even potentially, be brought into conflict with his duties as a trustee, since these duties are "fiduciary" (of utmost honesty and good faith). This principle is so strictly applied that the question as to whether or not any conflicting contract was fair or unfair is not taken into account. The rule applies not only to trustees in the narrower sense but also to agents, guardians, company directors, partners and anyone whose position is fiduciary. One of the most famous cases on conflict of interest must be *Aberdeen Railway Company v Blaikie Bros*,[43] involving Sir Thomas Blaikie, sometime Lord Provost of Aberdeen. Blaikie, the managing partner of Blaikie Bros, iron founders in Aberdeen, was also a director of the Aberdeen Railway Company. Blaikie Bros brought an action against the railway company for implementation of a contract in which the latter had agreed to purchase a large quantity of iron materials. In the House of Lords, the original contract was declared to be voidable. Blaikie, as a director of the railway company, was in a position of trust and was thus precluded from entering into a contract on its behalf with a firm of which he was himself a partner. It was not suggested, nor implied, that he had acted fraudulently.

Other cases also provide good examples. In *Cherry's Trustees v Patrick*,[44] a trustee was a supplier of alcoholic liquor. He made certain profits by trading with public houses forming part of the trust estate. It was

---

[37] Trusts (Scotland) Act 1921 s.32.

[38] *Scott v Occidental Petroleum*, 1990 S.L.T. 882.

[39] *Hay v Binny* (1861) 15 D. 362.

[40] *Martin v Edinburgh DC*, 1988 S.L.T. 329.

[41] Trusts (Scotland) Act 1921 s.4A, inserted by Charities and Trustee Investment (Scotland) Act 2005 s.94.

[42] Trusts (Scotland) Act 1921 s.4B, inserted by Charities and Trustee Investment (Scotland) Act 2005 s.94.

[43] *Aberdeen Railway Company v Blaikie Bros* (1853) 1 Macq. 461.

[44] *Cherry's Trustees v Patrick*, 1911 S.L.T. 313.

held that these profits could not be retained by him but must be accounted for to the trust estate. In *Clark v Clark's Executors*,[45] executors agreed to sell heritable property forming part of the executry estate to a third party. The third party then agreed to convey the property to one of the executors in her personal capacity. As this executor was clearly *auctor in rem suam*, the sale was reduced.

(6)   The office of trustee is gratuitous and no trustee has the right to be paid for his work, however skilled or arduous, unless there is express power to do so in the trust deed.[46] The definition of "payment" includes indirect payments and commission, and so in *Henderson v Watson*[47] it was held that a solicitor acting as trustee was not entitled to keep his share of payments made to the firm in respect of legal work performed. A trustee would be able to transact with the trust or the beneficiaries if such transactions were explicitly authorised by the trust deed or the beneficiaries, in full knowledge of their rights. The burden of proof would be on the trustee to show that he had acted in a fair and honest manner and that full information and value had been given.[48] That said, it is nowadays commonplace for provisions to be included in the trust deed allowing professionals such as solicitors and accountants to be paid for their services, and the explicit power to appoint one of the trustees as a law agent has been held to imply a power to pay remuneration.[49] If a trustee gains some personal benefit by being a trustee, he must declare it, since such benefit is really held on constructive trust for the beneficiaries. **12–11**

(7)   It is unlikely to come as a surprise that trustees are expected to keep proper and adequate records of their intromissions both with capital and income.[50] This is appropriate to the responsibility that they have been entrusted with. A beneficiary has the right to see any documentation kept in relation to administration of the trust, the most significant of which are the trusts accounts.[51]

(8)   Common law and statute law come together in a particularly important duty, to keep the trust funds properly invested. The trust deed itself will frequently give wide powers to trustees or give fairly specific directions. At common law and in the absence of directions, trustees were restricted to certain fixed interest securities, feu duties, ground annuals and heritable securities. Even if a truster directs that certain investments are to be retained, it seems that the trustees are under a duty to ensure that such investments continue to be in the best interests of the beneficiaries, even if that means disposing of investments and reinvesting the proceeds.[52]

Where there were no directions given in the trust deed (which would be unusual in a professionally drafted document) the Trustee Investment Act 1961 used to apply. This Act was intended to widen significantly the

---

[45] *Clark v Clark's Executors*, 1989 S.L.T. 665.
[46] *Fegan v Thomson* (1855) 17 D. 1146.
[47] *Henderson v Watson*, 1939 S.C. 711.
[48] *Johnston v Macfarlane*, 1987 S.L.T. 593.
[49] *Lewis' Trustees v Pirie*, 1912 S.C. 574.
[50] *Ross v Ross* (1896) 23 R. (HL) 67.
[51] *Murray v Cameron*, 1969 S.L.T. (Notes) 76.
[52] *Thomson's Trustees v Davidson*, 1947 S.C. 654.

investment powers of trustees. In practice its provisions were found to be administratively irksome and it was repealed by the 2005 Act. Under Pt 3 of the 2005 Act, trustees generally have the same powers of investment as if they were beneficial owners.[53] This includes power to invest in heritable property.[54] These provisions apply to all trustees, not just charity trustees. The fact that the trustees have taken advice does not relieve them of their basic duty of care. Their overarching duty in investment is to secure the best possible return to the trust, and so should be motivated by this above anything else.[55]

Powers of trustees

12–12 It is fair to say that there is considerable overlap between "powers" and "duties", since discharge of the latter will often necessitate exercise of the former. However, some additional commentary on the nature and sources of a trustee's powers are appropriate to supplement the considerations already outlined.

In answering any question of whether or not a trustee enjoys a certain power, it is perhaps obvious that the first place to look is the trust deed itself. Where the deed is silent, the trustees have powers implied by both common law and statute. The Court of Session may also exercise its *nobile officium* to give further powers to the trustees where the trust is unworkable.

The most basic common law power of trustees is to administer the trust on a day to day basis. The TSA 1921 and TSA 1961 both set out certain powers—which are granted to all trustees—except where explicitly restricted and provided they are not at variance with the provisions of the trust deed. These include the power to sell the estate, to grant leases, borrow money on the security of the estate, appoint agents and solicitors and grant all necessary deeds.

Unless there is only one trustee, the right to exercise the powers belongs to the majority of the surviving and accepting trustees. All trustees must be given the full opportunity to attend meetings and to participate in the administration of the trust. Sometimes, the deed of trust itself may provide for a quorum. In the absence of such a provision, the TSA 1921 provides that a majority of accepting and surviving trustees is a valid quorum.[56]

Under the terms of the TSA 1961, the validity of the sale by trustees of heritable property to a third party may not be challenged on the ground that such sale is contrary to the terms of the trust, provided the third party acted in good faith and for value.[57] Thus anyone buying heritable property from trustees does not require to satisfy himself that they have power to sell, unless there is anything to put him on his guard. These provisions do not affect the relationship between the trustees and the beneficiaries. Thus, even although trustees can grant a valid title to a third party when, in fact, they have no power to sell, they open themselves to an action for damages on the grounds of breach of trust at the hands

---

[53] Trusts (Scotland) Act 1921 s.4(1)(ea), inserted by Charities and Trustee Investment (Scotland) Act 2005 s.93.

[54] Trusts (Scotland) Act 1921 s.4(1)(eb), inserted by Charities and Trustee Investment (Scotland) Act 2005 s.93.

[55] See, e.g. *Cowan v Scargill* [1985] Ch. 270.

[56] Trusts (Scotland) Act 1921 s.3(c).

[57] Trusts (Scotland) Act 1961 s.2.

of an aggrieved beneficiary. If the third party had not acted in good faith, the beneficiary would be able to follow the particular investment and reclaim it.

Liability of trustees

Again, certain of the liabilities applicable to trustees have already been alluded to when considering duties. The focus in that context was liability to beneficiaries, the most significant of which is liabilities for incorrect distribution of trust funds. It is a trustee's nightmare to make a major mistake in the disbursement of assets by, say, paying the wrong beneficiary or overpaying the correct one. It used to be thought that, as a very general rule of thumb, if a wrong payment was made due to an error of fact, it could be recovered, but not so if there was an error of law. The situation has, however, shifted so as to be somewhat more complicated, perhaps even moving towards a reversal of the old rule, and that state of affairs has been achieved by way of a somewhat circuitous route. The development began in the courts, with the Inner House case of *Morgan Guaranty Trust Company of New York v Lothian Regional Council*,[58] where it was held by a bench of five judges that a remedy was available irrespective of whether the mistake made was due to an error of fact or an error of law. The same principles have been applied in recent cases.[59] There was recently an additional statutory protection introduced whereby a trustee will have no personal liability for errors in distribution made due to errors of fact regarding the existence, or non-existence, of a person or relationship which is relevant to the purposes of the trust, provided he has made reasonable enquiries and has acted in good faith.[60] This could apply where, for example, property has been distributed and it later emerges that there was someone not contemplated by the trustee who should have been entitled to receive a benefit.

12–13

It is also appropriate to consider certain matters relating to a trustee's liability in relation to parties outwith the boundaries of the trust, i.e. to third parties. This is a potentially confusing term, since a trust already involves three parties, but "third party" is used here in its general legal meaning of an external creditor.

It is often, quite wrongly, assumed that trustees incur no personal liability for debts incurred in their administration of the trust. This is not so; as a very broad rule, trustees are potentially personally liable for debts arising as a result of any contract entered into with a third party.[61] It is, however, possible to exclude this liability by express agreement, but the courts historically at least have required explicit wording to be used in the contract.[62]

As mentioned earlier in this chapter, a testamentary trust does not have a distinct personality in law. Most trusts are unincorporated bodies, although public trusts and charities are increasingly incorporated as companies limited by guarantee. Subject to that exception, trustees are personally liable, jointly and severally, for the debts they incur in the course of their administration. However, they are entitled to reimbursement in full from the trust estate, provided the debts

12–14

---

[58] *Morgan Guaranty Trust Company of New York v Lothian Regional Council*, 1995 S.L.T. 299.

[59] See, e.g. *Alliance Trust Savings Ltd v Currie* [2016] CSOH 154.

[60] Trusts (Scotland) Act 1921 s.29A, inserted by the Succession (Scotland) Act 2016 s.23.

[61] See, e.g. *Brown v Sutherland* (1875) 2 R. 615.

[62] Compare, e.g. the decisions in *Gordon v Campbell* (1842) 1 Bell App 428 and *Lumsden v Buchanan* (1865) 3 M. (HL) 89.

have been properly incurred. In most cases, this personal liability does not cause problems. The result would be otherwise if the assets of the trust estate were insufficient to cover the debts. In *Muir v City of Glasgow Bank*,[63] a shareholder died, leaving his estate in trust. Among the trust assets was stock in the City of Glasgow Bank, an unlimited company. The stock was transferred into the names of his two children as trustees. The bank crashed in 1878, leaving its shareholders with unlimited liability for its vast debts. Only 254 of its 1,819 shareholders remained solvent. The two trustees argued that their liability was limited to the extent of the trust estate. The House of Lords held that they were personally liable to meet all legitimate calls in full.

An executor is not generally liable for debts beyond the value of the estate at his disposal. If executors (or testamentary trustees) discover that the inherited debts exceed the value of the estate, in their own interests they should take steps to have the estate sequestrated. If they do not take this possibly painful step, their own intromissions may count as vitious, leaving them with personal liability for the debts of the deceased.

A trustee who is in breach of trust may well have to pay back all the loss this breach has caused to the trust estate. "Breach" can cover a wide variety of omissions and commissions, from fraud to negligence and in varying degrees. It would be breach of trust to fail to make proper provisions for investment of funds or to delay unreasonably in paying beneficiaries. As stated above, trustees have joint and several liability, although breach by one trustee, without the knowledge or acquiescence of the others, does not make them liable if they have acted reasonably.[64]

It is not unusual for a trust deed to include an indemnity clause stating that the trustees are not to be held personally liable for omissions, error or neglect. The courts have tended to interpret such clauses restrictively and have not allowed them to protect a trustee who is blatantly in breach of duty.[65]

Assumption, resignation and removal of trustees

12–15   There are a number of circumstances that might necessitate a change regarding who is occupying the office of trustee. It could be that the responsibility has become too onerous for one person, or it could be that a trustee has decided to leave office. There are also more serious situations, such as death or loss of capacity of a trustee; there are also a variety of reasons for which a trustee would require to be removed.

Unless the trust deed provides to the contrary, new trustees can be appointed or assumed by existing trustees. From the practical point of view, such assumptions would normally be in writing and the TSA 1921 provides appropriate styles.[66] If there are two existing trustees, both must sign the deed of assumption. If there are more than two, a quorum is sufficient but, in practice, the signature of all trustees is desirable. An executor-dative counts as a trustee with

---

[63] *Muir v City of Glasgow Bank* (1879) 6 R. (HL) 21.
[64] Trusts (Scotland) Act 1921 s.3(d).
[65] See, e.g. *Knox v Mackinnon* (1888) 15 R. (HL) 83.
[66] Trusts (Scotland) Act 1921 Sch.B.

broadly the same rights as a gratuitous trustee at common law and under the TSA 1921 and the TSA 1961, but he does not have the right of assumption.[67]

At common law a trustee had no power to resign, but under the TSA 1921 is entitled to do so, subject to important exceptions:

(1)   A sole trustee cannot resign unless he has assumed new accepting trustees or the court has either appointed new trustees or a judicial factor.
(2)   If a trustee accepts office on condition of a legacy or remuneration, he will require the permission of the court to resign and he may be required to make appropriate repayment.
(3)   The holders of certain offices exercising the functions of a trustee do not have a power to resign, e.g. judicial factors.[68]

For his own protection, a resigning trustee should execute a formal minute of resignation to avoid any possible personal liability for the future acts of his co-trustees. Again, the TSA 1921 provides an appropriate style.[69] Frequently, such a minute is incorporated into a deed of assumption of a new trustee. It is good practice to register such a document in the Books of Council and Session.

The court will normally, as a matter of course, remove a trustee on the grounds of loss of mental capacity, seriously debilitating disability, prolonged absence or disappearance. The court also has the general power to remove a trustee on such grounds as gross negligence, wilful breach of trust or fraud. An extreme example can be found in *Wishart, Petitioners*,[70] where a trustee was removed from office after absconding with trust funds. In general, however, this is a power that historically has been used only sparingly. Negligence itself is not necessarily sufficient, even if it causes loss to the trust estate; in *Dick, Petitioners*,[71] a trustee who had refused to co-operate with his co-trustees, to the detriment of the trusts estate, was *not* removed after he gave an undertaking that he would co-operate in future. In contrast, removal was granted in *MacGilchrist's Trustees v MacGilchrist*,[72] where it was held that a trustee continuously neglecting his duties was difficult to reconcile with the duty of good faith. Generally, the courts are reluctant to remove a trustee who *has* been acting in good faith even if his interpretation or administration has fallen short. If there is a deadlock among trustees, the courts may appoint a judicial factor, which will suspend the powers of trustees for as long as his appointment lasts. A judicial factor may also be appointed if the situation arises that there are no surviving trustees.

Judicial factors

A judicial factor is really a special kind of trustee. At one time a judicial factor was appointed only by the Court of Session under its *nobile officium*, but the right of appointment is now well established in the sheriff court. Although a judicial

12–16

---

[67] Succession (Scotland) Act 1964 s.20.
[68] Trusts (Scotland) Act 1921 s.3.
[69] Trusts (Scotland) Act 1921 Sch.A.
[70] *Wishart, Petitioners* (1910) 2 S.L.T. 229.
[71] *Dick, Petitioners* (1899) 2 F. 316.
[72] *MacGilchrist's Trustees v MacGilchrist*, 1930 S.C. 635.

factor is a trustee within the meaning of the TSA 1921,[73] in essence he is an official of the court whose rights and duties are regulated by statute.[74] A judicial factor is appointed by and answerable only to the court. He always functions on his own and is only permitted to resign from office with the authority of the court. The rules in respect of bonds of caution also apply. The person whose funds are in his care is called the "ward".

The very basic function of a judicial factor is to look after estates where some element of protection is required or a degree of fair play has to be ensured. Examples relevant to this particular area would be where trustees are in deadlock or where all original or assumed trustees have died. In terms of succession more broadly, it is also possible for creditors of a deceased to apply for appointment of a judicial factor where no trustee to the estate has been appointed, or where those appointed have declined office.[75] The court will appoint a judicial factor as a result of a petition stating the grounds, the property to be taken into his charge and the name of the person to be appointed. An interim appointment may be obtained in the case of urgency.

The judicial factor's authority to intromit with the estate is the extract decree of appointment that has a similar effect to an executor's confirmation. Unlike most trustees, a judicial factor would not normally complete title to the property of the ward but has power to intromit with the estate in the ward's name, under the general superintendence of the Accountant of Court. Normally a judicial factor has all the general powers of a trustee although, as shown in Ch.8, he is unable to exercise dispositive discretion.

TERMINATION OF TRUSTS

12–17 Traditionally, English law has considerable suspicion of anything that appears to make a trust perpetual. In Scotland, we tend not to see this as such a great problem. There are trusts that have existed in Scotland for generations and are still in good heart. Nevertheless, most trusts come to an end sooner or later. As has already been mentioned, in a mortis causa trust the testator can validly revoke the provisions in the trust disposition and settlement at any time up to his death. Termination of an inter vivos trust is more complicated.

Termination by the truster

12–18 It has already been observed several times that the law, very broadly, favours freedom in the treatment of one's property, and in accordance with this principle a truster is generally able to revoke an inter vivos trust. However, he will be prevented from doing so if two conditions apply. The first is that there must be an ascertained beneficiary other than the truster himself. In *Bertram's Trustees v*

---

[73] Trusts (Scotland) Act 1921 s.2.
[74] See, e.g. the Judicial Factors (Scotland) Act 1880, as amended and the Judicial Factors (Scotland) Act 1889, as amended.
[75] Judicial Factors (Scotland) Act 1889 s.11A, amended most recently by the Bankruptcy (Scotland) Act 2016.

Bertram,[76] an unmarried man assigned to trustees stocks and shares of considerable value, to be held for his benefit during his lifetime and thereafter for the benefit of his widow, should he marry, and lawful issue, should he have any. The court held that he was entitled to revoke it in the absence of anyone being ascertained to either of the two positions that could be occupied by potential beneficiaries. The second condition is that the ascertained beneficiary must have a *jus quaesitium* or "immediate beneficial interest". This in essence means that the beneficiary's interest must be unconditional, or conditional on nothing other than him surviving until a specified date.[77] If the beneficiary's interest is dependent on a particular event taking place, it is not immediate and the trust is therefore revocable. For example, in *Bulkeley-Gavin's Trustees v Bulkeley-Gavin's Trustees*,[78] the benefit was contingent on the wholesale nationalisation of land; this was an event that might never occur, and the court held that the trust was revocable.

Termination by trustees or beneficiaries

Trustees can normally only terminate a trust by administering the trust according to its stated purposes and making a final and total distribution ("denuding") in favour of the beneficiaries. If the trust assets were distributed to the wrong beneficiaries, the trust would not be at an end even though the trustees had denuded.

12–19

Beneficiaries have limited powers to request termination of a trust. Potentially, it is possible, provided they all consent and it does not prejudice the trustees in their proper administration or interfere with any alimentary rights. In *De Robeck v Inland Revenue*,[79] the trustees had arranged to pay estate duty in instalments; it was held that the trust could not be terminated until the estate duty was paid off, since to do so would prejudice the arrangement. As discussed in Ch.6, a beneficiary may also request termination where the remaining trust purposes are only of an administrative nature and the beneficiary has a full vested right of fee.[80]

Discharge of trustees

Trustees who have carried out their duties under the trust properly are entitled to be discharged from any future liability arising from the trust. It is common sense, therefore, for trustees to ask for a discharge before a final distribution is made to beneficiaries. Normally trustees will not denude until a discharge has been granted but, once it has been, they are bound to do so.[81] To put it another way, a trust is not really at an end until the trustees are discharged.

12–20

The discharge can only cover what is within the knowledge of the party granting it. If a beneficiary grants a discharge unaware that a trustee has carried out a major fraud, he could still bring a challenge at a later date when the facts

---

[76] *Bertram's Trustees v Bertram*, 1909 S.C. 1238.
[77] *Robertson v Robertson's Trustees* (1892) 19 R. 849.
[78] *Bulkeley-Gavin's Trustees v Bulkeley-Gavin's Trustees*, 1971 S.C. 209.
[79] *De Robeck v Inland Revenue*, 1928 S.C. (HL) 34.
[80] *Miller's Trustees v Miller* (1890) 18 R. 301.
[81] *Mackenzie's Executor v Thomson's Trustees*, 1965 S.C. 154.

come to light. If, however, a beneficiary was aware that a breach of trust had taken place yet signed a discharge he would be personally barred from founding on the breach at a later date.[82]

Whilst each individual trustee is entitled to a discharge, one discharge in favour of all trustees is common. The trust deed itself may lay down the actual format of the discharge, in which case the instructions will be followed. Since the Requirements of Writing (Scotland) Act 1995 came into effect, a document is formally valid if subscribed by the granter. Accordingly, a simple signature on a discharge is adequate, but it is common practice for the discharge to be self-proving and for it to be registered in the Books of Council and Session. The strict legal effect of granting a discharge is to protect trustees from future liability under the trust and to close off any challenge to their intromissions. This does not mean that trustees who have been discharged are beyond all possible challenge. The correct approach would be for the aggrieved party to raise an action of reduction in respect of the discharge, e.g. that it was granted as a result of fraud, essential error or breach of trust.[83] Such actions in respect of trustees are, fortunately, rare in practice.

---

[82] *Johnstone v Mackenzie's Trustees*, 1911 S.C. 321.
[83] See, e.g. *Campbell v Montgomery* (1822) 1 S. 484.

Appendix: Example of a Full Trust Disposition and Settlement

The trust disposition and settlement outlined below is provided as an example of **App1–01** what one might expect to receive having instructed a solicitor regarding the succession to one's estate. It is based on an actual will prepared in the early 2000s, but all names and addresses have been anonymised. The style is fairly typical and the provisions contain a number of elements of "good practice" that would be expected from a professionally drafted document. That is not to say that it is perfect, nor that it would definitely escape legal contention; the astute reader will have surmised that succession is an area fraught with unforeseen problems, in which the seemingly best laid schemes can, and often do, go awry!

To comment briefly on the contents, then, it can be seen that the wishes and intentions of the testator are perfectly clear, including the express revocation of all prior testamentary documents by clause one and an instruction to give effect to subsequent testamentary writings in clause five. There is clear appointment of trustees and executors by clause two, and appointment of a firm of solicitors as law agents to the trustees by the final clause. Clause three dispones the testator's whole estate to the trustees, but expressly for the purposes outlined thereafter only. In terms of the various legacies, these identify the subjects and objects leaving little to obviously necessitate interpretation, though as mentioned above in practice specific complications cannot always be predicted. It is also worth noting that provision has been made for the possibility of a beneficiary failing to survive the testator, with suitable substitute beneficiaries identified. Provision is also made for beneficiaries lacking capacity by clause 11, and the powers of the trustees are outlined in clause 12.

In order that the document be both formally valid and self-proving, the testing clause at the end would, of course, require to be completed with a signature by the testatrix and the named witness, with the testatrix also signing on every preceding page.

TRUST DISPOSITION AND SETTLEMENT OF EDWINA DOUGLAS

I, [*Mrs Edwina Douglas*], residing at [*Two Hundred and Forty Eight East Main* **App1–02** *Street, Sauchen, Aberdeenshire*], wishing to settle the succession to my means and estate in the event of my death provide as follows:

(1)   I revoke all prior wills and testamentary writings.

(2)   I appoint my daughter, [*Mrs Mary Leadingham*], residing at [*One Hundred and Eleven Meadowbank Gardens, Sauchen, Aberdeenshire*] and my son, [*Mr Clarke Douglas*], residing at [*Ninety Seven Skene House Park, Aberdeen*] to be my trustees and executors (hereinafter referred to as "my trustees").

(3)   I dispone, convey and make over to and in favour of my trustees my whole means and estate, real and personal, which shall belong to me at the time of my death but that is in trust only for the following purposes.

(4)   I direct my trustees to make payment of all my debts and funeral expenses.

(5)   I direct my trustees to give effect to any writings of a testamentary nature left by me however informal such writings may be, provided always that they are clearly indicative of my intentions and signed by me and dated the same day as, or subsequent to, the date of signing of this settlement.

(6)   I direct that my trustees are to find homes for any cats or dogs looked after by me.

(7)   I direct my trustees to sell any heritable property owned by me at the date of my death and to divide the proceeds equally among the said [*Mrs Mary Leadingham*] as an individual and as her own absolute property, the said [*Mr Clarke Douglas*] as an individual and as his own absolute property, [*Mrs Sybil Proctor*], residing at [*Eighty Nine Shafton Avenue, Glasgow*], and [*Mr Arnold McLeish*], residing at [*Ninety One Broomhouse Road, Edinburgh*]; declaring that in the event of any of the foregoing beneficiaries predeceasing me leaving issue who shall survive me, then such issue shall take equally between or among them *per stirpes* if more than one the share to which their parent would have succeeded had such parent survived me.

(8)   I direct my trustees to pay and make over the sum of [*Twenty Five Thousand Pounds*] (£[*25,000*]) Sterling and that free of government taxes and duties payable upon my death but without interest to date of payment to the said [*Mrs Mary Leadingham*] as an individual and as her own absolute property, whom failing her issue who shall take equally between or among them *per stirpes* if more than one.

(9)   I direct my trustees to pay and make over the sum of [*Twenty Five Thousand Pounds*] (£[*25,000*]) Sterling and that free of government taxes and duties payable upon my death but without interest to date of payment to the said [*Mr Clarke Douglas*] as an individual and as his own absolute property, whom failing his issue who shall take equally between or among them *per stirpes* if more than one.

(10)   I direct my trustees to divide the whole residue and remainder of my estate into four equal parts and to pay and make over one part to each of the following:

(First) [*Mr Daniel Proctor*], residing at [*Eighty Nine Shafton Avenue, Glasgow*];

(Second) [*Miss Emma Proctor*], residing at [*Eighty Nine Shafton Avenue, Glasgow*];

(Third) [*Miss Julia McLeish*], residing at [*Ninety One Broomhouse Road, Edinburgh*];

(Fourth) [*Mr Andrew McLeish*], residing at [*Ninety One Broomhouse Road, Edinburgh*] aforesaid; declaring that, in the event of any of the foregoing beneficiaries predeceasing me, his or her share shall be divided equally between the said [*Mrs Mary Leadingham*] as an individual and as her own absolute property, whom failing her issue, and the said [*Mr Clarke Douglas*] as an individual and as his own absolute property, whom failing his issue.

(11) If any part of my estate is held for a beneficiary who lacks full legal capacity my trustees shall have full power either to pay or apply the whole or any part of the income or capital falling to such beneficiary for their behalf in any manner my trustees may think proper, or to retain the same until such capacity is attained accumulating income with capital, or to pay over the same to the legal guardian or the person for the time being with whom the beneficiary has residence whose receipt shall be sufficient discharge of my trustees.

(12) My trustees shall have the fullest powers competent to gratuitous trustees in Scotland including without prejudice to the foregoing generality, power to retain my estate in the form in which they may find it at the date of my death or to vary or realise the whole or any part thereof and to invest the proceeds in securities which may include heritage and which may be other than those authorised by the Trusts (Scotland) Act 1921, the Trustee Investments Act 1961 or any similar enactments from time to time in force regulating the investment powers of trustees all as my trustees in their sole discretion may decide; My trustees shall not be held liable for any loss that may result by their so acting provided always that they have acted honestly and to the best of their abilities.

(13) I declare that my domicile is Scottish and that the law of Scotland shall apply to the administration of my estate.

(14) I appoint [*Leachem & Goode*], Advocates in [*Aberdeen*] to be law agents to my trustees: IN WITNESS WHEREOF these presents consisting of this and the preceding pages are signed by me at [*Sauchen, Aberdeenshire*] on the [*Fourth day of November, Two Thousand and Twelve*] before [*Dr Derek Mitchell-Smith, General Practitioner of Inverurie Health Centre, Inverurie, Aberdeenshire*].

INDEX

All references are to paragraph number

Abatement
  legacies, 6–07
Accession
  heritable property, 3–03
Accretion
  generally, 10–14
  rules of accretion, 10–16—10–17
  vesting and, 10–15
Accumulations of income
  restraints on testamentary freedom, 6–22—6–23
Actio injuriarum
  rights in respect of cadaver, 2–08
Additions
  wills, 7–02
Ademption
  special legacies, 6–08
Age
  capacity to make testamentary documents, 5–05
Agreement
  revocation of wills, 7–13
Alimentary liferents
  testamentary provisions, 6–12
Alterations
  wills, 7–02
Alternative substitutionary devices
  donations mortis causa, 9–13
  generally, 9–09
  insurance policies, 9–11
  marriage contracts, 9–12
  nominations, 9–10
Annuities
  testamentary provisions, 6–09
Appointment of executors
  bond of caution, 11–05
  executors-dative, 11–04
  generally, 11–03
Approbate
  legal rights and, 6–27—6–28
Assumption of trustees
  administration of trusts, 12–15
Attested wills
  validity, 5–13—5–14
Aunts
  intestate succession, 4–51

Bank accounts
  drafting inventory, 11–14
Bankruptcy
  insolvent estates, 3–13
Beneficiaries
  meaning, 1–04
  termination of trusts by, 12–19
Bond of caution
  executors, 11–05
Burials
  disposal of human remains, 2–09
Business assets
  drafting inventory, 11–12
Capacity
  testamentary documents
    age, 5–05
    generally, 5–04
    mental incapacity, 5–06
Cash in house
  drafting inventory, 11–10
Cessation of office
  executors, 11–27
Children
  intestate succession, 4–48
Civil partners
  intestate succession, 4–50
Claimants
  meaning, 1–04
Codicils
  alteration of wills, 7–03—7–04
Cohabiting couples
  intestate succession
    introduction, 4–56
    prior to Family Law (Scotland) Act 2006,
      4–57
    under Family Law (Scotland) Act 2006, 4–58
Collaterals
  intestate succession, 4–04, 4–05
Collation inter haeredes
  intestate succession, 4–06
Collation inter liberos
  examples, 4–39
  generally, 4–38